Modernisation of Indian Army: Still a Far Cry

Modernisation of Indian Army : Still a Far Cry

Mohd. Wasim

Commandant (Retd.)

Prashant Publishing House

DELHI - 110094 (INDIA)

PRASHANT PUBLISHING HOUSE
C-34, 28 Foota Road, Gali No. 3
West Karawal Nagar, Delhi-110094
Phone : 9810396373, 22963970

Modernisation of Indian Army : Still a Far Cry

First Published : 2010

ISBN : 978-93-80565-05-7

PRINTED IN INDIA

Published by Mr. R. K. Jha M/s. Prashant Publishing House, Delhi and Printed at H.S. Offset Press, Delhi.

Preface

For over a decade the Indian Army's efforts to modernise have been thwarted due to political neglect and lack of adequate budgetary support. The defence budget for Financial Year 2008-09 increased 10 per cent in nominal terms, barely adequate to keep up with inflation and the fall in the value of the rupee against the US dollar, but decreased to less than 2.0 per cent of India's projected GDP. A sum of US $12 billion was provided for capital acquisitions (US $9 billion for the army), but of this US $0.6 billion (Rs 3,000 crore) is expected to be surrendered as unspent.

The images of field guns firing in Kargil in 1999 with a devastating effect at the target end are still afresh in the mind of the Indian public. That was also the time when India was recovering from the economic crisis of the early 1990s when the foreign exchange reserves had dwindled to dangerous lows to even think of acquiring defence equipment through imports. The Kargil crisis compelled the politico-military establishment to reassess the country's defence and security policies, not just to replace the Soviet vintage equipment with the Armed Forces but in terms of their modernization. In the subsequent years as part of its overall modernization effort, a Field Artillery Rationalisation Plan was introduced; the same also formed basis for the Artillery modernization plans.

It presents not only a comprehensive overview of the record of armed forces but also gives a useful survey to the problems, pressures and opportunities to the nations in all the continents. As such it is clearly written and well-informed book. It gives a forceful introduction to a subject which is vital for the future defence of all nations and peoples. The book gives a unique account of the defence craftsmanship and modernisation of Indian Army.

—*Editor*

Preface

Contents

Contents

1

Introduction to Indian Army

Structure of the Indian Air-Force

Recruitment and Training

Recruitment is through three military related academies. These include the National Defence Academy, Indian Military Academy and Officers Training Academy. For entrance, one must display that they are both physically and mentally fit to be in the military by sitting examinations and undergoing medical checkups. The complete list of institutions training Indian army were listed in Military academies in India section.

Indian Army

Strength: During a conflict, the air-arm of the Indian army plays a crucial role in providing essential supplies and air cover to the ground forces. Shown here is the Indian Army's HAL Dhruv.

Indian Army Statistics

Active Troops	1,325,000 (2nd)
Artillery	7100
Battle Tanks	5010
Aircraft	52 squadrons of helicopters
Surface-to-air missiles	90,000+

The Indian Army is the world's second largest army in terms of military personnel (after China). It is a completely voluntary service, the military draft having never been imposed in India.

The army has rich combat experience in diverse terrains, due to India's diverse geography, and also has a distinguished history of serving in United Nations peacekeeping operations.

The force is headed by the Chief of Army Staff, currently General Deepak Kapoor. The highest rank in the Indian Army is Field Marshal, but it is a largely ceremonial rank and appointments are made by the President of India, on the advice of the Union Cabinet of Ministers, only in exceptional circumstances. General S.H.F.J. Manekshaw and the late General K.M. Cariappa are the only two officers who have attained this rank. The Indian Army has seen military action in the Indo-Pakistani War of 1947, the Indo-Pakistani War of 1965, the Indo-Pakistani War of 1971, and others such as Operation Polo in 1948, the Sino-Indian War in 1962 over the McMahon Line, and the Kargil War against Kashmiri insurgents and the Pakistan military personnel

Currently, the Indian army has dedicated one brigade of troops to the UN's standby arrangements. Through its large, sustained troop commitments India has come in for much praise for taking part in difficult operations for prolonged periods. The Indian Army has participated in several UN peace-keeping operations, including the ones in Cyprus, Lebanon, Congo, Angola, Cambodia, Vietnam, Namibia, El Salvador, Liberia, Mozambique and Somalia. The army also provided a paramedical unit to facilitate the withdrawal of the sick and wounded in Korea.

Indian Navy

The Indian Navy is the naval branch of the armed forces of India. With 55,000 men and women, including 5,000 naval aviation personnel and 2,000 Marine Commandos (MARCOS), it is the world's fifth largest navy. The Indian Navy currently operates more than 155 vessels, including the aircraft carrier INS Viraat. The navy is considered to have blue-water capabilities. It is fairly advanced in terms of technology and is in control of one of two Asian aircraft carriers. Two more aircraft carriers are on order and will be joining the Indian Navy. The ships of the Indian Navy are of Indian and foreign origin. In its maritime doctrine, the Indian Navy establishes its role in providing support to maritime neighbours during natural disasters. This was demonstrated during the Asian tsunami crisis during which the Indian Navy sent 35 ships to support relief efforts in neighbouring countries. The Indian navy has taken part in UN missions in the coast of Somalia and has provided security to an African Union summit held in Mozambique. India uses its navy to enhance its international relations through joint exercises, port visits, and humanitarian missions, including disaster relief. The Indian Navy is increasing its capabilities as a true blue-water navy; the Indian Navy's doctrine states that this is for the collective good of nations.

Indian Air Force

The Indian Air Force is the fourth largest air force in the world. In its history, it has generally relied on Soviet technology to support its growth. However, in recent times, India has begun building its own original aircraft, including the HAL Tejas, which is a 4.5 generation fighter. Also India and Russia are currently building a 5th generation stealth aircraft jointly. India has also developed UAV called Nishant and HAL Dhruv, an advanced light helicopter. Recently it has completed a test of long range BVR air to air missile named Astra and also conducted a successful test of Anti ballistic missile defence system and hence became the 4th country after US, Russia and Israel to do so.

Paramilitary forces of India

Indian Nuclear Power

It is estimated that India possesses around 200-250 nuclear warheads which could be deployed at short notice.

Nuclear Doctrine

The Indian military possesses nuclear weapons and sufficient means — by means of missiles and aircraft — to deliver anything over long distances. However, India has a *nuclear no-first-use* and no use against non-nuclear weapons state policy. It also maintains a non-nuclear doctrine based on *credible minimum deterrence*. India is not a signatory to the Nuclear Non-proliferation Treaty (NPT), arguing that it unfairly favours the established nuclear powers:

While the treaty places restrictions on the non-nuclear weapons states, it does little to curb the modernization and expansion of the nuclear arsenals of the nuclear weapons states; it provides no provision for complete nuclear disarmament.

Gallantry Awards

The highest wartime gallantry award given by the Military of India is the Param Vir Chakra (PVC), followed by the Maha Vir Chakra (MVC) and the Vir Chakra (VrC). Its peacetime equivalent is the Ashoka Chakra. The highest decoration for meritorious service is the Param Vishisht Seva Medal.

Future

Several reports have mentioned that the Indian military will be an even greater force to reckon with in the future given the twin advantage of economic growth and an increasing population. Analyses of the Central Intelligence Agency indicates that India is projected to possess the fourth most capable concentration of power by 2015. According to a report published by the US Congress, India is the developing world's leading arms purchaser.

Army

The army numbers about one million personnel and fields 34 divisions. Designed primarily to defend the country's frontiers, the army has become heavily committed to internal security duties in Kashmir and the Northeast. In 2002 the Indian Army had 980,000 active troops, along with an Army Reserve consisting of: 300,000 first line troops (those within five years of full time service), and another 500,000 second line troops (subject to recall to service until 50 years of age). The Territorial Army numbered 40,000 first line troops (and 160,000 second line troops). In 1994 the army had approximately 940,000 men and women on active duty, and another 36,000 in the Territorial Army. As of 1998 the Army had a sanctioned troop strength of 1,045,000, but there was a shortage of about 59,000 troops.

At the beginning of World War II there were 170,000 soldiers in the Indian Army all regulars, but by June of 1948 there were 2,000,000. This was the reason British Officers were needed to help train and form new units. Each Battalion needed eight British Officers to take command, as all the lower ranks were manned by Indian Viceroy Commissioned Officers, and NCOs. The army is headquartered in New Delhi and is under the direction of the chief of the army staff, always a full general. The chief of the army staff is assisted by a vice chief, two deputy chiefs, a military secretary, and the heads of four main staff divisions: the adjutant general, the quartermaster general, the master general of ordnance, and the engineer in chief.

The Army consists of a number of arms and services. These are: Armoured Corps, Regiment of Artillery, Corps of Engineers, Corps of Signals, Mechanised Infantry, Infantry, Army Service Corps, Military Nursing Service, Army Medical Corps, Army Dental Corps, Army Ordnance Corps, Corps of Electrical and Mechanical Engineers, Remount and Veterinary Corps, Military Farms Service, Army Education Corps, Intelligence Corps, Corps of Military Police, Judge Advocate General Department, Army Physical Training Corps, Pioneer Corps, Army Postal Service Corps and Defence Security Corps. In addition, the Army has its own Recruiting Organisation, Record Offices, Depots, Boys Establishments and Selection Centres and training institutions. These units are organized in twelve corps-level formations.

The army has five tactical area commands: the Northern Command headquartered at Udhampur in Jammu and Kashmir, the Western Command headquartered at Chandimandir in Chandigarh, the Central Command headquartered at Lucknow in Uttar Pradesh, the Eastern Command headquartered at Calcutta, and the Southern Command headquartered at Pune in Maharashtra. Each command is headed by a lieutenant general. In the Indian context, Command Headquarter can be likened to a Field Army or even an Army Group Headquarter with a General Officer Commanding-in-Chief presiding over matters in the rank of a (three-star) Lieutenant General. Next the line are the Corps Headquarters, which are Field Army Headquarters elsewhere. The Indian Army's combat formations are now grouped and tailored under many such Corps Headquarters (with some forces being retained under static Area Commands). As with the American Army, all Corps have numerical designations. They also have names, by which they are more commonly known. These names may derive from the city in which they are headquartered [XVI Corps / Nagrota Corps], or they may be evocative [IV Corps is Gajraj Corps, meaning "King Elephant."

The field force is grouped into Corps. Some of these are defensively oriented and have, over the years, acquired an unofficial-'Holding'. The others are called reserve or, unofficially again, 'Strike' Corps. The former is really a misnomer since these contain ample offensive potential. Corps Headquarters are designed to. handle an all-arms field army-of three to five divisions or their equivalents. Army Headquarters reserves could be mammoth-size or small, but powerful in either case. Heavy-tracked-Corps are an instance of the former, and the three parachute commandos (battalion-size units), which perform special forces duties, of the latter. Airborne, Air Assault or Parachute troops are usually held centralized. The mounts', in all cases, are provided by the Indian Air Force.

The Division and Independent Brigade Group are the lowest (or the highest, depending on the viewpoint) individual formations. They integrate in themselves all arms and services for sustained independent operations. There is great flexibility in their force mix, and in 'grouping for tasks'. Brigade (regiment in some armies) size combined-arms groups can be shed or added on at will. Standard Tables of Organization and Equipment do exist, but these are taken lightly for accounting purposes only. Divisions and independent brigade groups are designated by function, terrain of operation, or by their equipment mix. The Army has in its Order of Battle, mountain divisions, infantry divisions, armoured divisions (in which tank units predominate) and mechanized divisions (in which mechanized infantry units predominate). An Infantry Division typically has about 15,500 combat troops, with 8,000 support elements (artillery, engineers, etc).

It consists of 3 to 5 Infantry Brigades, an Armoured Regiment and an Artillery Brigade. A Brigade is commanded by a Brigadier, and an Infantary Brigade consists of three Infantry Battalions. A regiment can be a type of battalion (eg. in the Artillery/Engineers) or a grouping of a number of battalions of the same type (eg. The

Rajput Regiment). The approximate strength of an infantry battalion, commanded by a Colonel, may be taken as 900-1,000 personnel. A battalion may consist of three to four companies, and may be commanded by a Lieutenant Colonel or a Colonel. A company normally consists of 100-120 men and is commanded by a Major.

Independent brigade groups, as the name suggests, are vested with limited capability to carry out an independent mission. Independent brigade groups or independent brigade-sized formations may be armoured, mechanized, air defence (missile or gun), parachute, engineer, field artillery, electronic warfare or even standard infantry and mountain. These form 'Corps/Army troops', that is, they are held at Corps and Army levels for balancing out missions and task forces. At these levels, one would find heavy logistic support units in terms of supply, transport, field ordnance depots, and medical facilities. An extensive body of schools and centres supports army operations. The officer corps is largely drawn from the National Defence Academy at Khadakvasla, Maharashtra, a joint services training institution that provides educational equivalents to the bachelor of arts or bachelor of science degrees to cadets for all three service arms.

Cadets spend their first three years at the National Defence Academy and then are sent to their respective service academies for further training before being commissioned in the armed forces. A preparatory school, the Rashtriya Indian Military College, at Dehra Dun, Uttar Pradesh, provides education to candidates for the National Defence Academy. After completing their studies at the National Defence Academy, army cadets are sent to the Indian Military Academy at Dehra Dun. Other Indian Military Academy cadets are graduates of the Army Cadet College or are direct-entry students who have qualified by passing the Union Public Service Commission Examination.

They spend between twelve and twenty-four months at the Indian Military Academy before being commissioned in the army as second lieutenants. Still other officer training occurs at the Officers' Training Academy in Madras, Tamil Nadu, where a forty-four-week session is offered to university graduates seeking a short-service commission.

In addition to the Indian Military Academy, the army runs a number of military education establishments. The more prominent ones include the College of Combat at Mhow, Madhya Pradesh; the High Altitude Warfare School at Gulmarg, Jammu and Kashmir; and the Counter-Insurgency and Jungle Warfare School at Vairengte, Mizoram. The army also operates the Defence Services Staff College at Wellington in the Nilgiri Hills in Tamil Nadu, which provides master of science-level joint-service training for mid-level staff appointments and promotes interservice cooperation.

In 1994 it was reported that there were 200 women in the armed forces. In the army, which employs women as physicians and nurses, the participation of women is small but growing. The Indian Military Nursing Service was formed in 1926 and has eight nursing schools (five army, two navy, and one air force) and one nursing college in Pune. Bachelor of science graduates are commissioned as lieutenants in the Medical Nursing Service and attached to the various components of the armed forces.

Ranks as high as colonel can be attained by career officers. In the mid-1990s, a small but increasing number of women officers were being assigned to nonmedical services. In 1994, there were fifty women nonmedical army officers and another twenty-five in training. They are university graduates who have been put through rigorous training and are reported to be eager for combat unit assignments.

Development and Modernisation of Indian Army

The Indian Army is the largest branch of the armed forces of India and bears responsibility for land-based military operations. Its primary objectives include defending India from external aggression, maintaining peace and security within the country, patrolling borders and conducting counter-terrorist operations. It also conducts rescue and humanitarian operations during calamities and other disturbances. The President of India is the Commander-in-Chief of the Indian Army. With more than 1,130,000 soldiers in active service and about 1,800,000 reserve troops, the Indian Army is the world's second largest. It is a completely voluntary service and although a provision for military draft exists in the Indian constitution, it has never been imposed.

The Indian Army was formed soon after India gained independence in 1947 and retained most of the regiments of the British Indian Army. The Army is deployed in many of the world's conflict zones as a part of the United Nations Peacekeeping forces. The force is currently headed by the Chief of Army Staff, General Deepak Kapoor. Field Marshal is the highest attainable rank in the Indian Army and is conferred by the President of India, on advice of the Union Government, only in exceptional circumstances. Two officers have attained this rank so far.

Objectives

The Indian Army doctrine defines the role of the Indian Army as-"The Indian Army is the land component of the Indian Armed Forces which exist to uphold the ideals of the Constitution of India." As a major component of national power, along with the Indian Navy and the Indian Air Force, the roles of the Indian Army are as follows :

- Primary: Preserve national interests and safeguard sovereignty, territorial integrity and unity of India against any external threats by deterrence or by waging war.
- Secondary: Assist Government agencies to cope with 'proxy war' and other internal threats and provide aid to civil authority when requisitioned for the purpose."

History

Upon India gaining independence in 1947, the British Indian Army was divided into two parts to serve the newly created nations of Union of India and Islamic Republic of Pakistan. Most units went to India; four Gurkha regiments were transferred to the British Army while the rest went to India.

First Kashmir War (1947)

Almost immediately after independence, tensions between India and Pakistan began to boil over, and the first of three full-scale wars between the two nations broke out over the then princely state of Kashmir. Upon the Maharaja of Kashmir's reluctance to accede to either India or Pakistan, an impatient Pakistan sponsored a 'tribal' invasion of parts of Kashmir. The men included Pakistan army regulars. Soon after, Pakistan sent in more of its troops to annex the State.

The Maharaja, Hari Singh, appealed to India, and to Lord Mountbatten, the Governor General, for help. He signed the Instrument of Accession and Kashmir acceded to India (a decision ratified by Britain). Immediately after, Indian troops were airlifted to Srinagar and repelled the invaders. This contingent included General Thimayya who distinguished himself in the operation and in years that followed, became a Chief of the Indian Army. An intense war was waged across the state and former comrades found themselves fighting each other. Both sides made some territorial gains and also suffered significant losses. An uneasy UN sponsored peace returned by the end of 1948 with Indian and Pakistani soldiers facing each other directly on the Line of Control, which has since divided Indian from Pakistani-held Kashmir. Tensions between India and Pakistan, largely over Kashmir, have never since been entirely eliminated.

Participation in UN peace-keeping operations

Presently, the Indian army has dedicated one brigade of troops to the UN's standby arrangements. The large number of sustained troop commitments made by India has been praised for taking part in long and difficult operations. The Indian Army has participated in several UN peace-keeping operations, including the ones in Angola, Cambodia, Cyprus, Congo, El Salvador, Namibia, Lebanon, Liberia, Mozambique, Rwanda, Somalia, Srilanka & Vietnam. The army had also provided a paramedical unit to facilitate the withdrawal of the sick and wounded in Korea.

Inclusion of Hyderabad (1948)

After the partition of India, the State of Hyderabad, a princely-state under the rule of a Nizam, chose to remain independent. The Nizam, refused to accede his state to the Union of India. The following stand-off between the Government of India and the

Nizam ended on 12 September 1948 when India's then deputy-Prime Minister Sardar Vallabhai Patel ordered Indian troops to secure the state. Within 5 days of intense fighting, the Indian Army, backed by the Indian Air Force, successfully defeated Hyderabad State forces. The following day, the State of Hyderabad was proclaimed as a part of the Union of India. Major General Joyanto Nath Chaudhuri, who led the Operation Polo was appointed the Military Governor of Hyderabad (1948-1949) to restore law and order.

Goa, Daman and Diu Operation (1961)

Even though the British and French vacated all their colonial possessions in the Indian subcontinent, Goa, Daman and Diu remained under Portuguese control. On 12 December, 1961, after repeated Portuguese refusals to negotiate their leaving, New Delhi launched Operation Vijay and ordered a small contingent of its troops to invade the Portuguese territories and secure them. Unable to withstand the assault that lasted twenty-six hours, Goa, along with Daman and Diu (enclaves lying to the north of Maharashtra) joined India.

Sino-Indian Conflict (1962)

Since 1959, India followed a "forward policy" under which Indian border patrol units continuously pushed their posts forward deep into territory claimed by the People's Republic of China (PRC). Small-scale clashes between the Indian and Chinese forces broke out as India insisted on the disputed McMahon Line being regarded as the international border between the two countries. Despite heavy casualties, Indian troops did not retaliate the cross-border firing by Chinese troops. China's misinterpretation of India's true intentions in Tibet created more rifts between the two countries.

Buoyed by the success of its military operations in Hyderabad and Goa, India took a more aggressive stance towards its border disputes with China. In 1962, the Indian Army was ordered to move to the Thag La ridge located near the border between Bhutan and Arunachal Pradesh and about three miles (5 km) north of the disputed McMahon Line. Meanwhile, Chinese troops too had made incursions into Indian-held territory and tensions between the two reached a new high when Indian forces discovered a road constructed by China in Aksai Chin. After a series of failed negotiations, People's Liberation Army attacked Indian Army positions at the Thag La ridge. This move by China caught India by surprise and by October 12, Nehru gave orders for the Chinese to be expelled from Aksai Chin. However, poor coordination among various divisions of the Indian Army and the late decision to mobilize the Indian Air Force in vast numbers gave China a crucial tactical and strategic advantage over India. On October 20, Chinese soldiers attacked India in both the North-West and North-Eastern parts of the border and captured vast portions of Aksai Chin and Arunachal Pradesh.

As the fighting moved beyond disputed territories, China called on the Indian government to negotiate, however India remained determined to regain lost territory. With no peaceful agreement in sight, China unilaterally withdrew its forces from Arunachal Pradesh. The reasons for the withdrawal are disputed with India claiming various logistical problems for China and diplomatic support to it from the United States, while China stated that it still held territory that it had staked diplomatic claim upon. The dividing line between the Indian and Chinese forces was christened the Line of Actual Control.

The poor decisions made by India's military commanders, and, indeed, its political leadership, raised several questions. The Henderson-Brooks committee was soon set up by the Government of India to determine the causes of the poor performance of the Indian Army. The report of committee apparently faulted much of the command of Indian Armed Forces and severely criticized the executive government for its failures on several fronts.

The committee found that the major reason for the defeat was low deployment of troops on India's border with China even after hostilities began and also criticized the decision to not allow the Indian Air Force to target Chinese transport lines out of fear of Chinese aerial counter-attack on Indian civilian areas. Much of the blame was also targeted at the incompetence of then Defence Minister, Krishna Menon who resigned from his post soon after the war ended. Despite frequent calls for its release, the Henderson-Brooks report still remains classified.

Second Kashmir War (1965)

A second confrontation with Pakistan took place in 1965, largely over Kashmir. Pakistani President Ayub Khan launched *Operation Gibraltar* in August 1965 during which several Pakistani paramilitary troops infiltrated into Indian-administered Kashmir and tried to spark an anti-India rebellion. Pakistani leaders believed that India, which was still recovering from the disastrous Sino-Indian War, would be unable to deal with a military thrust and rebellion. However, the operation was a major failure since the Kashmiri people showed little support for such a rebellion and India quickly moved forces to drive the infiltrators out. Within a fortnight of the launch of the Indian counter-attack, most of the infiltrators had retreated back to Pakistan. Battered by the failure of Operation Gibraltar and expecting a major invasion by Indian forces across the border, Pakistan launched Operation Grand Slam on September 1, invading India's Chamb-Jaurian sector. In retaliation, the India's Army launched major offensive throughout its border with Pakistan, with Lahore as its prime target. Though the Indian Army's break through of the final phases of Pakistani defence was considerably delayed due to logistical issues, the conflict was largely seen as a debacle for the Pakistani Army.

Initially, the Indian Army met with considerable success in the northern sector. After launching prolonged artillery barrages against Pakistan, India was able to capture three important mountain positions in Kashmir. By September 9, the Indian Army had made considerable in-roads into Pakistan. India had its largest haul of Pakistani tanks when the offensive of Pakistan's 1 Armoured Division was blunted at the Battle of Asal Uttar which took place on September 10 near Khemkaran. Six Pakistani Armoured Regiments took part in the battle against three Indian Armoured Regiments with inferior tanks. By the time the battle had ended, the 4th Indian Division had captured about 97 Pakistani tanks in either destroyed, or damaged, or in intact condition. This included 72 Patton tanks and 25 Chafees and Shermans. 32 of the 97 tanks, including 28 Pattons, were in running condition. In comparison, the Indians lost only 32 tanks at Khemkaran-Bhikkiwind. About fifteen of them were captured by the Pakistan Army, mostly Sherman tanks. Pakistan's overwhelming defeat at the decisive battle of Assal Uttar hastened the end of the conflict.

At the time of ceasefire declaration, India reported casualties of about 2,000 were killed. On the other hand, it was estimated that about 3,800 Pakistani soldiers were killed in the battle, 9,000 were wounded and about 2,000 were taken as prisoners of war. About 300 Pakistani tanks were either destroyed or captured by India and an additional 150 were permanently put out of service. India lost a total of 190 tanks during the conflict and about 100 more had to undergo repair. In all, India lost about half as many tanks as Pakistan lost during the war. Given India's advantageous position at the end of the war, the decision to return back to pre-war positions, following the Tashkent Declaration, caused an outcry among the polity in New Delhi. It was widely believed that India's decision to accept the ceasefire was due to political factors, and not military, since it was facing considerable pressure from the United States and the UN to stop hostilities.

Bangladesh Liberation War (1971)

An independence movement broke out in East Pakistan which was brutally crushed by Pakistani forces. Due to large-scale atrocities against them, thousands of Bengalis took refuge in neighboring India causing a major refugee crisis there. In early 1971, India declared its full-support for the Bengali rebels, known as Mukti Bahini, and Indian agents were extensively involved in covert operations to aid them.

On November 20, 1971, Indian Army moved the 14 Punjab Battalion and 45 Cavalry into Garibpur, a strategically important town near India's border with East Pakistan, and successfully captured it. The following day, more clashes took place between Indian and Pakistani forces. Wary of India's growing involvement in the Bengali rebellion, the Pakistan Air Force (PAF) launched a pre-emptive strike on Indian military positions near its border with East Pakistan on December 3. The aerial operation, however, failed to accomplish its stated objectives and caused India to declare a full-scale war against Pakistan the same day. By midnight, the Indian Army, accompanied by Indian Air Force, launched major military thrust into East Pakistan. The Indian Army won several battles on the eastern front including the decisive of battle of Hilli, which was the only front where the Pakistani Army was able to buildup considerable resistance. India's massive early gains was largely attributed to the speed and flexibility with which Indian armored divisions moved across East Pakistan.

Pakistan launched a counter-attack against India on the western front. On December 4, 1971, the A company of the 23rd Battalion of India's Punjab Regiment detected and intercepted the movement of the 51st Infantry Division of the Pakistani Army near Ramgarh, Rajasthan. The battle of Longewala ensued during which the A company, though being outnumbered, thwarted the Pakistani advance until the Indian Air Force directed its fighters to engage the Pakistani tanks. By the time the battle had ended, 34 Pakistani tanks and 50 armored vehicles were either destroyed or abandoned. About 200 Pakistani troops were killed in action during the battle while only 2 Indian soldiers lost their lives.

Pakistan suffered another major defeat on the western front during the battle of Basantar which was fought from December 4 to 16th. By the end of the battle, about 66 Pakistani tanks were destroyed and 40 more were captured. In return, Pakistani forces were able to destroy only 11 Indian tanks. None of the numerous Pakistani offensives on the Western front materialized. By December 16, Pakistan had lost sizable territory on l oth eastern and western fronts.

Under the command of Lt. General J.S Aurora, the three corps of the Indian Army, who had invaded East Pakistan, entered Dhaka and forced Pakistani forces to surrender on 16 December, 1971, one day after the conclusion of the battle of Basantar. After Pakistan's Lt. General A.A.K. Niazi signed the Instrument of Surrender, India took more than 90,000 Pakistani prisoners of war, which included about 38,000 armed forces personnel and 52,000 militia and bureaucrats of West Pakistani origin. At the time of the signing of the Instrument of Surrender, 9,000 Pakistani soldiers were killed-in-action while India suffered only 2,500 battle-related deaths. In addition, Pakistan lost 200 tanks during the battle compared to India's 80.

In 1972, the Simla Agreement was signed between the two countries and tensions simmered. However, there were occasional spurts in diplomatic tensions which culminated into increased military vigilance on both sides.

Siachen Conflict (1984)

The Siachen Glacier, though a part of the Kashmir region, is not officially demarcated. As a consequence, prior to the 1980s, neither India nor Pakistan maintained permanent military presence in the region. However, Pakistan started hosting a series of mountaineering expeditions to the glacier during the 1950s. By early 1980s, the government of Pakistan was granting special expedition permits to mountaineers and United States Army maps deliberately showed Siachen as a part of Pakistan. This practice gave rise to the contemporary meaning of the term *oropolitics*.

An irked India launched Operation Meghdoot in April 1984 during which the entire Kumaon Regiment of the Indian Army was airlifted to the glacier. Pakistani forces responded quickly and clashes between the two followed. Indian Army secured the strategic Sia La and Bilafond La mountain passes and by 1985, more than 1000 sq. miles of territory, claimed by Pakistan, was under Indian control.

The Indian Army continues to control more than 2/3rd of the glacier. Pakistan made several unsuccessful attempts to regain control over Siachen. In late 1987, Pakistan mobilized about 8,000 troops and garrisoned them near Khapalu, aiming to capture Bilafond La. However, they were thrown back after engaging the Indian Army personnel guarding Bilafond. During the battle, about 23 Indian soldiers lost their lives while more than 150 Pakistani troops perished. Further unsuccessful attempts to reclaim positions were launched by Pakistan in 1990, 1995, 1996 and 1999.

India continues to maintain a strong military presence in the region despite extremely inhospitable conditions and the conflict over Siachen is regularly cited as an example of mountain warfare. The highest peak in the Siachen glacier region, Siakangri, is strategically important for India because its immense altitude and proximity to the Karakoram Highway enables the Indian forces to keep check on any Pakistani or Chinese movement in the region. Maintaining control over Siachen poses several logistical challenges for the Indian Army. Several infrastructure projects were constructed in the region, including a helipad 21,000 feet (6,400 m) above the sea level. In 2004, Indian Army was spending an estimated US$2 million a day to support its personnel stationed in the region.

Counter-insurgency activities

The Indian Army has played a crucial role in the past, fighting insurgents and terrorists within the nation. The army launched Operation Bluestar and Operation Woodrose in the 1980s to combat Sikh insurgents. The army, along with some paramilitary forces, has the prime responsibility of maintaining law and order in the troubled Jammu and Kashmir region. The Indian Army also sent a contingent to Sri Lanka in 1987 as a part of the Indian Peace Keeping Force.

Kargil Conflict (1999)

In 1998, India carried out nuclear tests and a few days later, Pakistan responded by more nuclear tests giving both countries nuclear deterrence capability. Diplomatic tensions eased after the Lahore Summit was held in 1999. The sense of optimism was short-lived, however, since in mid-1999 Pakistani paramilitary forces and Kashmiri insurgents captured deserted, but strategic, Himalayan heights in the Kargil district of India. These had been vacated by the Indian army during the onset of the inhospitable winter and were supposed to reoccupied in spring. The regular Pakistani troops who took control of these areas received important support, both in the form of arms and supplies, from Pakistan. Some of the heights under their control, which also included the *Tiger Hill*, overlooked the vital Srinagar-Leh Highway (NH 1A), Batalik and Dras.

Once the scale of the Pakistani incursion was realized, the Indian Army quickly mobilized about 200,000 troops and Operation Vijay was launched. However, since the heights were under Pakistani control, India was in a clear strategic disadvantage.

From their observation posts, the Pakistani forces had a clear line-of-sight to lay down indirect artillery fire on NH 1A, inflicting heavy casualties on the Indians. This was a serious problem for the Indian Army as the highway was its main logistical and supply route. Thus, the Indian Army's first priority was to recapture peaks that were in the immediate vicinity of NH1a. This resulted in Indian troops first targeting the Tiger Hill and Tololing complex in Dras. This was soon followed by more attacks on the Batalik-Turtok sub-sector which provided access to Siachen Glacier. Point 4590, which had the nearest view of the NH1a, was successfully recaptured by Indian forces on June 14.

Though most of the posts in the vicinity of the highway were cleared by mid-June, some parts of the highway near Drass witnessed sporadic shelling until the end of the war. Once NH1a area was cleared, the Indian Army turned to driving the invading force back across the Line of Control. The Battle of Tololing, among other assaults, slowly tilted the combat in India's favor. Nevertheless, some of the posts put up a stiff resistance, including Tiger Hill (Point 5140) that fell only later in the war. As the operation was fully underway, about 250 artillery guns were brought in to clear the infiltrators in the posts that were in the line-of-sight. In many vital points, neither artillery nor air power could dislodge the outposts manned by the Pakistan soldiers, who were out of visible range. The Indian Army mounted some direct frontal ground assaults which were slow and took a heavy toll given the steep ascent that had to be made on peaks as high as 18,000 feet (5,500 m). Two months into the conflict, Indian troops had slowly retaken most of the ridges they had lost; according to official count, an estimated 75%–80% of the intruded area and nearly all high ground was back under Indian control.

Following the Washington accord on July 4, where Sharif agreed to withdraw Pakistani troops, most of the fighting came to a gradual halt, but some Pakistani forces remained in positions on the Indian side of the LOC. In addition, the United Jihad Council (an umbrella for all extremist groups) rejected Pakistan's plan for a climb-down, instead deciding to fig ıt on. The Indian Army launched its final attacks in the last week of July; as soon as the Drass subsector had been cleared of Pakistani forces, the fighting ceased on July 26. The day has since been marked as *Kargil Vijay Diwas* (Kargil Victory Day) in India. By the end of the war, India had resumed control of all territory south and east of the Line of Control, as was established in July 1972 per the Shimla Accord.

By the time all hostilities had ended, the number of Indian soldiers killed during the conflict stood at 527 while more than 700 regular members of the Pakistani army were killed. The number of Islamist fighters, also known as *Mujahideen*, killed by Indian Armed Forces during the conflict stood at about 3,000.

Corps

Field Formation

A Corps is an army field formation responsible for a sector within a Command. There are 3 types of Corps in the Indian Army: Strike, Holding & Mixed. A Command generally consists of 2 or more Corps. A corps has Army Divisions under its command. The Corps HQ is the highest field formation in the army.

Regimental Organisation

In addition to this (not to be confused with the Field Corps mentioned above) are the Regiments or Corps or departments of the Indian Army. The corps mentioned below are the functional divisions entrusted with specific pan-Army tasks.

Arms

1. Indian Infantry Regiments
2. Armoured Corps Regiments-The Armoured Corps School and Centre is at Ahmednagar.
3. Regiment of Artillery-The School of Artillery is at Devlali near Nasik.
4. Corps of Engineers-The College of Military Engineering is at Dapodi, Pune. The Centres are located as follows-Madras Engineer Group at Bangalore, Bengal Engineer Group at Roorkee and Bombay Engineer Group at Khadki, Pune.

5. Corps of Army Air Defence-Center at Gopalpur in Orissa State.
6. Mechanised Infantry-Regimental Center at Ahmednagar.
7. Corps of Signals
8. Army Aviation Corps(India)

Services

1. Army Dental Corps
2. Army Education Corps-Center at Pachmarhi.
3. Army Medical Corps-Center at Lucknow.
4. Army Ordnance Corps-Centres at Jabalpur and Secunderabad (HQ).
5. Army Postal Service Corps
6. Army Service Corps-Center at Bangalore
7. Corps of Electrical and Mechanical Engineers-Centres at Bhopal and Secunderabad.
8. Corps of Military Police-Center at Bangalore
9. Intelligence Corps-Center at Pune.
10. Judge Advocate General's Deptt.-Institute of Military Law kamptee,Nagpur.
11. Military Farms Service
12. Military Nursing Service
13. Remount and Veterinary Corps
14. Pioneer Corps

Arms and services

Other Field Formations

- Division: An Army Division is an intermediate between a Corps and a Brigade. It is the largest striking force in the army. Each Division is headed by [General Officer Commanding] (GOC) in the rank of Major General. It usually consists of 15,000 combat troops and 8,000 support elements. Currently, the Indian Army has 34 Divisions including 4 RAPID (Re-organised Army Plains Infantry

Divisions) Action Divisions, 18 Infantry Divisions, 10 Mountain Divisions, 3 Armoured Divisions and 2 Artillery Divisions. Each Division composes of several Brigades.

- Brigade: The Brigade is smaller than the Division and generally consists of 3 Infantry Battalions along with elements of various Combat & Support Arms & Services. It is headed by a Brigadier equivalent to a Brigadier General. The Indian Army also has 5 Independent Armoured Brigades, 15 Independent Artillery Brigades, 7 Independent Infantry Brigades, 1 Independent Parachute Brigade,3 Independent Air Defence Brigades, 2 Independent Air Defence Groups and 4 Independent Engineer Brigades. These Independent Brigades operate directly under the Corps Commander (GOC Corps).
- Battalion: A Battalion is commanded by a Colonel and is the Infantry's main fighting unit. It consists of more than 900 personnel.
- Company: Headed by the Major, a Company comprises 120 soldiers.
- Platoon: An intermediate between a Company and Section, a Platoon is headed by a Lieutenant or depending on the availability of Commissioned Officers, a Junior Commissioned Officer, with the rank of Subedar or Naib-Subedar. It has a total strength of about 32 troops.
- Section: Smallest military outfit with a strength of 10 personnel. Commanded by a Non-commissioned officer of the rank of Havildar Major or Sergeant Major.

Regiments

Infantry Regiments

There are several battalions or units under the same formation in a Regiment. The Gurkha Regiment, for instance, has several battalions. All formations under a Regiment are battalions of the same arms or Corps (i.e., Infantry or Engineers). Regiments are not exactly field formations; they mostly do not make a formation. All Regiments of the Gurkha's for instance would not fight together as one formation, but can be dispersed over various Brigades or Corps or even Commands.

Artillery Regiments

The Regiment of Artillery constitutes a formidable operational arm of Indian Army. Historically it takes its lineage from Moghul Emperor Babur who is popularly credited with introduction of Artillery in India, in the Battle of Panipat in 1526. However evidence of earlier use of gun by Bahmani Kings in the Battle of Adoni in 1368 and King Mohammed Shah of Gujrat in fifteenth century have been recorded.

Indian Army Staff

Strength

Indian Army statistics

Active Troops	1,300,000
Reserve Troops	1,200,000
Indian Territorial Army	200,000**
Main Battle Tanks	4,500
Artillery	12,800
Ballistic missiles	100 (Agni-I,Agni-II)
Ballistic missiles	>500 (Prithvi-I)
Cruise missiles	200BrahMos
Aircraft	10 squadrons of helicopters
Surface-to-air missiles	90,000

* includes 3,00,000 1st line troops and 5,00,000 2nd line troops

** includes 40,000 1st line troops and 160,000 2nd line troops

Statistics

- 4 RAPID (Reorganised Army Plains Infantry Divisions)
- 18 Infantry Divisions
- 10 Mountain Divisions
- 3 Armoured Divisions
- 2 Artillery Divisions
- 13 Air Defence Brigades + 2 Surface-to-Air Missile Groups
- 5 Independent Armoured Brigades

- 15 Independent Artillery Brigades
- 7 Independent Infantry Brigades
- 1 Parachute Brigade
- 4 Engineer Brigades
- 14 Army Aviation Helicopter Units

Sub-Units

- 63 Tank Regiments
- 7 Airborne Battalions
- 200 Artillery Regiments
- 360 Infantry Battalions + 5 Para (SF) Battalions
- 40 Mechanised Infantry Battalions
- 20 Combat Helicopter Units
- 52 Air Defence Regiments

Rank Structure

The various rank of the Indian Army are listed below in descending order:

Commissioned Officers

- Field Marshal
- General (the rank held by Chief of Army Staff)
- Lieutenant-General
- Major-General
- Brigadier
- Colonel
- Lieutenant-Colonel
- Major
- Captain
- Lieutenant

Junior Commissioned Officers (JCOs)

- Subedar Major/Honorary Captain
- Subedar/Honorary Lieutenant

- Subedar Major
- Subedar
- Naib Subedar

Non Commissioned Officers (NCOs)

- Regimental Havildar Major2
- Regimental Quarter Master Havildar2
- Company Havildar Major
- Company Quarter Master Havildar
- Havildar
- Naik
- Lance Naik
- Sepoy

Combat Doctrine

The current combat doctrine of the Indian Army is based on effectively utilizing holding formations and strike formations. In the case of an attack, the holding formations would contain the enemy and strike formations would counterattack to neutralize enemy forces. In the case of an Indian attack, the holding formations would pin enemy forces down whilst the strike formations attack at a point of Indian choosing. The Indian Army is large enough to devote several corps to the strike role. Currently, the army is also looking at enhancing its special forces capabilities.

Equipment

Most of the army equipment is imported, but efforts are being made to manufacture indigenous equipment. All Indian Military Firearms guns are manufactured under the umbrella administration of the Ordnance Factory Board, with principal Firearm manufacturing facilities in Ishapore, Cossipore, Kanpur, Jabalpur and Tiruchirapalli.

Indian National Small Arms System (INSAS) rifle, which is successfully inducted by Indian Army since 1997 is a product of Rifle Factory, Ishapore. While ammunition is manufactured at Khadki and possibly at Bolangir.

Aircraft

The Indian army had projected a requirement for a helicopter that can carry loads of up to 75 kg heights of 23,000 feet (7,000 m) on the Siachen Glacier in Jammu and Kashmir. Flying at these heights poses unique challenges due to the rarefied atmosphere. The Indian Army chose the Eurocopter AS 550 for a $550 million contract for 197 light helicopters to replace its ageing fleet of Chetaks and Cheetahs, some of which were inducted more than three decades ago. The deal has however been scrapped amidst allegations of corruption during the bidding process.

Recipients of the Param Vir Chakra

Listed below are the most notable people to have received the Param Vir Chakra, the highest military decoration of the Indian Army.

Future developments

India is currently reorganising its mechanised forces to achieve strategic mobility and high-volume firepower for rapid thrusts into enemy territory. India proposes to progressively induct as many as 1,657 Russian-origin T-90S main-battle tanks (MBTs), apart from the ongoing upgradation of its T-72 fleet. The Army recently placed an order for 4,100 French-origin Milan-2T anti-tank guided missiles (ATGMs). Defence ministry sources said the Rs 592-crore (USD 120 million approx.) order was cleared after 26/11, with the government finally fast-tracking several military procurement plans.

2

Modernising the Indian Army

For over a decade the Indian Army's efforts to modernise have been thwarted due to political neglect and lack of adequate budgetary support. The defence budget for Financial Year 2008-09 increased 10 per cent in nominal terms, barely adequate to keep up with inflation and the fall in the value of the rupee against the US dollar, but decreased to less than 2.0 per cent of India's projected GDP. A sum of US $12 billion was provided for capital acquisitions (US $9 billion for the army), but of this US $0.6 billion (Rs 3,000 crore) is expected to be surrendered as unspent. Nothing exemplified the army's lack of preparedness for war more than the fact that 155 mm ammunition for the Bofors howitzer had to be imported from South Africa during the Kargil conflict in 1999. Had the conflict not been confined to the 150 km frontage of the Kargil sector, T-72 and 130mm medium gun ammunition too may have run short and it would have been politically embarrassing for the government as well as the army.

Not only that, in the plains the army would have had to fight with obsolete Vijayant tanks and several other vintage equipment that were unsuitable for combat. Even though A.K. Antony, the Defence Minister, has said, 'We need to cut down on the unnecessary procedures, bottlenecks and red tape in our procurement mechanism,' the Ministry of Defence has been unable to give modernisation of the armed forces the priority that it deserves. The Army Chief's modernisation vision is to 'adapt to high-end technology, improve night-fighting capability... (and) information technology, information warfare and network centric warfare.' The indigenously designed Arjun main battle tank (MBT) has been in the pipeline for over two decades. Though the tank has many good features, it has consistently failed to meet the army's GSQR for an MBT and orders have been placed for only 124 tanks to be manufactured. The lack of progress on the Arjun MBT has significantly slowed down the pace of armour modernisation. In the year 2000 India signed a deal with Russia to acquire 310 T-90S tanks. Subsequently, India began to assemble these tanks at Avadi. It has recently been reported that in addition to these, India has decided to acquire another 347 T-90S tanks and assemble them within the country.

The first Indian assembled T-90S (Bhishma) rolled off the production line on 8 January 2004. Meanwhile, a large number of T-72M1 (Ajeya) tanks are still awaiting modernisation. The lack of a suitable fire control system and night fighting capability are major handicaps.

In a future conventional war that will be fought under the nuclear shadow, manoeuvre will be extremely limited. This restriction will lead to much greater emphasis being placed on firepower to achieve the laid down military aim. Hence, it is imperative that artillery modernisation is undertaken with alacrity so as to generate firepower asymmetries on the future battlefield. The last major acquisition of towed gun-howitzers was that of about 400 pieces of 39-calibre 155mm FH-77B howitzers from Bofors of Sweden in the mid-1980s. This gun had proved its mettle in the Kargil conflict. Just when a contract for 120 tracked and 180 wheeled self-propelled (SP) 155mm guns was about to be concluded after years of protracted trials, South African arms manufacturer Denel, a leading contender for the contract, was alleged to have been involved in a corruption scam in an earlier deal for anti-material rifles (AMRs).

Since January 2008, the Ministry of Defence (MoD) has issued three global tenders for 155mm guns and howitzers for the mountains, the plains and self-propelled guns for the deserts. Summer and winter trials were expected to be held in 2009-10, but so far the bids received are still being evaluated. The artillery modernisation programme is bound to see further delays. The probability of the next conventional war breaking out in the mountains is far higher than that of a war in the plains. With this in view, the artillery recently conceptualised a requirement for a lightweight towed howitzer of 155mm calibre for employment in the mountains. Neither the present Bofors howitzer nor its 52-calibre replacement will be capable of effective operations in the mountains. A lightweight 45-calibre 155mm howitzer weighing less than 5,000 kg, with a light but adequately powered prime mover, is ideal for the mountains. In January 2008, the MoD floated a Request for Proposal (RfP) for 140 pieces of ultra-light 39 calibre 155mm towed howitzers for use by the Indian Army's mountain formations. Presumably, these will also be employed by its rapid reaction divisions – as and when they are raised – as the howitzers will be easy to transport by air.

India has floated a global tender for the purchase of 400 52-calibre 155mm towed artillery guns for the army, to be followed by indigenous manufacture of another 1,100 howitzers. An RfP has also been issued for 180 wheeled self-propelled guns for around Rs 4,700 crore for employment by mechanised forces in the plains and semi-desert sectors. Approximately 180 pieces of 130mm M46 Russian medium guns have been successfully 'up-gunned' to 155mm calibre with ordnance supplied by Soltam of Israel. The new barrel length of 45 calibres has enhanced the range of the gun to about 40 km with extended range ammunition.

A contract for the acquisition of two regiments of the 12-tube, 300mm Smerch multi-barrel rocket launcher (MBRL) system with 90 km range was signed with Russia's Rosoboron-export in early 2006. This will be a major boost for the long-range firepower capabilities of the army. Extended range (ER) rockets are being introduced for the 122 mm Grad MBRL that has been in service for over three decades. The ER rockets will enhance the weapon system's range from 22 to about 40 km. A Rs 5,000 crore (US $1billion) contract has also been signed for the serial production of the Pinaka MBRL weapon system, another DRDO project plagued by time delays and completed with help from Larsen and Toubro and the Tatas.

Since the Bofors 155mm Howitzer was introduced into service, the indigenously designed and manufactured 105 mm Indian Field Gun (IFG) and its (not so) light version, the Light Field Gun

(LFG), have joined the 75/24 Indian Mountain Gun, the 100mm Russian field gun and the 122mm Russian howitzer on the obsolescence list.

Counter-bombardment (US term counter-fire) capability is also being upgraded, but at a slow pace. At least about 40 to 50 weapon locating radars (WLRs) are required for effective counter-bombardment, especially in the plains, and only a dozen have been procured so far. In addition to the 12 AN-TPQ 37 Firefinder WLRs acquired from Raytheon, USA, under a 2002 contract worth US $200 million, Bharat Electronics Limited is reported to be assembling 28 WLRs. These radars will be based on both indigenous and imported components and have been approved for introduction into service after extensive tests. The radar is expected to match the capabilities of the Firefinder system and will have a detection range of about 40 kilometre.

The BrahMos supersonic cruise missile (Mach 2.8 to 3.0), with a precision strike capability, very high kill energy and range of 290 km, was inducted into the army in July 2007. It is a versatile missile that can be launched from TATRA mobile launchers and silos on land, aircraft and ships and, perhaps in future, also from submarines. 50 BrahMos missiles are expected to be produced every year. Efforts are underway to further increase its strike range. BrahMos Aerospace has orders worth Rs 3,500 crore (US $0.65 billion) from the army and the navy, which has opted for the anti-ship as well as the land attack cruise missile (LACM) versions. These terrain hugging missiles are virtually immune to counter measures due to their high speed and very low radar cross section and are far superior to subsonic cruise missiles like Pakistan's Babur.

Despite its large-scale employment on border management and extensive commitments in IS and CI operations, infantry modernisation had been languishing for several decades when the Ministry of Defence (MoD) finally cleared a visionary plan to modernise the army's infantry battalions by according 'in principle' approval in the form of Modification 4B to the war establishment (WE) of a standard infantry battalion in 1998. However, no funds were specially sanctioned for this purpose till the NDA government approved the expenditure of Rs 3,500 crore (US $0.6 billion) in

September 2003. The army has initiated a project for a Future Infantry Soldier as a System (F-INSAS). 'F-INSAS basically aims at "converting an infantryman into a fully-networked all-terrain, all-weather, weapons platform with enhanced lethality, survivability, sustainability, mobility and situational awareness" for the digitised battlefield of the future.'

While 250 Kornet-E anti-tank guided missiles (ATGMs) with thermal imaging sights have substantially increased the anti-tank capability of infantry battalions, most efforts to modernise the equipment held by infantry and Rashtriya Rifles (RR) units are aimed at enhancing their capability for surveillance and target acquisition at night and boosting their firepower for precise retaliation against infiltrating columns and terrorists holed up in built-up areas. 200 hand-held BFSRs with practical ranges up to seven to eight km where clear line of sight is available, 2,000 hand-held thermal imaging devices (HHTIs) with ranges up to 2,000 metres for observation at night and stand-alone infrared, seismic and acoustic sensors with varying capabilities have enabled infantrymen to dominate the Line of Control so completely that infiltration has come down to almost a trickle.

The newly acquired weapons, which complement these surveillance and observation devices, include: 1,500x 84 mm rocket launchers, including some disposable ones; 1,000 AMRs (anti-material rifles); 8,000 UBGLs (under-barrel grenade launchers); 4,000 new generation carbines; 300 bullet proof vehicles; and, several hundred accurate sniper rifles. However, the numbers acquired and the ammunition stocks are still inadequate and need to be made up more rapidly. While the INSAS 5.56 mm assault rifles have now been in service for almost 10 years and proved to be effective, the light machine gun (LNG) version is still facing teething problems and the carbine version for close quarter battle has not found favour with the army. New 5.56 mm assault rifles of bull-pup design with an integrated laser range finder and grenade launcher are under development. Efforts are also being made to provide infantry platoons and sections with integrated GPS-based navigation system, secure lightweight walkie-talkie radio sets and better protective gear with a helmet that incorporates a built-in head-up display.

The mechanised infantry is now equipped with the BMP-2 ICV Sarath of which over 1,000 have been built since 1987. A new variant is the 81 mm Carrier Mortar Tracked Vehicle (CMTV) that is based on the chassis of the Sarath ICV and has been indigenously developed to enhance the integral firepower available to mechanised infantry battalions. Other variants include a command post, an ambulance, armoured dozer and engineer and reconnaissance vehicles. Mechanised reconnaissance and support battalions need better surveillance radars, fire-and-forget ATGMs and effective night fighting capability.

A new DRDO project that is reported to be ongoing aims to equip future soldiers with lightweight force multipliers. Soldiers of the future will have miniaturised communication and GPS systems, small power packs, weapon platforms and smart vests with fibre-optic sensors. For over 350 infantry battalions, plus about 150 Rashtriya Rifles, Assam Rifles and Territorial Army battalions, these major changes will be extremely costly to implement and will spill over at least 10 to 12 years – that is, if the funds can be found. Without modernising this cutting edge of its sword, the army will soon begin to resemble the armies of India's lesser neighbours.

Another DRDO project that is way behind schedule is the Nag anti-tank missile system. The antiquated Jonga-mounted SS-11 B1 anti-tank guided missile (ATGM) system has been replaced in missile battalions by MILAN shoulder-fired ATGMs. However, a vehicle-mounted missile system like the Nag is definitely necessary for reconnaissance and attrition tasks and for anti-tank screens. The experimental Plan AREN tactical communications system for strike formations needs early replacement. The ability to carry broadband data needs to be enhanced in particular. Even the more recent static communications network called ASCON lacks ISDN capability for the real-time transmission of maps and streaming video.

The Defence Minister, A.K. Antony, recently admitted that there are gaps in India's air defence coverage. While the allusion was primarily to the lack of sufficient radar coverage to detect aerial threats to India's air space, the air defence (AD) of field formations continues to be given a much lower priority than it deserves. With the DRDO's indigenous Akash medium-range and Trishul short-range surface-to-air (SAM) missile projects not making major headway, it is time to start looking at substitutes from abroad. The air defence of mechanised forces is another area that is crying for attention. The SAM-6 and SAM-7 Kvadrat-Strela medium range missile system, the backbone of AD for strike formations since the early 1970s, is now ageing and needs urgent replacement.

The Tungushka and the OSA-AK (SA-8) missile systems are on the obsolescence list and the 23mm, multi-barrelled Schilka tracked air defence gun system is already obsolete. In fact, the assets of the Army Air Defence corps are grossly inadequate to provide high quality low-level air defence to the field formations. Hence, forward combat echelons will lack effective protection against enemy aircraft during a future war. The young Army Air Defence corps requires substantial capital infusion to really come into its own.

For the future, the Defence Research and Development Organisation (DRDO) is planning to develop an integrated air defence system with exo-atmosphere (above 40 km altitude) and endo-atmosphere (below 30 km) capabilities by 2009-10. The system may also have built-in features to double up as a tactical missile, apart from functioning as an extended air defence system to engage target aircraft beyond 100 km. This was stated by V.K. Saraswat, Chief Controller, DRDO R&D (Missiles and Strategic Systems), after the successful test launch of a high-altitude interceptor missile from the Wheeler Island in December 2007. This programme will also lead to the development of an indigenous ballistic missile defence (BMD) capability.

An automated command and control and decision support system for use by the General Staff is still far from becoming a reality, as also supporting systems like the battlefield surveillance system and air space management system. The urgent requirement of real-time satellite reconnaissance systems has still not been operationalised despite the nuclear overhang under which the armed forces now operate. Even though the cameras on India's remote sensing and cartographic satellites now have sharply enhanced resolutions, less than one metre, military-grade photographs of still better resolution are needed to be purchased from the open market. These sources may dry up quickly during war.

A 'system of systems' approach must be followed so that scarce RSTA and communications resources can be synergistically configured and optimally exploited, based on the concept of 'network-centric warfare' in which surveillance sensors, targeting systems and 'shooters' are fused together in a seamless 'system of systems' that reduces response time between the acquisition of a target and its destruction to 15-20 minutes.

Though some modern frequency hopping radio sets with integral encryption devices have been introduced into service in recent years, networked communications, which form the backbone of an effective C4I2SR system, need substantial upgradation. The tactical-level Tac C3I system for field formations is in urgent need of an upgrade. The Plan AREN system has been in service for almost three decades and is based on outdated and bulky technologies. The ASCON communication system for voice and data links between static HQ and those in peacetime locations, still has some years of service left as it is of modular design and can be upgraded to a limited extent. However, its capability to provide data links is rather limited as data requirements have grown by leaps and bounds over the last decade or so. A tri-service Defence Communication Network (DCN) is in an advanced stage of planning.

While some Stentor long-range BFSRs have been in service for over a decade, medium-range radars are still to be acquired. Israeli Searcher-I and Heron unmanned aerial vehicles (UAVs) have been introduced into service but these are few in number and it will be a long time before they really make a difference by providing a real-time surveillance capability so that ground forces can initiate action even as a fresh input is received. Only a small number of Searcher-II UAVs, with an upper ceiling that makes them suitable for the mountains, have been acquired.

PGMs are increasingly gaining currency as weapons of choice in conflict on land, however, the Indian artillery does not have

PGMs in quantities large enough to matter. Only limited quantities of the Russian Krasnopol PGM have been imported for the Bofors 155mm howitzer. Among others, the Bofors Bonus PGM is a suitable candidate, subject to successful trials in the deserts and mountains.

Despite a Long-term Integrated Perspective Plan (LTIPP) and five-year Defence Plans, approval has to be sought on file for each new weapon system or piece of equipment on a 'case-by-case' basis. It is by now well-known how each such case chronicles the saga of an uphill struggle to get approval first from the MoD, then MoD (Finance), the Ministry of Finance (MoF) and, finally, the Cabinet Committee on Security. All this is only possible after the DRDO has first certified that the weapon system or equipment in question cannot be developed and manufactured indigenously and such a certificate is hard to come by. Gradually these archaic procurement and acquisition procedures are being reviewed and improved. The Defence Procurement Procedure (DPP) 2008 was promulgated recently.

The approach to army modernisation must be more focused; the priorities need to be clearly established and then adhered to. The government must give a firm commitment in terms of funds and the MoD should streamline its procedures and processes for speedy procurement of high priority weapons and equipment. It is time to institute a rolling, non-lapsable defence modernisation fund of Rs 25,000 crore (US $5 billion) as a viable method of ensuring that defence procurement is not subjected to the vagaries of annual budgets. The present situation is disturbing and, if allowed to go on indefinitely, will seriously compromise the army's preparedness to fight the next border war that inimical neighbours like Pakistan can be expected to thrust on India. The MoD 'has assured the army of full support for its around 600 modernisation schemes, worth about Rs 70,000 crore in the 11th Plan (2007-2012) period,' but it remains to be seen whether this will actually materialise.

MILITARY MODERNIZATION

The military modernization begun in the late 1970s had three major focuses. First, under the political leadership of Deng Xiaoping, the military became disengaged from civilian politics and, for the most part, resumed the political quiescence that characterized its pre-Cultural Revolution role. Deng reestablished civilian control over the military by appointing his supporters to key military leadership positions, by reducing the scope of the PLA's domestic nonmilitary role, and by revitalizing the party political structure and ideological control system within the PLA.

Second, modernization required the reform of military organization, doctrine, education and training, and personnel policies to improve combat effectiveness in combined-arms warfare. Among the organizational reforms that were undertaken were the creation of the state Central Military Commission, the streamlining and reduction of superfluous PLA forces, civilianization of many PLA units, reorganization of military regions, formation of group armies, and enactment of the new Military Service Law in 1984. Doctrine, strategy, and tactics were revised under the rubric of "people's war under modern conditions," which envisaged a forward defence at selected locations near China's borders, to prevent attack on Chinese cities and industrial sites, and emphasized operations using combined-arms tactics. Reforms in education and training emphasized improving the military skills and raising the education levels of officers and troops and conducting combinedarms operations. New personnel policies required upgrading the quality of PLA recruits and officer candidates, improving conditions of service, changing promotion practices to stress professional competence, and providing new uniforms and insignia.

The third focus of military modernization was the transformation of the defence establishment into a system capable of independently maintaining a modern military force. As military expenditures remained relatively constant, reforms concentrated on reorganizing the defence research-and-development and industrial base to integrate civilian and military science and industry more closely. Foreign technology was used selectively to upgrade weapons. Defence industry reforms also resulted in China's entry into the international arms market and the increased production of civilian goods by defence industries. The scope of

PLA economic activities was reduced, but the military continued to participate in infrastructure development projects and initiated a program to provide demobilized soldiers with skills useful in the civilian economy.

Civil-Military Relations

Lines between civilian and military leadership and institutions in China are indistinct. All high-ranking military leaders have high-level party positions, and many high-ranking party officials have some military experience. When military leaders participate in national policy making, therefore, it is not clear whether their positions reflect PLA corporate interests or the interests of groups that cut across institutional lines. In general, in times where there was national leadership consensus on national policy, such as in the 1950s, the PLA was politically quiescent. Once the PLA was drawn into civilian politics during the Cultural Revolution, the military became divided along the lines of civilian factions. As long as the national leadership remained divided on a number of policy issues, the PLA, fearing factional struggles and political instability, was reluctant to leave the political scene. When Deng Xiaoping was rehabilitated in 1977, however, the stage was set for the withdrawal of the military from politics and a partial return to the PLA's previous political passivity.

Political Role of the People's Liberation Army

Deng Xiaoping's efforts in the 1980s to reduce the political role of the military stemmed from his desire to reassert civilian control over the military and to promote military modernization. To accomplish his objectives, Deng revitalized the civilian party apparatus and leadership and built a consensus on the direction of national policy. He also established personal control over the military through personnel changes, and he reduced the scope of the PLA's domestic political, economic, and social roles. Finally, he strengthened party control over the military through institutional reforms and political and ideological education. The revitalization of the party and the establishment of a consensus on national policy assured top military leaders of political stability and a vigorous party capable of handling national and regional affairs without extensive military participation. Deng's personal political control was established over the military through his assumption of the position of chairman of the party Central Military Commission in June 1981 and through his appointment of his supporters to key positions in the party Central Military Commission, Ministry of National Defence, and the PLA's General Staff Department, General Political Department, and General Logistics Department. Occasional replacement of military region and military district commanders also strengthened Deng's hand. Military leaders who objected to Deng's policies were replaced with more amenable personnel.

The creation of the state Central Military Commission in 1982 aimed to further strengthen civilian control over the military by stressing the PLA's role as defender of the state and by establishing another layer of supervision parallel to party supervision. The civilianization of several PLA corps and internal security units reduced the size of the PLA and the scope of its involvement in civilian affairs. The placement of defence industries under civilian control and the transfer or opening up of military facilities, such as airports and ports, to civilian authorities also limited the PLA's influence in economic and political matters. Propaganda using the PLA as a model for society also diminished, and emphasis was placed on the PLA's military rather than political role.

Party Control

In addition to making personnel changes, Deng revitalized party control over the PLA and diffused the military's political power by designating provincial-level, municipal, district, and county party committee secretaries to serve concurrently as the first political commissars of their equivalent-level units in the regional PLA. The percentage of PLA personnel permitted to join the party was limited by restricting party membership to military academy graduates. Political and ideological training stressed the military rather than the social, ideological, or economic role of the PLA. Special effort was made to discredit the PLA's role in the Cultural Revolution; the PLA's support for the left was described as incorrect because it caused factionalism within the military. While emphasizing the necessity and appropriateness of reforms to modernize the military, political education also sought to guarantee military support for Deng's reform agenda. Beginning in 1983 a rectification campaign (part of the party-wide rectification campaign aimed primarily at leftists) reinforced this kind of political and ideological training.

Beginning in the late 1970s, Deng Xiaoping succeeded in decreasing military participation in national-level political bodies. Military representation on the Political Bureau fell from 52 percent in 1978 to 30 percent in 1982, and military membership in the party Central Committee declined from 30 percent in 1978 to 22 percent in 1982. Most professional military officers shared common views with the Deng leadership over military modernization and the fundamental direction of national policy, and they willingly limited their concerns to military matters. Nonetheless, some elements in the PLA continued to voice their opinions on nonDefence matters and criticized the Deng reform program. Dissent centered on prestigious military leaders, notably Ye Jianying, who feared that ideological de-Modification, cultural liberalization, and certain agricultural and industrial reforms deviated from Marxist values and ideals. The Deng leadership contained these criticisms with the help of the personnel changes, political education, and the rectification campaign just mentioned. In this way it was able to keep military dissent within bounds that did not adversely affect civil-military relations.

Popular Attitudes Toward the People's Liberation Army

Starting in the late 1970s, popular attitudes toward the PLA also underwent considerable changes. In the 1950s and 1960s, the military's prestige was very high because of its wartime exploits, because it was held up as a role model for society, and because of its participation in civilian construction projects. But the power gained by the PLA during the Cultural Revolution reawakened civilian resentment of military privileges and abuses of power. By the early 1980s, with the circumscription of the PLA's domestic role and the implementation of agricultural reforms offering greater opportunities for rural youth, the PLA's reputation as a prestigious, elite, Marxist-model organization and a promising channel for social mobility was severely tarnished. Society's perception of the military appeared to be returning to the traditional viewpoint that "one doesn't make nails out of good iron; one doesn't make soldiers out of good men." To restore this damaged image in the late 1980s, the media extolled the PLA's martial virtues and the great strides made in military modernization in recent years.

Modernizing Artillery : Retrospect and Prospect

The images of field guns firing in Kargil in 1999 with a devastating effect at the target end are still afresh in the mind of the Indian public. That was also the time when India was recovering from the economic crisis of the early 1990s when the foreign exchange reserves had dwindled to dangerous lows to even think of acquiring defence equipment through imports. The Kargil crisis compelled the politico-military establishment to reassess the country's defence and security policies, not just to replace the Soviet vintage equipment with the Armed Forces but in terms of their modernization. In the subsequent years as part of its overall modernization effort, a Field Artillery Rationalisation Plan was introduced; the same also formed basis for the Artillery modernization plans.

Consequent to the experience in Operation Parakaram, the Indian army revised its doctrine in 2004 to respond to the realities of a tough neighbourhood. As a result, a Cold Start doctrine was articulated which had several premises. Evidently, a doctrine draws from experiences of previous wars and can be aspirational as it defines the objectives that should be chosen for the future and the operational concepts to be followed to attain goals. In this mode, a doctrine drives the nature of organization, force structure and training.

The Cold Start doctrine enunciated by the Indian Army rests on rapid mobilization, concentration and launch of operations in a seamless continuum. The other planks of the doctrine are:

- Multiple thrusts with divisional sized integrated battle groups.
- Broad front, shallow depth, limited objectives.
- Pivot corps offensives supplemented with available Integrated Battle Groups from Strike Corps resources.

- Strike reserve largely uncommitted.
- Aims at attrition and capture of territory.
- Cognizant of possible nuclear thresholds.
- All weather, day night operations; air drops and heliborne operations; IW and EW; massed firepower ('100 guns' concept); operational fires.

Massing of accurate and heavy volume of firepower, coordinated with combined arms operations including the air support would be a necessary condition for achieving the objectives of a Cold Start doctrine in real-time. The Artillery doctrine no doubt will flow out of the conceptual and doctrinal issues for combined arms operations emanating from the Cold Start precepts.

Lack of adequate artillery firepower would definitely restrict the freedom and movement of own forces whereas enhanced enemy artillery fire power will also add to difficulties of own forces' manoeuvre. The Cold Start doctrine requires a massive artillery support ab initio to neutralise the enemy defences in the shortest possible time without giving him much reaction time.

Further, the India Army Chief has recently talked about the changing geo-political and strategic environment and the need to be prepared for a range of security threats and challenges including the possibilities of a need to deal with two fronts. He also reflected upon the Out of Area Contingencies which may necessitate employment of forces. Therefore the gaping voids in our field artillery need to be filled up in a hurry to meet the likely threats to the defence of the realm. The artillery rationalization plan's key objective was to standardize the equipment profile from a multitude of caliber of guns to a single caliber. There are advantages to be gained in terms of streamlined logistics, easy maintenance and repairs including standardization of ammunition.

While, this plan was outlined at the turn of the century with ambitious goal of implementing it in three to four plan periods of Five Year Defence Plans, no progress could be made due to several contextual factors. The major factor being the ghost of Bofors (payoff allegations in their mid-1980s deal) exacerbated further by allegations of corruption in some of the subsequent potential artillery acquisition deals.

However, as a first step towards modernization of field artillery almost over a decade after enunciation of FARP, there is silver lining on the cloud. Finally, the government has decided to buy 145 M777 ultralight howitzers from the US-based entity of the BAE Systems through the government-to-government Foreign Military Sales (FMS) route. The FMS route avoids all the ills and impediments associated with India's Defence Procurement Procedure which has been continually revised but has not delivered especially on the artillery procurement. A Fast Track Procedure is also part of the DPP but that has also not helped meet India's burgeoning defence acquisition needs.

An indication that the above deal of 145 light Howitzers may be clinched was a notification by the Pentagon to the US Congress in the second half of January 2010 of a possible sale of 145 state-of-the-art lightweight towed Howitzers to India.

The Defence Security Cooperation Agency rationalized to the Congress, "India intends to use the howitzers to modernise its armed forces and enhance its ability to operate in hazardous conditions. The howitzers will assist the Indian Army to develop and enhance standardisation and to improve interoperability with US Soldiers and Marines who use the M777 as their primary means of indirect fire. India will have no difficulty in absorbing these weapons into its armed forces." That it also makes a good commercial sense and an important breakthrough in the Indian defence bazaar can not be mentioned in the solemn note to the Congress.

There are reports however, on another level, that the deal may not come through as a result of the recent strategic side-lining of India in the London Conference on the Afghanistan imbroglio. There are unconfirmed reports that the Indian policy establishment is considering as to what strategic leverages India has to ensure its meaningful role in unfolding scenarios in Afghanistan where the dominant discourse is being dictated by the US, notably the Pentagon. Some years back, before the Indo-US defence Framework Agreement was signed in 2005 and the Ministry of Defence had drawn out ambitious defence acquisition plans, a retiring Defence Secretary had remarked that defence purchases from abroad should be used a strategic leverages in consonance with our policy objectives. If such recourse is adopted it would further delay the process of procurement.

But then this is not the end of the massive requirements of Indian field artillery for either ultra light howitzers or for that matter other type of guns. There are four other types of 155 mm guns which are to be acquired as part of the long-term artillery modernization plans.

While the acquisition of 145 Howitzers would be sufficient only to equip seven artillery regiments after catering for General staff reserves and would fill existing voids or provide replacements for mountain artillery units to be converted to 155 mm caliber as part of FARP, additional requirements have also arisen because of the governments decision to raise two mountain divisions and a fourth artillery division to support operations in the mountainous areas. This would translate into a requirement of ultra light howitzers for four mountain artillery brigades which would mean acquisition of additional 290 pieces that would have to be spread over 12th, 13th and 14th Five Year Defence Plans.

As part of the first phase of FARP, besides the 145 pieces, a requirement of 158 Towed and wheeled guns, 100 tracked guns to support the mechanized formations and 180 wheeled guns with armour protection has been spelt out. Hopefully, these guns would be acquired in the current 11th Five Year Plan (2007-2012). Last year, the Defence Acquisition Council had included a fifth category classified as Mounted Gun Systems. These howitzers, mounted on wheeled chassis, would have a shoot and scoot capability with the crew remaining mounted on the vehicle.

Looking at the overall requirements the estimates of the number of guns to be inducted to complete the rationalization plan range from 2700 to 3600 guns in the long term perspective of 15 to 20 years costing between Rs 22,000 crores to Rs 30,000 crores. These demands are based on the total number of artillery regiments which are 200 or so, and the additional artillery units planned to be raised. Such mammoth requirements also predicate that India has to indigenize the production of 155 mm guns as it can remain an importer if it has any pretensions of becoming a major power. Defence Minister A K Antony though has already stated that the policy now was to acquire every important system with Transfer of Technology (ToT). Indian artillery immediately needs 400 towed 155 mm guns as no such guns have been acquired since the Bofors were inducted in 1987. Induction of these guns would be followed by indigenous production of 1580 guns of this type.

The acquisition process was suspended after dealings with Singapore's ST Kinetics (and six other companies) were put on hold due to allegations of corruption involving Ordnance Factories Board (OFB)'s top executive. That in fact led to a single vendor situation, and that is best avoided, according to the procurement manual.

The results of the investigations (by India's Central Bureau of Investigation, or CBI) are not known but till the companies involved are not cleared of the allegations or suspicions, no contracts would be signed by them. However, pending the completion of the process, the procedural system has okayed that the trials of equipment offered by these companies could go on so as not to cause further delay. A deal could and would be signed only after these companies are cleared of any charges of wrong-doing.

Accordingly, the government has approved the trials of the Towed guns from SK Kinetics and BAE Systems with the caveat that trials are subject to clearance of allegations of corruption (in the case of SK Kinetics). Indian Army Chief Gen Deepak Kapoor (a gunner himself) had admitted the development to be of a particular concern as the Army has not been able to purchase a single gun in the last 23 years. Earlier Denel of South Africa was blacklisted on similar charges which led to the current re-tendering process. The second category is of Tracked guns mounted on tank chassis for supporting the mechanized formations for five artillery regiments to be acquired to the extent of 100 155mm/52 caliber guns to replace the existing 130mm Catapult and 105 mm Abbot Guns.

There is the third category of wheeled 155 mm guns mounted on a six-wheeled vehicle with armour protection to the extent of

180 (as mentioned earlier). The fourth category of ultralight howitzers has already been discussed above. And the last and the fifth category is the mounted gun system, The artillery modernization includes off-the-shelf purchase of 200 155mm/52-calibre mounted gun systems to be followed by indigenous manufacture of another 614 such howitzers under transfer of technology. The 17-tonne motorized howitzers will arm 40 regiments. A rough glance would suggest that the overall requirement would easily surpass a figure of 3000 guns.

Concerned about fast depleting stocks including war wastage reserves of field artillery, the Army Headquarters has mooted a proposal for the induction of 80-100 pieces of 130 mm medium guns from old stocks lying with former Soviet Republics, as a desperate last resort, to have something at least ASAP.

Though of World War II vintage, the 130 mm gun was imported and inducted into the Indian artillery in the 19060s. It is a rugged and a reliable gun which has seen action in all the terrains as obtaining in India including the Sia Chen Glacier base, high altitude areas and deserts. However, it lacks the sophistication and mobility of the modern artillery guns, and has a limited range of the types of ammunitions it can fire.

The Army headquarters is being forced to adopt such a measure for earliest making up of critical deficiencies and building already depleted war wastage stocks. It needs to be underscored that except for upgradation of a limited number of 130 mm guns to 155mm by Soltam of Israel, a project that received mixed reviews, the Indian army has not inducted or upgraded an artillery gun for nearly three decades. In fact, OFB tried to sell the upgunned 130mm to the Gulf countries, but there was no interest in an old system here.

With indigenous production at standstill, in the Artillery faces a real precarious situation and hence this desperate and some say counterproductive measure. It is learned that the issue was discussed in recent Defence Acquisition Council meeting with final decision still pending.

Enunciation of the Cold Start doctrine could not have served its purpose of strategic communication to our potential adversaries unless the voids in fire power are made up in double quick time. The acquisition decisions on procurement of 155 mm 52 caliber towed howitzers, SP tracked and wheeled guns, and mounted gun systems as also ultralight howitzers must be taken on priority for the Artillery to play its role in a future war imposed on India.

Indian Navy: Challenges Beyond The Horizon

The Currency of Power

In the mid-1980s many commentators predicted the end of the role of military force as the "currency of power". Subsequent decades were however marked by global changes that significantly altered the distribution of international power. Radical shifts in the status of erstwhile subjugated states, the empowerment of newly developed and developing nations, and the displacement of totalitarian regimes across Europe, have altered the perception of the influence of military power in determining the course of global events. The freeing up of economies, which became the norm by the mid-1990s, resulted in a rise in expectations in many parts of the world. The spread of information made the disparities in living standards more glaring and national, political or ethnic groupings became assertive of their right to a share of the global wealth. As changing tectonic conditions result in periodic earthquakes which enable the earth's crust to adjust to the altered conditions, this instability created violent upheavals involving the use of military force to realign political or economic power. Predictions of the demise of military force as a currency of power were thus belied by the unilateral exercise of the military option in Central Europe and in West Asia. Far from the imagined era of stability (which is largely interpreted as the maintenance of the status quo) and the much vaunted "end of history" theory, the last two decades have been the most violent in history.

Apart from its being used as a means of forcibly redistributing political power within and between nations, military power is also being applied to further economic interests. The attack on Iraq by the US, and the current imbroglio in that unhappy country, had as much to do with the perceived energy requirements of the US as with any real or imaginary weapons of mass destruction.

Similarly, it has been argued that Iraq's plans to trade its oil wealth in euros threatened the primacy of the dollar as the global currency, and the attack on Iraq was a measure to safeguard vital US economic interests. It is apparent therefore, that far from becoming irrelevant, or even waning in importance, military power is still considered a legitimate and viable option by countries that wish to impose their vision of the international order on recalcitrant lesser states. It is equally an unavoidable conclusion that states that wish to retain their freedom of manoevre in global affairs, must possess a sound economy, backed by a robust (even if defensive) military capability. Clearly the age has not yet arrived when nations can dispense with their armed forces. If anything, recent events would indicate the opposite-that failure to invest in national defence capability could cost a country dear.

The Nature of Future Wars

While it is fairly clear that nation states will continue to resort to military force, and we will need to maintain armed forces for the foreseeable future, it is much less clear, what size and shape and capabilities those forces will need to have. Warfare has begun to evolve away from the historical pattern, and massive wars on a global scale between evenly matched and industrialised opponents are generally accepted to be a phenomena of the past. Major influences on the nature of future warfare will be exerted by three main factors-economic interdependence and globalization, redistribution and realignments of international power, and technology.

With the collapse of the USSR, socialist economic doctrines were rapidly discarded by all countries and they have embraced the free market philosophies of the West. The resultant free flow of capital, the increase in global movement of labour, and the offshoring of industrial production have bound countries together in a variety of ways-economic, social and cultural. It would be impossible under these conditions for a country to inflict severe or lasting damage to another with which it has close economic ties without itself suffering in the process. Globalization has thus curtailed the freedom of the more powerful nations to act with impunity against weaker nations with well-developed economies, and with which they have economic relationships. The nature of conflict between such countries would necessarily be of brief durations and be focused on the achievement of narrow and specific (mainly economic) objectives.

The changed distribution and alignment of international power has various facets. The US, and under its leadership NATO, have resorted to military actions decisively against several countries in the last two decades. The object states of these actions are countries that are characterised by poor economic levels, political instability, and the absence of democratic forms of government. It is hard to see similar actions being taken against countries with a stable and democratic system in place, and which have well developed economic, social and cultural international linkages. Although the US has emerged as the sole superpower, it has been forced to become increasingly heedful to international opinion. Thus, while the end of the Cold War resulted in the emergence of a single super power, the economic globalization that followed has swung the pendulum slightly back, resulting in a moderation of the superpower status. The spread of satellite television brought distant wars to the homes of viewers, and the developed countries are finding it increasingly difficult to justify the loss of human life. The political cost of casualties in war has increased to the point where risk avoidance has become an important factor that impinges on war tactics in Western countries.

These factors permit the following conclusions:

- Wars of the future are likely to brief and focused on economic objectives.
- They will be more in the nature of specific operations against unequal and weak states with poorly developed and insular economic and political systems.
- They will not be waged with equally industrialised or advanced countries.
- They will be increasingly subject to world opinion and approval.
- Risk avoidance will result in the use of long range weapons and aerial bombardment with precision weapons.

The Revolution in Military Affairs

The factors discussed above will have a profound effect on the framework and rules by which wars will be fought. They will determine under what circumstances nations, even powerful ones, will resort to military action against other states, and with the passage of time, will increasingly circumscribe the kind of targets that will be acceptable for attack. In contrast, the third factor, i.e. technology, will have its greatest impact on the means and methods in which future wars will be fought, and on the weapon systems and platforms of military and naval forces.

In the mid-1990s it was realised that the rapid growth of information technology and digital communications made possible the transmission of huge amounts of battle theatre data in real time. This happened at a time when the demise of the Soviet Union suddenly knocked out the core of the US Navy's strategy, which was centred on tracking, outmaneuvering and pre-empting the Russian forces at sea. The US Navy was quick to recognise the need to shift its strategy to one based on joint operations with other forces, on and over land. This shift was only possible because of the emergence of technology to back it up. The new concept of operations is based on data being uploaded on to a network which can be accessed by all combatant commanders, and the scenario perceived by individual units can be integrated in real time to give all commanders a total perspective on the overall operational scenario. It has thus become possible for a unit to bring to bear its fire power on a target, even if it does not even have it on its radar or other sensors.

Western military scholars define a revolution in military affairs as a rapid change in the warfare paradigm brought about by technology or new concepts, which are usually accompanied by new organisational structures. Unlike earlier such revolutions in naval warfare in the past such as the advent of steam, the invention of the submarine, the invention of the radar, the development of the aircraft carrier and nuclear power, the current RMA is different in that it is likely to affect not only one service and its combat methods, but will have its impact on all armed forces and their operational doctrines.

The Future Navy

Specifically for the Navy, the current RMA will impinge on one of its basic traditional characteristics-the isolation of the naval commander at sea and the corresponding degree of freedom he had to make operational and tactical decisions. The published opinion is that the new scenario will enable rapid dissemination of operational information and decentralise decision-making, but there is another aspect which may have the opposite effect; the operational commander's superior too will have the total picture and will in a sense be alongside the fleet commander, which will considerably curtail his initiative!

Notwithstanding these areas of uncertainty, it seems inevitable that net-based war or network-centric warfare is the way naval warfare is headed, and our planners and designers will have to factor this into their template for the Navy of the future. The US and NATO have recognised this and have embarked seriously on a programme of "transformation" of their Navies to make them conform to the new roles and warfighting trends. New organisations have been set up with the specific task of conceptualizing and implementing the process of transformation and many decisions have already been taken to make the force structure of the future navy correspond to its predicted role and missions.

It goes without saying that the strategic imperatives of all countries vary, and notwithstanding recent writings and pronouncements about shared strategic interests and natural strategic partners, those of the US and Western powers are bound to be at divergence with several aspects of our own strategic perceptions. It is necessary for the current trends to be seen through the prism of national self-interest, and to make plans for the future structure of the Navy accordingly. One fact does seem evident-there is a need for transforming the Navy to one that will meet our requirements of the future.

The Indian Navy has no time to lose in instituting such a process. The concept of network-centric warfare has already been studied for several years, but the task of making the navy of the future capable of it has to be addressed now if the current discourse is not to remain an academic one. A few major thrust areas could be:

- Design and production of an indigenous net platform on which the network-centric operations will be based. This would have two or three versions with differing capabilities for different classes of ships.
- Commonalisation of procedures between the Air Force and the Navy to enable joint operations followed by standardization of communication and sensor systems for networking compatibility.
- Reduction in the number of types of warships, to reduce logistic complexity and improve ship availability. The Quadrennial Defence Review of 2006 for the US Navy envisages four types of ships for a total of 143 major surface combatants. In contrast, the 21 principal surface combatants we have in the Navy today belong to seven different types.
- Institution of a programme for integration of the submarine force into the network; this will require a major effort to equip submarines with real time communication systems with minimal loss of stealth. It will also require a changed mindset in the operating philosophy of submarines wherein submarines are given the minimum essential operational intelligence and directives before deployment and thereafter left pretty much to themselves for the duration of hostilities.
- Institution of a development programme for precision guided weapons.
- Development of a modern and interoperable radar system network between all combatant units.

This is probably a minimalist approach, and it has not considered the major efforts required in associated areas, particularly in education and training. But the point to be emphasised is an often-stated truism: it takes a lifetime to build a Navy, and if we are to transform the Navy of today into one that meets the task of (say) 2025, then the time to act is already upon us. It is interesting to observe that in the US context, two of the most ship innovative design decisions, the Littoral Control Ship and the conversion of the Ohio class, were thrust from above upon the US Navy. The Indian scene is different, and the Navy will have to wage a long struggle to get approval for its every proposal. The scenario is complicated by the fact that technology is advancing at an exponential rate, and this increases the cost of upgradations, and brings in its wake the spectre of rapid obsolescence. The preparation of a blueprint for the future Navy, the setting in motion of the development of the technologies required, and the steering of the concept and its implementation will require a dedicated organisation at a high level. Such an organisation will need to study the problem in a comprehensive manner, and cover the entire range of issues from the analysis of technology to finance and design, construction and training. More importantly they will have to convince the Government and many within the Service itself of not only the need, but also the urgency of such measures.

Modernisation of warfare strategies and techniques, and adoption of technologically advanced concepts are futile exercises if the basic structure of the Navy is not given the timely attention that is due. The creation of a balanced maritime defence force is an essential aspect of any modernisation, and the shortfall in our fleet units and submarines has to be made good by the political commitment to a sustained building programme rather than by sporadic inductions. In conclusion it needs to be said that the entire premise in this chapter has been that the equipment and system needed for net-based warfare will be developed and built in India, as dependence on foreign sources for such crucial systems will create an unacceptable vulnerability.

It has also been based on the hope that the process of production and acquisition and for obtaining government approvals will also be modernised along with the equipment and systems for the armed forces.

Military Organization

By 1987 changes in military organization indicated the importance Chinese leaders attached to structural reform in building military forces capable of waging modern, combined-arms warfare. These reforms included the creation of the state Central Military Commission parallel to the party Central Military Commission, reduction in force, reorganization of military regions, formation of group armies, enactment of the new Military Service Law, and reorganization of defence industries.

State and Party Central Military Commissions

At the apex of Chinese military organization stood two bodies—the state and party Central Military Commissions. The 1982 state Constitution created the state Central Military Commission as the state organ subordinate to the National People's Congress responsible for "directing the country's armed forces". The state Central Military Commission was the state's decision-making body in military affairs and directed and commanded the armed forces. The state Central Military Commission consisted of the chairman, who was commander in chief of the armed forces, an executive vice chairman, two vice chairmen, and four other members.

The party Central Military Commission, elected by the party Central Committee, exercised de facto, authoritative policy-making and operational control over the military. In addition to the chairman, the party Central Military Commission in 1987 included a permanent vice chairman who was concurrently secretary general, two vice chairmen, and four deputy secretaries general. The leadership of the state and party Central Military Commissions was identical, but the membership of the party Central Military Commission below the top leadership was thought to include regional commanders and service chiefs. Because the PLA has been under party control since its inception, the leadership of the party over the military did not change with the establishment of the state Central Military Commission. Although parallel leadership blurred the distinction between the two groups, the party Central Military Commission retained its traditional, preeminent position in charge of military affairs.

Ministry of National Defence and NDSTIC

Beneath the two Central Military Commissions were the

Ministry of National Defence and the National Defence Science, Technology, and Industry Commission (NDSTIC), which separately took orders from the two Central Military Commissions but had no operational control over the PLA. The Ministry of National Defence was responsible for military modernization and provided administrative support for the PLA. It was responsible for planning, manpower, budget, foreign liaison, and training materials, but it possessed no policy-making or implementation authority. The NDSTIC—formed in August 1982 by merging the National Defence Science and Technology Commission, National Defence Industries Office, and Office of the Science, Technology, and Armaments Commission of the party Central Military Commission—was responsible for military research and development, weapons procurement, and coordination of the defence and civilian economic sectors.

Operational Control

In 1987 operational control of the PLA ran from the two Central Military Commissions to the PLA's three general departments: General Staff Department, General Political Department, and General Logistics Department. Below the department level ran parallel chains of command for operational, political, and logistical matters, each with its own separate communications facilities. Military policy originated in the party Political Bureau or the party Central Military Commission, became an operational order at the General Staff Department level, flowed through the military regions, and arrived at a main-force unit. Orders to regional forces also passed through the military district (provincial) level.

General Staff Department

The General Staff Department carried out staff and operational functions for the PLA and had major responsibility for implementing military modernization plans. Headed by the chief of general staff, the department served as the headquarters for the ground forces and contained directorates for the three other armed services: Air Force, Navy, and Strategic Missile Force.

The General Staff Department included functionally organized subdepartments for artillery, armored units, engineering, operations, training, intelligence, mobilization, surveying, communications, quartermaster services, and politics. Navy Headquarters controlled the North Sea Fleet, East Sea Fleet, and South Sea Fleet.

Air Force Headquarters generally exercised control through the commanders of the seven military regions. Nuclear forces were directly subordinate to the General Staff Department. Conventional main, regional, and militia units were controlled administratively by the military region commanders, but the General Staff Department in Beijing could assume direct operational control of any main-force unit at will. Thus, broadly speaking, the General Staff Department exercised operational control of the main forces, and the military region commanders controlled the regional forces and, indirectly, the militia.

General Political Department

The General Political Department was responsible for ideological indoctrination, political loyalty, morale, personnel records, cultural activities, discipline, and military justice, and it provided the party structure for the PLA. It also published *Jiefangjun Bao* (Liberation Army Daily), the PLA's influential newspaper. The General Political Department director was at the head of a system of political commissars assigned to each echelon in the PLA. One of the primary tasks of the political commissar was the supervision of the party organization through party committees at the battalion level and above or through party branches in companies.

Virtually all high-ranking officers in the military were party members. Until the early 1980s, when party membership in the PLA was restricted, an effort was made to have a party or Communist Youth League member in every unit down to the smallest maneuver element. Political commissars were equal in rank and authority to the commander of their echelon in peacetime but theoretically deferred to the commander during war. Commissars assumed many time-consuming chores, such as personnel problems, relations with civilians, and troop entertainment.

General Logistics Department

The General Logistics Department, headed by a director, was responsible for production, supply, transportation, housing, pay, and medical services. Historically, much of this support came from the civilian populace, and before the establishment of the General Logistics Department it was organized most often by commissars. PLA logistical resources in 1980 were far fewer than those of Western or Soviet forces; in the event of war the Chinese military would be heavily dependent upon the militia and civilians. In 1985 the General Logistics Department was reorganized, its staff cut by 50 percent, and some of its facilities turned over to the civilian sector.

Streamlining and Reduction in Force

Efforts began in the 1980s to streamline the PLA and organize it into a modern fighting force. The first step in reducing the 4.5-million-member PLA in the early 1980s was to relieve the PLA of some of its nonmilitary duties. The Railway Engineering Corps and the Capital Construction Engineering Corps were civilianized, and in 1983 the PLA internal security and border patrol units were transferred to the People's Armed Police Force.

In 1985 China reorganized its 11 military regions into 7 and began a 2-year program to reduce the force by 1 million. Eight military regions were merged into four—Chengdu, Jinan, Lanzhou, and Nanjing—and three key regions—Beijing, Guangzhou, and Shenyang—remained intact. The PLA accomplished its 1-million-troop cut by streamlining the headquarters staffs of the three general departments, the military regions, and the military districts; reducing the size of the Air Force and the Navy; retiring older, undereducated, or incompetent officers; and transferring county- and city-level people's armed forces departments, which controlled the militia, to local civil authorities.

The PLA also reorganized its field armies (main-force armies) into group armies to increase its capability to wage combined-arms warfare. Breaking with the previously triangular organization of military units, the group armies combined formerly independent arms or services into a comprehensive combat unit. Group armies consisted of infantry and mechanized infantry divisions, tank divisions or brigades, and a number of artillery, antichemical, air defence, engineer, signal, reconnaissance, electronic countermeasure, and logistics troops. In the late 1980s, some group armies also had helicopter, air support, or naval units.

In 1987 PLA strength was about 3 million. Ground forces numbered about 2.1 million—the world's largest standing army; the Navy about 350,000—including those assigned to Naval Aviation, Coastal Defence Forces, and Marine Corps; the Air Force about 390,000; and the Strategic Missile Force about 100,000. The PLA was supported by an estimated 4.3 million basic (armed and trained) militia and 6 million ordinary (poorly armed and trained) militia. According to the 1984 Military Service Law, the militia, which was being combined with a newly developed reserve system, and the People's Armed Police Force also formed part of the Chinese armed forces. In 1986 reserve forces were included officially in the organizational system.

Doctrine, Strategy, and Tactics

From the early 1950s until the mid-1970s, people's war remained China's military doctrine. The PLA's force structure, however, which came to include nuclear weapons as well as artillery, combat aircraft, and tanks, did not reflect the concept of people's war. In the late 1970s, Chinese military leaders began to modify PLA doctrine, strategy, and tactics under the rubric of "people's war under modern conditions."

This updated version of people's war lacked a systematic definition, but it permitted Chinese military leaders to pay tribute to Mao's military and revolutionary legacy while adapting military strategy and tactics to the needs of modern conventional and nuclear warfare. Elaborating on Mao's concept of active Defence—tactically offensive action with a defensive strategy—Chinese strategy was designed to defeat a Soviet invasion before it could penetrate deeply into China. Chinese strategists envisaged a forward Defence, that is, near the border, to prevent attack on Chinese cities and industrial facilities, particularly in north and northeast China. Such a Defence-in-depth would require more positional warfare, much closer to the border, in the initial stages of a conflict. This strategy downplayed the people's war strategy of "luring in deep" in a protracted war, and it took into account the adaptations in strategy and tactics necessitated by technological advances in weaponry. The PLA emphasized military operations using modernized, combined arms tactics for the dual purpose of making the most effective use of current force structure and of preparing the armed forces for more advanced weaponry in the future.

The doctrine of "people's war under modern conditions" also incorporated the use of strategic and tactical nuclear weapons. China's own nuclear forces, which developed a second-strike capability in the early 1980s, provided Beijing with a credible, if minimum, deterrent against Soviet or United States nuclear attack. China repeatedly has vowed never to use nuclear weapons first, but it has promised retaliation against a nuclear attack. Chinese strategists also evinced an interest in tactical nuclear weapons, and the PLA has simulated battlefield use of such weapons in offensive and defensive exercises.

Education and Training

Reforms in training and education constituted an important part of the military modernization program in the 1980s. Senior officials recognized that improving the military skills and raising the education levels of both officers and troops were necessary prerequisites for the utilization of more advanced weaponry and the conduct of combined-arms operations. The PLA leadership focused education reforms on the military academy system and altered training to emphasize the officer corps, mechanized warfare, and combined arms operations.

Revitalization of the Military Academy System

Beginning in 1978, the PLA began to revive the military academy system, which the Cultural Revolution had devastated. By 1984 the system had over 100 institutions and consisted of two kinds of schools: command schools and specialized technical training centres. The PLA increased funding for military education, incorporated the study of foreign military experiences into the curriculum, and expanded contacts with foreign military academies. The rejuvenation of the military academies highlighted the emphasis placed on officer training. The PLA stipulated that most new officers should be military academy graduates, set minimum education levels for all officers, and established special classes to help officers meet those standards. Education and military academy training thus became criteria for promotion, in addition to seniority, performance, and experience.

In 1986 the PLA introduced three measures that further strengthened the military academy system. First, at the top level the PLA's Military Academy, Political Academy, and Logistics Academy merged to form the National Defence University, China's senior military training and research institution. Second, a new, three-level training system for command officers was announced, whereby command officers would receive regular training at junior, middle, and higher military command academies. Third, noncommissioned officer (NCO) training entered the military academy system with the establishment of a naval academy for petty officers and an air force NCO academy and the creation of NCO classes in over forty ground force academies.

Training Reforms

Before the military modernization program began, PLA training was highly politicized and emphasized single-unit infantry troop training. Training reforms started with the depoliticization of training, whereby troops spent 80 percent of their time on military activities and 20 percent on political training. The scope of training then changed to concentrate on training officers capable of directing combined-arms warfare. Improved military education in the rejuvenated military academies provided some of this officer training. In addition, large-scale combined-arms exercises, which served to raise officer capabilities in commanding and coordinating combined-arms operations under combat conditions, occurred on a regular basis. These exercises stressed Defence against attacking tanks, paratroopers, and aircraft and on occasion involved the simulated use of tactical nuclear weapons. The PLA also began using simulation equipment in training and in 1985 held its first completely simulated combat exercise. In 1986 the PLA training system underwent further reforms that complemented changes in military organization. A combined-arms tactical training center was created for training the newly formed group armies (former field armies) on a rotational basis. The training center coordinated group army exercises and utilized laser devices and simulation equipment in its training. The PLA also established a systematic training program for new recruits, replacing the old system in which inductees received basic training in their units. Under the new system, before new recruits were assigned to PLA units, they completed four months of training by a training regiment attached to a group army. The training regiments also trained squad leaders.

Personnel

Defence modernization brought changes to military personnel policies and practices. Personnel reforms emphasized upgrading the quality of recruits, improving conditions of service, altering promotion practices to stress professional competence over seniority or political loyalty, and providing new uniforms and insignia. The 1984 Military Service Law codified some of the changes in personnel policies and set the stage for further changes, such as the restoration of ranks.

Recruitment

The Military Service Law provided the legal basis for conscription, and it combined compulsory and voluntary service. All citizens between eighteen and twenty-two, regardless of sex, nationality, profession, family background, religion, or level of education, were obliged to perform military service. Almost 10 million men reached conscription age each year, but the PLA chose less than 10 percent of those eligible. A very small number of women were inducted annually. In the 1980s the PLA attempted to upgrade the quality of its inductees by changing recruiting practices. The PLA previously drew its recruits from rural youth of politically acceptable families. But the Military Service Law, the introduction of rural reforms offering greater economic opportunities for rural youth, and the PLA's requirements for higher educational levels caused recruitment to draw more recruits from better educated urban youth. Officers were drawn from military academy graduates; enlisted men and women who completed officer training in officially designated institutions and passed officer fitness tests; graduates of universities and special technical secondary schools; and civilian cadres and technical personnel recruited by nonmilitary units in the PLA. As a result of the new conscription and officer recruitment practices, the level of education in the PLA was much higher than that of the general population.

Conditions of Service

The Military Service Law stipulated changes in conditions of service. Compulsory terms of service were three years for the ground forces and four for the Air Force and Navy. Soldiers could elect another term of one or two years in the ground forces and one year in the Navy and Air Force. After completing five years of compulsory service, a soldier could switch to voluntary service and could serve an eight-to twelve-year term until the age of thirty five. The conscription law also made provisions for limited preferential treatment of service personnel and their families. However, military service was regarded by some as a hardship because of low pay, poor food, lowered marriage prospects, and difficulties in finding jobs after demobilization. To alleviate the unattractive aspects of military service and to help local economic development, the PLA instituted a program of dual-use training, whereby soldiers learned skills useful in civilian life in addition to military training.

Promotion

In the late 1970s, the PLA began altering its promotion practices to reflect the new emphasis on professional competence. Previously, there had been no retirement system in effect, and junior and field-grade officers had remained at their posts for many years with little opportunity for advancement. When promotion occurred, it was based on seniority, political rectitude, or a patron-client relationship. Officers advanced up a single chain of command, remaining in the same branch or service for life. In 1978 the PLA reinstituted the retirement system established by the 1955 Military Service Law and promulgated officer service regulations, which set retirement ages for military officers. Thus the PLA began a two-pronged effort to retire older officers and to promote younger, better educated, professionally competent officers. Older officers, including many over seventy years of age, were offered generous retirement packages as inducements to retire. The PLA also formulated new promotion standards that set minimum education levels for officers and emphasized education in military academies as a criterion for promotion. Officers below the age of forty had to acquire a secondary-school education by 1990 or face demotion. Furthermore, past promotion practices were to be discarded in favor of greater emphasis on formal training, higher education levels, and selection of more officers from technical and noncombat units. With the reduction in force begun in 1985, professional competence, education, and age became criteria for demobilization as well as promotion. By 1987 the PLA's promotion practices were based more on merit than they had been a decade earlier; nevertheless, political rectitude and *guanxi* (personal connections) continued to play an important role in promotion, and no centralized personnel system had been established.

Ranks, Uniforms, and Insignia

The 1984 Military Service Law also stipulated that military ranks would be reintroduced to the PLA. Military leaders justified the restoration of ranks as improving organization, discipline, and morale and facilitating coordinated operations among different arms and services, thus serving to modernize and regularize the military. The PLA's experience in the 1979 Sino-Vietnamese border war, in which the absence of ranks led to confusion on the battlefield, was another factor leading to the restoration of ranks. However, the rank system was not immediately implemented because "preparatory work" still needed to be done. Implementation was delayed by disputes in higher echelons in the PLA over who would receive what rank and by the long process of reducing the size of the military. In mid-1987 the PLA still had not restored its system of ranks. The ranks for officers reportedly were to be based on the 1955 rank system, which included one supreme marshal and ten marshals at the very top. Ground force and Air Force ranks were to be senior general,

general, lieutenant general, major general, senior colonel, colonel, lieutenant colonel, major, senior captain, captain, first lieutenant, and second lieutenant. Naval officer ranks were to be senior admiral, admiral, vice admiral, rear admiral, senior captain, captain, commander, lieutenant commander, senior lieutenant, junior lieutenant, and ensign.

Although the restoration of ranks was delayed, in 1985 PLA personnel were issued new uniforms and service insignia. Officers at and above regimental level wore woolen and blended woolen uniforms; officers at battalion level and below and soldiers wore cotton uniforms. All personnel wore visored military caps, new collar insignia, and shoulder boards. The cap emblem was round with a design of five stars and the ideographs *bayi* (August 1st, the anniversary of the 1927 Nanchang Uprising) surrounded by wheat ears and cog wheels. Uniform colors were olive green for the ground forces; dark blue in winter, and a white jacket and dark blue trousers in summer for the Navy; and an olive green jacket and dark blue trousers for the Air Force. Officer jackets had epaulets and golden buttons with the five-star and August 1st design. Collar badges were red for the ground forces, black for the Navy, and blue for the Air Force. Personnel of the intraservice Strategic Missile Force wore distinctive patches but otherwise retained the uniform of their parent service. The new uniforms replaced the baggy, green fatigue uniforms that had made it hard to distinguish between officers and soldiers. The change in uniforms served the needs of military modernization by raising morale, strengthening discipline, and facilitating command and organization.

3

Indian Army 2020

A nation's military is a major but unstated factor in international Realpolitik, howsoever moderated and underplayed, in acknowledgement of international sensitivities. Nevertheless, its existence and capabilities percolate into the public domain, domestic as well as international, and its presence, even unstated, becomes a background presence, which provides a sense of hard-edge backup to the national establishment for undertaking effective front line diplomacy. It is, therefore, essential in the national interest that the armed forces are upgraded and updated on an ongoing basis, something which governments have been traditionally loath to acknowledge and undertake, the Indian government perhaps more so than others in this respect. Historically, it is to the credit of the Indian Army that it has fulfilled its role as an organ of the state, and undertaken all assigned tasks successfully, except in the Sino-Indian border war of 1962 and reclamation of Indian territory in the Aksai Chin plateau, on the Sino-Indian border in Tibet, for which reasons have to be sought elsewhere. It has functioned effectively in every type of role, in spite of the general lack of a supportive government environment by way of adequate finances, resources, equipment, personnel policies, or higher political direction. The modernization and upgradation of the Indian Army to function in a 21st century environment is, therefore, a priority task for the present as well as successive governments to undertake.

The new millennium opened literally with a thunderclap, as the world witnessed America's new Day of Infamy on live media, with the demolition of the World Trade Centre in New York on

September 11, 2001, in an air-assault by Al Qaida fidayeen. In his speech to the Congress on September 20, 2001, President George W Bush proclaimed America's 'War on Terror'. In its aftermath, the tensions of the recently terminated Cold War appeared to revive in a different manifestation, which mutated almost seamlessly into the new conflict that spread rapidly outwards, and impacted Afghanistan and Iraq. In fact, the War on Terror seems to have replaced the earlier geo-political confrontation of the Cold War with another worldwide confrontation, this one an ethno-religious clash of cultures (if not of entire civilizations) between neo-con America and Jihadi Islam.

The doctrines of pre-emptive intervention and regime change by the military superpower and high intensity holy war by non-state terrorists are set to overwhelmingly shape the security environment of the new millennium, and will dominate India's perceptions and security stances in at least the middle term future. Numerous local and regional extensions and variations of the conflict have sprung up all over the world, extending from immigrant communities in Europe, all the way to Indonesia, Thailand, Malaysia and the Philippines in South East Asia, traversing enroute hotspots in Russia and Eastern Europe, Chechnya, Central Asia, Afghanistan, Pakistan, Kashmir, as well as other parts of India, and Bangladesh, with branch lines to Chinese Turkestan along the Silk Route. Some of these new wars have subsumed ongoing confrontations, others are taking the form of proxy wars, sub-ethnic insurgencies, terrorism, narcotics, organized crime, illegal migration, environmental poaching, as also high intensity flare-ups over disputed borders, and perhaps with others yet to come (who knows?) involving exclusive economic zones, oil, seabed and water resources. India's relationships with the Peoples' Republic of China, as well as its strategic surrogate Pakistan, have generally been adversarial, but now repairs to these traditional contentions are being attempted. But any attempts at reconstruction will have to take into account the wider context of the new realities of the War on Terror.

To India, these realities will include, amongst others, the massive and seemingly unstoppable 'peaceful rise' of the Middle Kingdom immediately next door, with its unspoken but implicit connotations of military super-capabilities in the not too distant future, the come-back of Islamic jihad in South and South East Asia, the emergence of 'Maobadi' militias in Nepal on India's doorstep, closely interlinked with their fraternal confederates of the newly consolidated Communist Party of India (Maoist) and other Naxalite affiliates in a nascent Compact Revolutionary Zone, which reaches deep into the Indian heartland. India, shining or not, is nevertheless on its way to be an emerging power whose pluralistic society is under direct attack by the new conflict, which demands the closest attention and can be ignored only at peril; whose ultimate dimensions are as yet unclear. Till that time, there are only wide open questions, difficult, if not impossible to forecast from the present perspective.

Thus, at one extreme, putting a way-out positive spin on the current trends in Indo-Pak and Sino-Indian relations, the possibilities of turning swords into ploughshares appear endless. For instance, with the current upsurge in people-to-people relationships between India and Pakistan and general improvement in the civil environment, could for example a South Asian Federation become a practical reality in 2020, just as the European Union is today, (including, necessarily, resolution of the Kashmir and Siachen problems to the satisfaction of all parties concerned)? Would such a solution emerge as a match winner, or would there still remain some warm embers of national interest, pride and resentments, which would continue to smolder, perhaps requiring to be extinguished later? Would an international border held only by paramilitary forces replace the Line of Control and Actual Ground Position Line?

Ultimately, what impact would all these developments have on the force structure of Army 2020 in terms of mechanized and holding forces for plains and desert warfare; holding forces for the Line of Control and Actual Ground Position Line, and also the ditch-cum-bund and other Defence assets and infrastructure painstakingly and painfully developed along the entire front with Pakistan? Also, if and when outstanding issues with the Peoples' Republic of China are resolved on a permanent basis, what would be the end results for forces holding the Line of Actual Control in Northern, Central and Eastern Commands, right from the Kara

Koram Pass in extreme northern Ladakh down to Kibithoo in extreme eastern Arunachal Pradesh? On a similar spin, if the internal security situation also improves to the same extent, will civil administrations manage without continuous recourse to the Army as at present, reducing these unpleasant, thankless, and irksome commitments in aid to civil power, perhaps with substantial savings in manpower in terms of the Rashtriya Rifles? Therefore, at the politically upbeat end of the scale, with conflicts, both domestic and international, being resolved, Army 2020 might well evolve into a minimalist organization, lean perhaps to the point of cadaverousness, based primarily on high technology and special forces, supported by airpower, which many today see as a classical model for the new world.

However, there are also more down market perceptions too, whose darker prognoses cannot be totally set aside. Amongst these are the massive and seemingly unstoppable 'peaceful rise' of the Middle Kingdom immediately next door, with its unarticulated but implicit connotations of military super-capabilities; the come-back of Islamic jihad on India's doorstep in the Islamic Republic of Pakistan, Afghanistan, Bangladesh and Southeast Asia; the emergence of 'Maobadi' militias in Nepal on India's immediate doorstep, with a corresponding Compact Revolutionary Zone of their fraternal confederates, the People's War Group established deep within the Indian heartland; could all suggest a 'Future History' in much deeper tones of sepia.

Taking an in-between perception of the two extremes, it would be realistic to assume that the world would perhaps continue to remain an uncertain and uneasy place, where the only certainty would be uncertainty. Threats would be undefined, unexpected and also omnipresent, in shapes and forms, which cannot be visualised clearly at present. Army 2020 will, therefore, have to be designed to function in an amorphous security environment with capabilities to operate across the entire spectrum of conflict from low intensity warfare to the ultimate unthinkable Kurukshetra of nuclear conflict.

Except in the unlikely event of a major reversal turnabout in India's traditional political worldview within the next decade or so, the role of the Defence forces in 2020 will remain unchanged from the traditional one of homeland Defence – protection of the territorial integrity of Indian territory by land, sea, or air. This will be consistent with the perceptions that all governments in office, regardless of their political philosophies or domestic policy, have taken all along since Independence, in which international military alignments through power blocs, mutual Defence treaties, or major expeditionary commitments overseas (except of course on United Nations missions) have been eschewed.

However, the perception of homeland Defence has never passively ruled out pro-active or pre-emptive interventions within or outside the country, wherever considered necessary in the national interest, as have been undertaken on numerous occasions earlier by the Indian Army. This cannot, and indeed must not be wished away or forgotten. Military intervention in the national interest, to consolidate and nurture the fledgling nation, commenced almost immediately after Independence and through the early years of the Republic, with operations in the (then) princely states of Kashmir, Hyderabad, and Junagadh. The historical process continued with the assimilation of Portuguese colonies in 1961, absorption of the Sikkim Monarchy, assistance and support to the brutalized people of East Pakistan – now Bangladesh – in 1971, attempted peacemaking in Sri Lanka in 1987-1990, the Maldives in 1988, or more recently, the carefully harmonised anti-insurgency operations with Myanmar and Bhutan against separatist elements along contiguous border areas. Similar contingencies may arise in the future as well, and there is no need to be in any manner apologetic about them, though some ventures can certainly be criticized for incoherent political direction and poor military planning. In addition, the Indian Army has also very successfully displayed its capabilities for operations other than war (OOW) in these regions by way of training missions and assistance in natural calamities, whenever requested by the host countries. Such contingencies could very well arise in future too.

Viewed from the final months of 2004, Indian Army 2020 is only fifteen years ahead on the timeline, within the current 15-Year Defence Perspective, and not really all that distant at all in terms of successive Five Year Defence Plans. The building of the New Army is, therefore, already in progress with the ongoing

Tenth, and the future Eleventh, Twelfth and Thirteenth Five Year Defence Plan series. If these proceed even approximately on schedule (which incidentally, has almost never been the case!), Army 2020 should be in place within the Thirteenth Five Year Defence Plan (2017-2022).

But Defence planning has traditionally been low on the scale of national priorities, with myriad hurdles in the process of planning, decision-making and production. Political decision-making and effective follow through action by the government have been glacial in terms of results actually achieved.

Desperate attempts to expedite the process, even during national emergencies like Kargil 1999, ultimately backfired into low grade, ill informed and crudely partisan political confrontations around the Tehalka sting operation, the CAG Report, and the so-called Coffin-gate scandals, which rocked the political firmament of the time.

Their spill-over effect severely inhibited the official decision-making process, and perhaps damaged it beyond repair. The evolution of Army 2020 will have to live with this and evolve as best as it can. The crux of the issue, as always, will be sustained availability of adequate finances.

Finance ministers controlling the nation's purse strings (including in the current dispensation) generally do not look benignly on resources diverted from the national kitty towards Defence, and dole them out grudgingly at the best of times. Plans for Indian Army 2020, integrated into the overall perspective of the Defence Services, are therefore, critically interlinked with the national effort in terms of resources likely to be allotted, as also to timely political and financial decision making.

This is likely to be a fluctuating process, very much influenced by the course of geo-political and economic developments, as well as political philosophies and attitudes of future governments regarding adequate and sustained financial support for Defence planning. All these imponderables would impact heavily on the Defence Plan series, and therefore, on the profile of Army 2020, but in what manner and to what effect, remain questions only the future can answer. Meanwhile, an almost continuous flow of revolutions in military affairs has been underway for over two decades now, which should certainly be incorporated into the profile of Army 2020.

The Indian Army has traditionally been manpower intensive, which many modern intellects disparage as a hangover from the Second or even the First World War era. But it must be understood that these apparent anachronisms linger on even at present, due to certain economic as well as operational compulsions. At one level, the inability of the Indian Army to shed manpower is due to lack of resources to replace it with high-end technologies, primarily because of the generally low priority accorded to Defence planning, and inadequate resource allotment.

In the absence of equipment, manpower intensive alternatives, somehow have to persist almost by default. The unsatisfactory hybridization, which created the current Reorganized Army Plains Infantry Division – RAPID – is a good example of this. In this case, the divisional structure was reduced by a brigade, on the assumption that manpower thus reduced would be replaced by force multipliers and surveillance.

Needless to say, the Army waited for these in vain, because the financial resources for the technological makeover were simply never allotted. It is to be seen whether these difficulties will persist in future as well. By present indications, it seems that they would still be around for quite some time.

At another level, mountain and jungle terrain in the northern and eastern regions combined with extensive deployments on counter insurgency, established operational imperatives for organizations with adequate manpower. Here, sheer technology, though helpful, was not the dominating factor, and there was no substitute for numbers of well-trained 'boots on the ground', as American forces in Iraq are painfully learning the hard way. So, in New Age organizations, manpower versus technology will have to be implemented carefully and judiciously. At present, there is an intense debate within the military and the rest of the strategic community on the shape of warfare in the future, and the type of army required to meet future threats. Will a traditional conventional army, even if technologically upgraded, be adequate to handle these when they occur? Now that the process of reconstruction is already under way, what kind of an Army 2020 should emerge at the end of it? How and to what extent will it or can it reflect the operational compulsions of that future time? The answer to these and other similar questions must be clearly understood, which is that Indian Army 2020 must retain the basic configuration of a conventional army, and not be mutated by radical doctrinal surgery into some kind of heavy constabulary.

The New Army must possess integral multi-role operational capabilities across the entire spectrum of conflict, whether nuclear, conventional, or low intensity. Any undue emphasis or insistence on a tailor-made orientation focusing primarily on any particular level of warfare would be dangerously misplaced.

To effectively undertake its task of land warfare for homeland Defence, India requires a large army, with an armory ranging from land-launched strategic weapons at the high intensity end of the spectrum, to special operations forces at the low intensity end. The middle levels will continue to be bulked out by conventional forces, with adequate manpower – armor, artillery, infantry, as well as integral army aviation, backed up by the requisite support and logistics elements. The basic organizations of the Army require extensive technological upgradation, but are otherwise stable and time-tested under a wide variety of environments. They are flexible enough for structured regrouping for various contingencies. Changes to the existing pattern should be introduced only after careful deliberation.

Amongst other emerging factors are strategic weapons systems, which are still a comparatively recent acquisition and whose command and control methodologies are yet to be fully stabilized. The Strategic Forces Command has been recently established as the designated inter-services agency for overall management of these high-end assets. The new organization is logical and was originally scheduled to function directly under the much awaited Chief of Defence Staff, but since this appointment is yet to be implemented, it has now been placed de facto under the Chiefs of Staff Committee, through the Integrated Defence Staff. It still remains to be seen how the final shape of the new

Command emerges, i.e. whether in the classical sense of a separate command with direct control of operational, logistics, and personnel, or as a functional command for operational employment of dedicated strategic components held with each individual Service. In the Indian context, perhaps the latter would be more practicable. However, whatever the command structure model ultimately adopted, it must also be optimally calibrated to fulfil the important aspect of 'command satisfaction' within its hierarchy, an aspect not often considered, or, if so, ignored or disregarded. Each Service operates in its own physical environment, and land-based strategic systems are within the Army's domain. Army 2020 must incorporate an integral component of strategic forces. which can be operationally emplaced under the Strategic Forces Command.

A word about Army Aviation, which must be another vital area of focus for Army 2020. Airpower dominates the battlefield, and must be employed to achieve maximum synergy. However, in the inter-services context, this eminently profound article of faith has been allowed to acquire an extended meaning of single service ownership of all air assets. To the Army, airpower is essentially firepower, surveillance and target acquisition from the sky in close or distant support of ground operations extending up to the operational depth of the tactical battle area. Given the advances in technology, these tasks can now be undertaken by manned as well as unmanned flight platforms, covering a range of unmanned air vehicles / remotely piloted vehicles (UAV / RPV), ground launched precision-guided missiles, and rotary wing ground combat aviation (attack and assault helicopters). These aerial platforms operate primarily in the environment of the land battle, either independently or in a supplementary role to the air battle, often without diverting high-end airpower from its primary tasks. Army 2020 will have to build up integral air resources for itself, particularly in rotary winged combat aircraft (attack and assault helicopters, airborne early warning, communications and medevac) integral to Army Aviation, which must become the primary agency of rotary wing airpower.

But for all this to be effective within the given timeframe raises the vital issue of the attitudinal and cultural reorientation of the Defence forces into a synergized joint-service environment. While acknowledging the supreme importance of individual Service identities and aspirations, by 2020, the Indian Army individually, as well as the Defence Forces collectively, must no longer be allowed to function as independent disconnected entities, without the required inter-service synergy for fullest exploitation of their respective capabilities. Army 2020 will, therefore, have to be organized, equipped, trained and culturally energized to take its place within an operational triad in conjunction with maritime and aerospace power, functionally interlinked through an integrated politico-military Higher Defence Organization, and a common framework of joint-service doctrines and joint command structures. It takes three to tango, but nevertheless unless the joint services environment is simultaneously developed and implemented, Army 2020 (as indeed Navy 2020 or Air Force 2020) cannot be employed to its fullest capability and effect. In some senses, provision of an enabling environment of jointmanship (a clumsy term!) and stamping them on the individual ethos and culture of each Service may well be the most challenging task, which should be accorded an overall priority higher than many other issues. In this context, the major area of reconstruction of Indian Army 2020 (and the other Services) might well be in reform of traditional mindsets and approach to battle.

2020 : Indian Army

National security, is that ambience, in which a nation is able to protect and promote its national values, pursue its national interests and aspirations, in spite of, or, in the absence of, external or internal threats, real or perceived. Threats to national security may impact on any aspect of a nation's life, ranging from its territorial integrity and internal cohesion to its economy, political structures and institutions, diplomacy, national leadership, national character, morale and so on. The armed forces of a nation have a vital role to play in meeting these threats.

India's National Interests

India's national interests, simply stated, are as follows :-

- National sovereignty.

- Unity and integrity of the country.
- Democratic and secular polity.
- Economic development.
- Social and economic justice.
- Favourable world order.
- Preservation and promotion of our values.

Our Strategic Vision

Nations adopt a national strategy in order to attain their national interests or goals. Clarity of strategic vision is very important if the national strategy is to take the nation on an optimal course to its desired national objectives. Let us, briefly, examine our strategic vision.

We are one of the oldest civilizations on Earth. Nearly, a sixth of the human race is Indian. Our country occupies a strategic location on the southern promontory of the Asian land mass and dominates large expanses of the Indian Ocean including the routes to the oil rich Gulf region, South East Asia and the Orient. These intrinsic attributes qualify, indeed demand, that India be a major player at the world stage.

By tradition, India has been a peace-loving and responsible nation. It has abjured aggression, espoused the doctrine of 'Ahimsa' or non-violence, led the non-aligned group of nations and played a constructive role as a member of the United Nations. This tradition clearly suggests that India should aspire to become a benign and moral superpower, rather than one, whose brute strength or wealth alone, confer on it, its place under the sun. Any examination of our strategic environment must be carried out against the backdrop of our strategic vision and the long term plans and strategies needed to realise that vision. By such an examination, we shall be able to predict the strategic environment of the decades ahead, and arrive at the appropriate force structure and equipment profile for our Army of the future.

Aim

The aim of this chapter is to visualise the likely national security environment in 2020 with special reference to the threats and challenges that may confront us at that time, and arrive at the most appropriate force structure and equipment profile for the Indian Army of 2020.

While the focus in this chapter is on the Army, it must not be construed that the Army can fulfil its missions without the active partnership of the Navy and the Air Force. Joint, or preferably, integrated tri-service functioning in war and peace will be an essential pre-requisite for success in all our operations. With this background, let us examine the geo-strategic environment we might face in 2020.

The Geo-Strategic Environment

Two major events, roughly a decade apart, have played a major role in shaping the current geo-strategic environment. The first being the demise of the Soviet Union. It brought the Cold War to an end, and conferred on the USA, an unchallenged pre-eminence in the world as the sole superpower.

The second was the '9-11 Event'-the 11th September 2001 terrorist attacks on targets in Washington DC and New York. This impelled the USA to declare 'War on Terrorism', and attack Afghanistan and Iraq with a 'coalition of like-minded countries', with the purpose of ousting their regimes, which were sponsors of terrorist groups like Al Quaeda and were hostile to the USA. The USA believed that Iraq was in possession of weapons of mass destruction (WMD).

The impact of these two events are now being clearly felt in international affairs and by all indications, appear to be long lasting. We need to take note of the following major ramifications, which are specially relevant to India :-

- The USA has become hegemonic. Her style of diplomacy is increasingly becoming peremptory and coercive.
- The UN has been sidelined by the USA, which, acts at will, ignoring the need for UN's sanction.
- The USA has adopted the doctrine of 'Preemptive Military Intervention'. In consonance with this doctrine-threats, whether real and present or, perceived, are not allowed to mature, by use of military force.

- The USA has drawn a list of countries, which are 'of concern' to it. Of these, it has dealt with Afghanistan and Iraq. North Korea and Iran await similar treatment by the superpower. Recently, India has voted in favour of a USA backed resolution against Iran possibly to secure military materials, nuclear technology and fuel for civilian purposes. If India resiles from her pro-USA stance in the late November 2005 voting, the USA may deny its expectations. This would amount to dictating India's foreign policy.
- China is neither amenable to coercion nor susceptible to being 'contained'. Besides, because North Korea is a protégé of China, the latter has a major role in USA's dealings with that country. The USA has also economically engaged China, as it provides a large market for US manufactured goods. The USA believes too, that as the USA-China trade gets increasingly intertwined, the likelihood of an armed conflict between the two will correspondingly reduce.
- The European Union, despite reservations on the part of some constituents, is for purposes of *realpolitik* pro-USA.
- Russia, because of her present economic debility, is supporting the USA or, at least, not opposing her. It may become more independent in its attitude as its economy recovers, a process that has already begun.
- Pakistan is a 'major non-NATO ally' of the USA and also its frontline state for the 'War on Terrorism'. The US has troops and aircraft on Pakistan's soil. It has been permitted to set up bases in return for huge subventions and to bail out Pakistan from the brink of a near-collapse economic situation. In effect, Pakistan has become a client state of the USA with a less than independent foreign policy.
- Terrorism, religious fundamentalism, nuclear and missile technology proliferation are pressing concerns for the US. It believes that these could ultimately pose danger to its 'homeland', something about which the USA is hypersensitive, or, even paranoid.

These are some of the ramifications of the two events i.e. the Soviet collapse and the 9/11 event, which shall continue to influence international relations in the next two decades or more. However, by 2020, some changes would have taken place with regard to the circumstances of the world's principal nations. These are enumerated below :-

- The USA will continue to be the preeminent power. Nevertheless, her 'edge' over China would have reduced to a small margin.
- China would be increasingly inclined to join issue with the USA, taking into account its envisaged near-superpower status. However, she would not risk her new found prosperity by being over-assertive with the USA and thus risk war.
- India would have caught up with China and achieved parity with China in many areas, but not military.
- Pakistan will continue to be the USA's client state, and in case the latter so presses, she may even enter into a comprehensive peace agreement with India. Otherwise, Pakistan would prefer to keep tensions alive with India in order to extract concessions and benefits from both China and the USA who will want an economically resurgent India to be reined in.
- The USA's 'War on Terrorism' may prove to be endless as, though the enemy has been rightly identified, the means being applied are all wrong, indeed, self-defeating.
- Radical religion will pose problems for the entire world as such. As radicalism flourishes in less developed countries, by 2020, there would also be a large number of very poor countries with radicalism well entrenched.

After this brief estimate of the geo-strategic environment in, 2020, let us turn to India's internal security environment.

India's Internal Security Environment, 2020

India is a rapidly developing country with a GDP growth of seven percent. It has a huge reserve of technical manpower and strong liberal political culture, a youthful population more than half of which will be below 30 years of age in 2020. It also has strong and apolitical armed forces. Our present concerns, which may persist in future are as under:-

- The present rate of population growth is 1.6 percent. It is imperative to bring it down to one percent by 2020-2025.
- The political culture in the country has deteriorated over the years. Communalism, sectarianism, regional parochialism, and sub-nationalism are on the rise. There is growing criminalisation of politics and a culture of 'vote banks' has taken root. Politicisation of the bureaucracy and the police, is well-established. The Armed Forces have, so far, been able to remain insulated from politics. Unless these evils are overcome, in 2020, we may have a nation whose internal security environment will be extremely unhealthy.
- Distributive justice with regard to sharing of revenues and the fruits of development is an imperative, if radical left movements, currently active in the country, are to be eliminated by 2015 or so.
- The separatist movements in the North-East and J & K must be amicably resolved.
- Black money and drug trafficking must be put to an end as they not only ruin the economy but also corrupt the youth.

Attention to the above areas of concern will enable India to achieve desired internal security by 2020. Let us now identify the threats and challenges India is likely to face in 2020.

Threats and Challenges to India : 2020

Military Threats

- India is not likely to face a military threat from the USA or China because of its strength, both military and economic.
- A medium level military threat may arise from Pakistan if it fails to make adequate economic and political progress, or, its leadership passes to radical elements, or, the country as such, fails and lapses into a state of anarchy.

- Bangladesh may pose a very low level threat if it decides to encourage demographic 'aggression' by using its over-sized armed forces in support.
- Threats of non-state groups armed with WMD could become a reality. They could be acting on their own initiative or, at the behest of a sponsor nation. This dimension of WMD would warrant war-like response from us.

Challenges. Apart from military threats, a number of non-military challenges may have to be faced by our Army in the 2020 time frame. These are as follows:-

- Human resources of appropriate quality may get drawn to the more lucrative civilian sector. The terms and conditions of service and satisfaction levels of personnel, must be made more attractive. We should also enroll more short service personnel than regular cadres to reduce pension liabilities and for better career management of officers.
- Funds allotted to the Armed Forces should be sustained at a level of three per cent of GDP for at least 12 to 15 years so as to ensure requisite modernisation and making good existing shortfalls.
- Defence Research and Development Organisation (DRDO) must be upgraded qualitatively and top quality scientists should be inducted into it. Rightfully, their expectations of pay and research facilities will be high. These must be met.
- Private sector participation in defence R & D and development of complete systems by them, must be facilitated. Government should fund their defence research projects and give them guarantees of sizeable orders to encourage their partnership with the DRDO.
- Scientific and technical manpower will be eagerly sought by other countries. To overcome this 'brain-drain', we should improve the working conditions and research facilities in our country.

- The IT driven revolution in military affairs requires that the Army 'manages' these changes in a systematic and smooth manner. We need to create an integrated force working in an 'unified battle space'; seamless communications; extensive exploitation of IT with excellent 'cyber security'; top quality space based and terrestrial surveillance systems and fully operationalised C4I2 systems. This convergence of various technologies and capabilities will bestow the forces with much enhanced force-multiplier benefits through Network Centric Warfare (NCW). We have a long way to go in this regard.
- Internal contingencies of various types could retard or block the Army's effort to achieve optimal development in the next 15 years. We need to be prepared with suitable contingency plans to overcome these 'drag' factors.

Extreme Contingencies. In the unlikely event of our prognosis being grossly in error, the following extreme contingencies could occur :-

- The USA, in a bid to prevent China from superseding her as the superpower, provokes China to a war with possible use of nuclear weapons.
- China, in frustration with the US-India Axis and to teach India a lesson, may declare war on us.
- Pakistan may join China in the war against India, or, allow to be used as a proxy to support China in a 'holding' mode.

Nature of Warfare in 2020

We have already seen that war with the USA and China (and, indeed, other advanced countries) is most unlikely. War with Pakistan may however occur, as also minor skirmishes with Bangladesh. Such engagements may have the following characteristics :-

- They will be of short duration, say, a week or less.
- Penetration in depth is unlikely to be attempted by either side.

- 'Cold Start' will be attempted whenever possible to achieve surprise and maximise gains.
- The entire border is likely to be activated with shallow thrusts, very heavy firepower and short span manoeuvres.
- Nuclear weapons may not be used; their use may, however, be threatened.
- Special Forces and coup-de-main forces will play a major role.
- Integrated action by all three services will be crucial for the enhancement of our combat power vis-à-vis the adversary's.
- Levels of technology employed in the wars will be higher than at present.
- Wars will end in stalemate, with little or no gain, and heavy losses to military as well as civilian targets.
- In the case of Bangladesh, the threat is of such a low level as to be non-serious. However in the skirmishing, the danger of casualties to unarmed civilians will be great and will need to be handled with firmness and imagination.

Vision : Indian Army: 2020

The foregoing threat assessment and the likely nature of any future war we may be required to fight, including the extreme contingencies we have listed, should give us the 'Vision' of the Indian Army, 2020. We may state this vision as follows:-"The Indian Army, 2020 will be an optimally equipped and weaponised force, with the capability to operate effectively in an integrated joint services environment, over the entire spectrum of conflict, in a regional context."

The vision statement spelt out above, is appropriate to the restrained aspirations of this huge and benign country, whose ethical values and traditions inhibit it from anything less modest than what has been stated. It also ensures that this country shall never again have to undergo the humiliation of foreign conquest, as in the past; hence the emphasis on optimal strength, under all conditions of warfare.

Role of the Indian Army

Armies are maintained by countries in order to safeguard their core values and national interests from external aggression and internal subversion. The Primary and Secondary roles of our Army are as under :-

- Primary Role. Deter external aggression and, if deterrence fails, defeat it by force.
- Secondary Role. Assist the Government in overcoming internal threats, foreign sponsored or indigenous, and aid the civil authority when requisitioned for the purpose.

Capabilities Entailed by the Role

The capabilities that the Army must posses to fulfil its role must be identified in accordance with our 'Vision' for the Army. The capabilities, thus identified are as under :-

- Deterrent Capability. The Army should be so strong in both conventional and nuclear weapons, that potential aggressors are deterred.
- War Fighting Capability. If deterrence fails, the Army should be able to fight a successful war against the enemy, over any terrain, and in conventional as well as NBC warfare situations.
- Internal Security Management Capability. The Army should be able to deal with and manage internal security situations of various types like insurgency, grave law and order situations; and also render aid to civil power, when requisitioned under various situations including disasters, both natural and man-made.
- Force Projection Capability. The Army should be capable of operating 'out-of-area' as part of an integrated task force, when ordered by the Government.
- Peace Keeping Operations Capability. The Army should be able to undertake UN Peace Keeping Missions in any part of the world and inter-operate with Army components of other countries in such operations.

Though we presently posses all these capabilities in some

measure, the desired level is yet to be realised in many areas. Resource inadequacy, lack of clear policy directions from the Government, frequent 're-thinks' on the part of the Army, failure of timely supplies of material and shoddy quality of what has been supplied, are some of the reasons attributable to the Army's inability to achieve and retain the desired level of capability at all times. Perhaps, even more important reason, is the knowledge driven Revolution in Military Affairs (RMA), which accelerates the process of obsolescence of equipment, doctrines and tactics. It is in this critical area of RMA that a lot of work needs to be done so that we can have adequate levels of the desired capabilities, at all times. Let us now examine whether the present structure of the Army needs to be altered to enable the Army to fulfil its assigned role better.

Structure of the Army : 2020

General. It is idle to claim that our organisations have 'stood the test of time and war' and, therefore, need not be tampered with. The nature of wars we are likely to face has changed. The battle zone is virtually transparent to surveillance devices. The range and lethality of weapons has increased many times over. Precision guided munitions have replaced the old area-neutralisation munitions. Means of mobility have increased. And the convergence of Information Technology, computers, all-weather sensors, communications and firepower resources has vested commanders at various levels, with unprecedented real-time knowledge of the situation as also the ability to alter it at will. These developments necessitates a review of our existing force structure.

Macro-level Restructuring. The Army has always been regretting the blunting of the 'Combat Edge' it had over its traditional adversary. The calculation of force ratios between the adversaries was hitherto done on a service to service basis-our Army versus the opponent's, our Navy and Air Force versus the opponent's. This gave us a skewed idea of the capability of our armed forces as a whole vis-à-vis our adversary. Wars are not fought service wise. All the services have to join during combat. In such a milieu, the three services should be integrated into one strong unified force with-unity of command and control, total synergy in operations, and much superior and economical employment of the resources available to the armed forces. There is bound to be great opposition to this idea, just as in the case of formation of the Andaman and Nicobar Command (ANC) in 2001-2002. There is no escaping the military logic of creating suitably constituted integrated theatre commands and functional (non-territorial) commands for the Armed Forces as a whole. The benefits that will accrue are : cohesion among the services, synergy leading to maximisation of combat power, better exploitation of the RMA brought about by C4I2 enabling Network Centric Warfare (NCW), strategic and intra-theatre flexibility in handling of resources and, above all, classic unity of effort. No specific solutions are offered for the creation of such integrated theatre commands. If the idea suggested above raises discussion on this important issue, our aim would have been achieved. Hopefully, this idea too, is NOT put into cold storage like the creation of the post of Chief of the Defence Staff!

Reorganising the Present Army for 2020. The resistance to change for macro level restructuring of India's Armed Forces, is likely to be stiff. It may, therefore, not be achievable in the 5-10 years timeframe. However, within the existing organisation of the Army some meaningful reorganisation can be brought about. The following suggestions could be considered :-

- Intelligence and surveillance organisations must be strengthened and modernised.
- Additional Special Forces (SF), patterned broadly on the present organisation, need to be raised. These units should be capable of functioning in very small groups, for prolonged periods, within or beyond the combat zone. Their tasks could include covert special reconnaissance; target specific raids; unconventional operations to organise resistance groups and conduct guerilla warfare in enemy territory; penetration of terrorist organisations for intelligence purposes; and counter-terrorism in all its manifestations including WMD. The personnel must be endowed with very high level of practical intelligence, initiative, mission orientation and excellent linguistic competence appropriate to the area where they are to operate.

- Special Rapid Action forces for offensive or reactive employment at the Corps level and an Army reserve with adequate airlift resources including for light tanks/ICVs, needs to be created.
- Information Warfare Units need to be created at each Corps to carry out psychological operations.
- An amphibious formation suitably grouped with other elements for out of area operations should be raised.
- As the proxy war and insurgencies abate, the existing RR force may be scaled down suitably and kept as a reserve force for the same tasks as before.
- Conventional forces, which are today considered to be 'holding' forces, should be enabled to take up 'cold start' offensives by grouping with them mechanised forces, airborne/ heliborne forces as the case may be. This will give the 'strike' forces a forward launch pad for their tasks.
- Strategic forces need to be built up to 'deterrent' levels against a major power like China. The more forbidding the weapon the more likely it is to deter the enemy. The nuclear arsenal must, therefore, be enlarged and diversified to include thermo-nuclear weapons. To ensure guaranteed second strike capability, submarines capable of launching thermo-nuclear weapons must be available.
- Air defence of the field force must be upgraded considerably.
- Army logistics must be improved by equipping transport units with high mobility vehicles. Heavy lift helicopter units of the Air Force should be made available to them on a guaranteed basis for training and operations.

We have suggested what could be done to better utilise the presently available forces to give us the desired capabilities. The question, whether the existing organisation of the field army into corps, division and brigades should be retained, or a more flexible organisation of 'task forces' directly controlled by a divisional or corps headquarters should be introduced, needs to be considered by the Army. The organisation so created should not only be tactically sound, it should also result in substantial savings in manpower for the Army. Overall, with a switch to the Task Force mode, significant savings of manpower can accrue even at present.

Equipment Profile

Mechanised Forces. T-90 tanks are likely to be the mainstay for the next two decades and after mid-life upgradation. The next generation of Infantry Combat Vehicles (ICV) should be in service by 2010 or so. Part of the ICVs should be wheeled. All mechanised forces should be NBC proof, better protected, and have greater speed and night fighting capability.

Artillery. Multiple Launch Rocket Systems (MLRS) with range in excess of 120 kilometers, SSMs of the Prithvi family with solid propellant, self-propelled guns (both tracked and wheeled) of the same calibre, some long range rifled mortars and a higher availability of precision guided munitions form the bulk of the Artillery 'wish list' for 2020. Better radio sets, better equipment (both radar and opto-electronic) for target acquisition and survey, upgraded computers for both gun and observer ends and advanced systems of fire direction and damage assessment are also needed. The use of remotely piloted aerial vehicles working in conjunction with long range MLRS will help shape the future battlefield in depths, hitherto not attained. It will also alter the battlefield into a non-linear one.

Infantry. The Infantry needs to be upgraded to produce very high volumes of fire using a range of weapons. Surveillance by radars and other sensors will give the Infantry added ability to 'kill' enemy tanks and other hard targets.

The next generation of ATGW should be in service by 2015, giving the Infantry greater lethality. With improved personal protective clothing, better night vision capability and the ability to shoot down attacking aircraft with section level anti aircraft guided missiles, the infantryman of Army 2020 will be a very formidable soldier indeed.

Doctrinal Changes

The following doctrinal changes/refinements are suggested for the Army in 2020:-

- Through superlative preparedness deter any country from engaging us in war.
- Every war in the future, must be fought in an integrated manner.
- Every war must be won with the fewest casualties and cost to us.
- Attack all the enemy's vulnerabilities, all at one time if possible, and create an adverse impact on his will to fight.
- Manoeuvre versus Attrition. Attrition involves heavy costs to the attacker, manoeuvre places the attackers at a relative advantage over the defender. Even in the mountains, it is only by manoeuvre that the formidable, fixed defences can be captured with the minimum cost to us. Aggressive use of airborne and heliborne/heli-landed troops in conjunction with unorthodox employment of tanks and ICVs after heavy bombardment, will enable manoeuvre in mountains.
- Leadership. Despite the vast inventory of high-tech machines and instruments available to the Army and the better educated soldier of 2020, good leaders will always be prized.

There is no mathematical exactness about when events will transpire and whether certain aspects we have assumed as being constant will actually be so or will alter radically, putting our prognosis into error. Notwithstanding this, a few points cannot be disputed. These are: India is progressing rapidly as an economic power; its natural endowments like strategic location, rich mineral resources and a large, industrious and hardy population, befit her for great power status. Its Army is large, disciplined, battle tested and renowned throughout the world for its professional quality. Such an army should be upgraded further in quality to serve India of 2020, in a befitting manner.

4

Modernisation Military Equipment of India

Agni (missile)

The Agni missile is a family of Medium to Intercontinental range ballistic missiles developed by India under the Integrated Guided Missile Development Program. As of 2008, the Agni missile family comprises three deployed variants:

1. Agni-I short range ballistic missile, 500-700 Km range.
2. Agni-II medium range ballistic missile, 2,000-3,000 Km range.
3. Agni-III intermediate range ballistic missile, 3,000-5,500 Km range.
4. There will not be an Agni-IV missile, with DRDO leapfrogging from intermediate range Agni-III to a standard ICBM possibly.
5. Agni-V intercontinental ballistic missile, 5000-6000 Km range (under development).

Agni-I was first tested at the Interim Test Range in Chandipur in 1989, and is capable of carrying a conventional payload of 1000 kg (2,200 lb) or a nuclear warhead. Agni missiles consist of one (short range) or two stages (intermediate range). These are rail and road mobile and powered by solid propellants. The Agni I has a range of 700-800 km while the Agni-II has a range of 2,000–2,500 km. They are claimed to be a part of the "credible deterrence" against China and Pakistan. The Agni-II can only reach most parts of western, central and southern China. With the successful test of Agni-III which has a range of 3500 km, it falls within the reach of most major Chinese cities, including Beijing and Shanghai.

Agni-III is the third in the Agni series of missiles. Agni-III was tested on July 9, 2006 from Wheeler island off the coast of the eastern state of Orissa. After the launch, it was reported that the second stage of the rocket had failed to separate and the missile had fallen well short of its target. Agni-III was again tested on April 12, 2007, this time successfully, from the Wheeler Island off the coast of Orissa.On May 7, 2008 India again successfully test fired this missile. This was the third consecutive test; it validated the missile's operational readiness while extending the reach of India's nuclear deterrent to most high-value targets of the nation's most likely adversaries.

It has been reported that the missile's Circular Error Probable (CEP) lies in the range of 40 meters, which, if confirmed, would make the Agni-III one of the most accurate strategic ballistic missiles of its range class in the world. This is of special significance because a highly accurate ballistic missile increases the "kill efficiency" of the weapon; it allows Indian weapons designers to use smaller yield nuclear warheads (200 Kiloton thermonuclear or boosted fission) while increase the lethality of the strike. This permits India to deploy a much larger nuclear force using less fissile/fusion material (Plutonium/Lithium Deuteride) than other Asian nuclear powers. Older, less accurate ballistic missiles, such as those deployed by earlier nuclear powers require larger yield (1-2 Megaton) warheads to achieve the same level of lethality. It has also been reported that with smaller payloads, the Agni-II can hit strategic targets well beyond 3500 km.

In May 2008 Indian scientists announced they had developed and patented a path-breaking technology that increases the range of missiles and satellite launch vehicles by at least 40%. The enhanced range is made possible by adding a special-purpose coating of chromium based material to a rocket's blunt nose cone. The material acts as a reactive-ablative coating that forms a thin low density gaseous layer at the tip of the rocket as it approaches hypersonic speeds; this super-heated gas layer reduces drag by 47% (at mach 7-8), thereby allowing range enhancements at least

40%. It has been announced that this technology will be incorporated in future Agni deployments after having undergone ranging and calibration tests.

Akash missile

Akash is India's medium range surface-to-air missile Defence system developed by the Defence Research and Development Organisation (DRDO) and Bharat Electronics Limited(BEL) as part of the Integrated Guided Missile Development Program. The missile can target aircraft up to 30 km away, at altitudes up to 18,000 m. Akash can be fired from both tracked and wheeled platforms. Akash is said to be capable of both conventional and nuclear warheads, with a reported payload of 60 kg. A nuclear warhead could potentially give the missile the capability to destroy both aircraft and warheads from ballistic missiles. The missile battery is described as being able to track and attack several targets simultaneously. An Akash battery comprises four 3D phased array radars and four launchers with three missiles each, all of which are interlinked. Each radar is able to track 16 targets simultaneously and control a launcher with 3 missiles. Hence it is reported to be able to track 64 targets and simultaneously attack any 12 of those targets at one time. The Akash system is comparable to the Patriot system, but unlike the Patriot, Akash is fully mobile and capable of protecting a moving convoy of vehicles. Like the Patriot, the Akash is really an air defence SAM which has been tested in a ballistic missile role. The system provides air defence missile coverage of 2,000km^2.

Along with India, a limited number of other countries including the US, Russia, Japan, Israel, and some EU countries have developed operational multitarget-handling surface-to-air missile systems. With the successful user trials of Akash, India has validated the technology and operational efficacy of this missile system. This system is claimed to be more accurate than the MIM-104 Patriot as it has thrust during the entire course of its flight compared to the Patriot that has thrust only for the first 12 seconds, after which the missile coasts, thus making it less accurate. Apart from that the Akash can be launched from static or mobile platforms, including a battle tank.

Development and History

The first test flight of Akash missile was conducted in 1990, with development flights up to March 1997.

Two Akash missiles intercepted two fast moving targets in simultaneous engagement mode in 2005. 3-D Central Acquisition Radar (3D-CAR) group mode performance is also fully established. The Akash Project has most expensive missile project ever undertaken by theftgfdaghof India in the 20th century. Total development costs for the missile and associated radars and systems was almost $120 million to the taxpayers.

Description of Missile

Akash is a surface-to-air missile with an intercept range of 30 km. It has a launch weight of 720 kg, a diameter of 35 cm and a length of 5.78 metres. Akash flies at supersonic speed, reaching around Mach 2.5. It can reach an altitude of 18 km can be fired from both tracked and wheeled platforms. An on-board guidance system coupled with actuator system makes the missile manoeuvrable up to 15g loads and a tail chase capability for end game engagement.

A digital proximity fuse is coupled with a 55 kg pre-fragmented warhead, while the safety arming and detonation mechanism enables a controlled detonation sequence. A self-destruct device is also integrated. It is propelled by Integrated Ramjet Rocket Engine. The use of ramjet propulsion system that enables sustained speeds without deceleration throughout its flight. The Missile has command guidance in its entire flight.

The design of the missile is somewhat similar to that of SA-6 with four long tube ramjet inlet ducts mounted mid-body between wings. For pitch/yaw control four clipped triangular moving wings are mounted on mid-body.

For roll control four inline clipped delta fins with ailerons are mounted before the tail. However, the internal schema shows a different layout with an onboard digitial computer, no Semi-active seeker, different propellant, different actuators and command guidance datalinks. The Akash carries an onboard radio-proximity fuse.

System

Each Akash battery consists of 4 self propelled Launchers (3 Akash SAMs each), a Battery Level Radar-the Rajendra, and a Command post (Battery Control Centre). 2 batteries are deployed as a Squadron (Air Force), while up to 4 form an Akash Group (Army configuration). In both configurations, an extra Group Control Centre (GCC) is added, which acts as the Command and Control HQ of the Squadron or Group. Based on a single mobile platform, GCC establishes links with Battery Control Centres and conducts air defence operations in coordination with air defence set up in a zone of operations.

For early warning, the GCC relies on the Central Acquisition Radar. However, individual batteries can also be deployed with the cheaper, 2-D BSR (Battery Surveillance Radar) with a range of over 100 km.

Each Akash battery can engage up to 4 targets. Each battery has 4 launchers with 3 missiles each, with each Rajendra able to guide 4 missiles in total, with a maximum of 2 missiles per target. Up to a maximum of 4 targets can be engaged by a typical battery with a single Rajendra if one missile is allotted per target.

Communications between the various vehicles are a combination of wireless and wired links. The entire system is designed to be set up quickly and to be highly mobile, for high survivability.

The Akash system can be deployed by rail, road or air.

Radars

The missile is guided by a phased array fire control radar called 'Rajendra' which is termed as Battery Level Radar (BLR) with a tracking range of about 60 km.. It can track 64 targets in range, azimuth and height and guide eight missiles simultaneously towards 4 targets. The Rajendra derivative on a BMP-2 chassis and to be used by the Indian Air Force is known as the Battery Level Radar-II whereas that for the Army, is based on a T-72 chassis and is known as the Battery Level Radar-III.

A single Akash missile has an 88% Probability of kill. Two

missiles can be fired, five seconds apart, to raise the Probability of Kill to 98.5%. Long range target acquisition is performed by the 3D Central Acquisition Radar (3D CAR), which is a long range surveillance radar that can track 150 targets in Track while Scan mode at a range of 180 km.

Platforms

The Army's radar and launchers are based on the T-72 chassis to accompany the Army's fast moving armoured formations. The Air Force versions use a combination of tracked and wheeled vehicle. The Air Force Akash launcher consists of a detachable trailer which is towed by an Ashok Leyland truck, and which can be positioned autonomously. Both the Army and Air Force launchers have three ready-to-fire Akash missiles each. The launchers can slew in both elevation and azimuth.

Propulsion

The Akash,like the Russian 2K12 Kub (SA-6 Gainful), utilizes an integrated ramjet-rocket propulsion system, which provides thrust for the missile throughout its entire flight. "Because this missile has an integrated ram-rocket, manoeuvrability is highest. The engine is 'on' throughout the flight. The thrust is on till the missile intercepts the target. Most other surface-to-air missiles, including the U.S. Patriot and the Russian S-300 series, use solid-fuel rocket propulsion.

Status

Each missile is expected to have starting costs below US$ 500,000, i.e. under Rs.20 million, which is less than half the cost of similar Western missiles which usually cost between US$ 1.2-1.5 million (Rs. 50-60 million) each.. It is expected that this cost will further decrease due to the economies of scale achieved as production ramps up.

Indian Air Force

In December 2007, the Indian Air Force completed user trials for this missile. The trials, which were spread over ten days were declared successful after the missile hit the target on five occasions.

Multiple targets handling capability of Akash weapon system was demonstrated by live firing in C4I environment. Before the ten day trial at Chandipur, ECCM Evaluation tests were carried out at Gwalior Air force base and mobility trials were carried out in Pokhran. The IAF had evolved the user Trial Directive to verify the Akash's consistency. The following trials were conducted: Against low flying near range target, long range high altitude target, crossing and approaching target and ripple firing of two missiles from the same launcher against a low altitude receding target. The Indian Air force was satisfied with the performance of Akash after extensive flight trials and has decided to induct the weapon system. An order for two squadrons were placed initially, with these being inducted in 2009. The IAF found the missile performance to be satisfactory and was expected to place orders for 16 more launchers to form 2 more squadrons for India's northeast theater. On March 30, 2009 Tata Power's Strategic Electronics Division (Tata Power SED) announced that it had bagged the INR 1.82 Billion order for the 16 additional Akash launchers to be delivered in the next 33 months. However, in January 2010 it was revealed that the Indian Air Force had ordered for six additional squadrons (48 launchers, 750 missiles) of the Akash system. The Indian Air Force (IAF) ordered the additional 750 Akash medium-range surface-to-air missiles (SAMs) from state-run defence behemoth Bharat Electronics Ltd (BEL) at a cost of Rs 42.79 billion ($925 million).

More orders are expected from the Indian Army in addition to the above orders. IAF orders may also rise as it phases out its Pechoras and if the Indo-Israeli JV to develop a MRSAM (Medium Range SAM) for the IAF continues to be put on hold, while a similar program for the Indian Navy proceeds unimpeded.

In February 2010, the Indian Air Force accepted the Akash missile system as a substantial part of its arsenal, raising orders to eight squadrons of the type.

Indian Army

After long delays, the Indian Army has warmed up to the Akash missile, and is considering ordering several Akash squadrons for its strike forces.

Other

It was also reported that Malaysia had shown interest in purchasing the Akash missile system.

Astra missile

Astra is an active radar homing Beyond visual range air to air missile (BVRAAM) or a so called Beyond Visual Range missile developed by Defence Research and Development Organisation (DRDO), India. This is the first air-to-air missile developed by India; an advanced missile that enables fighter pilots to lock-on and shoot down enemy aircraft with a distance of more than 80 km away.

Development and Trials

Defence Research and Development Organisation (DRDO) is developing this advanced beyond visual range air-to-air missile (BVRAAM) to arm the Indian Air Force's Mirage 2000H, MiG-29, Sea Harrier, Su-30MKI, MiG-21 Bison and HAL Tejas fighter aircraft. Astra resembles an elongated Matra Super 530. It uses an in-house developed solid fuel propellant, though DRDO is believed to be looking at rocket/ramjet propulsion similar to that used in its Akash Surface to air missile project. This missile was successfully tested without control and guidance systems on May 9 to May 12, 2003. The missile was again successfully tested on 25 March 2007. On 27 March the vertical launch of the missile was carried out suggesting the use of the missile as a long range surface to air missile for the Indian Navy to arm its destroyers and frigates and for the Indian Air Force.

The ground testing of the Astra missile was successful. The missile was successfully tested on September 13, 2008. The missile will intercept the target aircraft at supersonic speed. The test flight of the missile from IAF Sukhoi-30 MKI fighter aircraft will be carried out before induction of the missile into service. Again On 11 January 2010, India successfully test-fired Astra in the Chandipur-on-sea area, off the Orissa coast. Initially planned to arm Jaguar, MIG-29 and indigenous light combat aircraft, Tejas, DRDO officials are now concentrating that after user's trial, the missile would be integrated with Indian Air Force's front line fighter aircraft like Sukhoi-30 MKIs and Mirage-2000.

The trial to test the dual mode guidance was carried out in May 2009. Captive flight trials of Astra missile carried out in November 2009. Another set of trials were conducted on 11 Jan 2010 at Balasore in Orissa.

Description

The maximum range of Astra is speculated to be 120 km in head-on chase and 25 km in tail chase.It will have an active homing range of 25 km. The missile has a pre-fragmented warhead and is fitted with a proximity fuze. A radar fuse already exists for the Astra, but the DRDO is currently working on a new laser fuse. The Mark 2 version of Astra will have a maximum range of 150 km and tail chase range of up to 35 km.

BEL Battle Field Surveillance Radar

The PJT-531 Battle Field Surveillance Radar-Short Range (BFSR-SR) is a man portable 2D short range Battle Field and Perimeter Surveillance Radar developed by the Indian Defence Research and Development Organization (DRDO). The BFSR has been designed by DRDO's Bangalore-based laboratory, the Electronics and Radar Development Establishment (LRDE) and is being manufactured by Bharat Electronics Limited (BEL).

BFSR has found use in the Indian border areas, especially along the Line of Control (LoC) in Jammu and Kashmir to prevent infiltration. Over 1100 units are in use by the Indian Army. Foreign Countries have also placed orders for the BFSR.

Development

In the aftermath of the Kargil War, and with the heightened levels of infiltration, the Indian Army started looking at electronic sensors to augment the surveillance capabilities. One of the technologies identified was a small, surveillance radar, and the Army projected its requirements to LRDE shortly after. Sanction was given to DRDO to develop an indigenous radar. In the meantime, some Battle Field Surveillance radars (SR) were imported from Israel at a cost of Rs. 80 Crores, pending completion of the project. This accompanied a large-scale induction of high tech equipment for the Indian Armed Forces.

The radar was designed and developed by LRDE, a DRDO unit, and manufactured by BEL. Initiated in 2000, the development was carried out in LRDE, with the Project Director being Dr. S. Varadarajan, and with BEL collaboration. The project was a systematic example of concurrent engineering, with the production agency involved through the design and development stage. This enabled the design to be brought into production quickly. A salient feature of the BFSR programme was the high level of involvement of the Indian private sector, a first for defence programmes in India. Private firms supplied the rotational assembly and tripod, the Control and display unit as well as electronics assemblies after design and technology transfer by LRDE. This has continued into the substantial production run.

The radar was ready for trials in early-2002, and after extensive trials in Rajasthan and Jammu and Kashmir, it was accepted in July 2002, 24 months after development work commenced.

Description

BFSR is a man portable, lightweight, battery operated, surveillance radar. Weighing around 30 kg, it can be carried and operated by two or three man teams. The BFSR is a fully coherent Pulse Doppler radar, operating with a 10% duty cycle, and a 5W peak power. The low peak power provides the radar a Low Probability of Intercept (LPI), making it difficult to detect by enemy sensors. The radar operates over 21 channels in J band (10 to 18/20 GHz). It can be operated in all weather conditions, and during day and night.

BFSR-SR components include a mounting tripod, an antenna/ electronics assembly, two 24 V batteries for power, and an integrated control and display unit (CDU). Targets are classified automatically using Doppler target classification, with output Doppler return being channelled to the operator through headphones for the Doppler audio.

The radar operates on two rechargeable 24 V batteries, which are carried separately by the soldiers. They are also be operated from AC mains. The batteries are suspended from the tripod to provide extra stability to the radar, although they can be kept separately.

Radar Array and Hardware

The radar array consists of J-band Transmit, receive and processing modules within the single array block. The signal processor is a single on-board FPGA-based chip, which has been tailored for very low power consumption.

The antenna array is made up of microstrip patch array antennas. The transmitter is a solid state transmit module, while the separate receiver is a super-heterodyne type receiver.

The radar algorithm incorporates Digital Pulse compression Technology, which improves the LPI characteristics, as well as making the radar more accurate. This technology was developed in-house by LRDE, which constituted a major breakthrough for Indian radar technology.

Display

The BFSR processing and display units, and control functions are integrated on a single, touch sensitive, portable IBM PC, called the Control and Display Unit (CDU). Some processing elements are also built in to the radar. The processed information is displayed on a high-resolution 10.4" LCD colour display.

The PC operates on a Windows NT-based, menu driven user interface, which makes operating the BFSR extremely simple.

A high resolution, north oriented, coloured radar picture is displayed on PC display. The radar display can either be in a Plan position indicators (PPI) display, or a B-Scope display. The display also has provision for digital geographic map overlay, which allows the target data to be integrated with tactical data for use by ground forces and commanders.

Different geographical maps can be overlaid on the radar display. A target position can be marked for further investigation, or combing of the area by ground forces. The interface between the radar and the CDU can be either RS232C or LAN connectivity. A light weight, rugged, standard army 2-wire field cable is used for communicating between the radar and CDU. This allows the operators to be positioned up to 100 m away from the radar, in the safety of trenches, bunkers, or hides. This provides them better security and safety, and allows for greater flexibility in deploying the radar at suitable spots to meet technical and tactical requirements. The use of wired interface also provides a better security from interception and lower noise, and does not require the radar and CDU to be within Line-of-Sight of each other.

Networking

The BFSR has a COTS-based built in networking and sensor fusion to increase the effectiveness of surveillance. Up to 10 radars may be networked at one time to provide greater area of coverage. All radars in a network can also be remotely controlled from a central hub.

Provision to Network various radars for wider area coverage has also been built into the BFSR.

Thermal Imager

A third generation thermal imager has also been configured for use on the BFSR and has been integrated with it (as shown in the image in the infobox). Operating in the Mid-wavelength Infrared (MWIR) spectrum (3-5 micrometre wavelengths), the imager has a single field of view (monocular sighting) This has given the BFSR day and night viewing capability.

All BFSR data and images, both radar as well as thermal data are combined and displayed on the common control and display unit (CDU). Thus, the radar can integrate its display with IR sensor output, which improves the overall efficacy of the system.

The radar continues to progress further in terms of integration with more features being added. To aid in sensor fusion, and increase the effectiveness of surveillance, newer variants are also being networked with the Indian Army's Hand-held Thermal Imagers (HHTIs) for visually tracking targets detected by the radar.

Operation

The BFSR has been designed for fast deployment, with a setup time of less than 5 minutes. The radar has an inbuilt GPS for self location and alignment with the digital map. It also has a built-in digital magnetic compass which can automatically align the radar to the North. This ensures that the precise location of targets is measured.

Modes of Operation

The radar can be operated in various modes-Surveillance/ Scanning ("Search"), acquisition, tracking/classification mode. The radar can also be operated manually, or put into an automated "Standby" mode. BFSR also has integrated calibration and maintenance modes, which aids in easy maintenance and testing on the field. Additionally, the radar also contains a built-in training simulator, which aids in the training of operators without the need to extensive training facilities. Further training modules can be easily loaded on to the PC.

The built-in test equipment (BITE) on the BFSR aids in increasing reliability and allowing for easy calibration and fault detection of the radar on the field.

The various modes are remotely configurable from the CDU by the operator, which allows for different modes of operations without any physical changes on the BFSR, and without needing the operator to expose himself to any danger. The operation can also be remotely controlled for networked radars.

In scanning mode, the radar can scan around a specified sector looking for any moving objects. It is also capable of "Track-while-Scan" (TWS) operation, and can track 50 targets in TWS acquisition mode. The speed of scan can also be adjusted by adjusting the speed of the antenna's rotation to either a low, medium or high rotational speed.

If a target is found, the operator can choose to track that target in the dedicated tracking mode. The Doppler return from the target is then processed, and fed into the operator's headphones to aid in classification. A classification algorithm in the radar also automatically classifies the into crawling target, single moving target, group of men, light vehicle, heavy vehicle and helicopter.

The radar can also be vehicle or mast-mounted, to increase the detection capabilities. For mobility, better range, and for overcoming obstructions and ground reflection, a vehicle mounted version of BFSR has been developed. The radar array is mounted on a 6 meter long telescopic mast on a jeep or truck platform.

Applications

BFSR is designed keeping in mind the requirements of border surveillance and intruder detection. Thus, it is an ideal tool for border surveillance and protection. It can also be used for battlefield surveillance and intelligence gathering by scouts, forward observers and Special Forces units. It can also be used as a low-cost solution for detection of low flying helicopters and boats by smaller infantry units, enabling in better protection in the absence of larger air-defence radars.

The BFSR has been mainly used by the Indian Army for surveillance of designated areas and borders, for the prevention of infiltration and illegal immigration. It can also be used for perimeter surveillance and protection of sensitive sites, industrial facilities, power plants and similar sites.

Status

BFSR-SR is currently being used extensively by the Indian Army, which has employed it in the border areas with Pakistan and Bangladesh for surveillance and prevention of infiltration. In 2004, 1176 units were ordered by the Indian Army for Rs. 551 Crores (USD 125 mn) and were delivered within 18 months. the Indian Border Security Force has also inducted these radars for border surveillance.

Foreign sales

BEL is heavily promoting the BFSR as a major product to foreign customers in order to improve its international defence presence. At Rs. 40-50 lakhs per unit, the BFSR costs a third of the price of comparable western systems. Officials have also stated that the BFSR has several superior features compared to radars from competing firms, such as Thales (France), Elta (Israel), BAe (UK), Raytheon (USA) and AMS (Italy).

The BFSR has also notched up foreign sales, with Indonesia ordering 100 units and Sudan ordering 10 radars. In fact, Indonesia was the first customer to receive the radars, even before the Indian Army. Mozambique has also bought some radars for trials. BEL is looking at Sri Lanka, Uzbekistan and some other countries for potential sales. There have been serious sales enquiries from at least 5 countries. BEL is in the process of offering the product for field evaluations in other countries.

BEL Weapon Locating Radar

The BEL Weapon Locating Radar (WLR) is a mobile artillery locating Phased array radar developed by India. This counter-battery radar is designed to detect and track incoming artillery and rocket fire to determine the point of origin for Counter-battery fire.

The WLR has been jointly developed by DRDO's Bangalore based laboratory, LRDE and the Government owned Bharat Electronics Limited (BEL). The sub-systems have been fabricated by BEL based on the DRDO designs and delivered to LRDE for integration.

History

The Indian army projected a requirement for fire-finding radars in the 1980s. As early as 1989, the Indian Army evaluated the American AN/TPQ-36/37 radars. However, these radars were not allowed to be sold, and the procurement process was stopped by the Government. In February 1995, a Request for Proposal (RFP) was issued to five companies for procurement of 4 WLRs. Only Hughes (now Raytheon) responded to the RFP. After trials, the radar was found to not be meeting the General Staff Quality Requirements (GSQRs) of the Indian Army, which were found to be too stringent, and were relaxed. At the same time, it was decided to consider development of an indigenous WLR by India's primary Defence contractor, DRDO.

In September 1998, an RFP was issued for the urgent purchase of WLRs-An/TPQ-36/37 from Hughes (USA), Thomson CSF (France) and ISKARA of (Ukraine). However, the American and French radars were withheld after sanctions were imposed after the Pokhran-II Nuclear tests, and negotiations with the Ukrainian manufacturers came to no conclusion. Additionally, DRDO was not authorized to begin development of a WLR. These lacklustre efforts to obtain a WLR system were severely criticized by the Parliamentary Standing Committee on Defence.

Efforts to acquire such a system intensified after the Kargil War, where the Indian Army was severely disadvantaged by its lack of firefinding radars. While the Pakistani forces were equipped with American AN/TPQ-36 Firefinder radars, India only had British Cymbeline mortar detecting radars, which were not suitable. Almost 80% of Indian casualties during the war resulted from enemy artillery fire, making such a radar critical.

To correct this weakness, in 2002, the Ministry of Defence issued an RFP to five manufacturers. With the lifting of sanctions in late-2001, the US Government offered to sell the AN/TPQ-37 radar to India under their Foreign Military Sales (FMS) programme for Rs. 68 Crores each. In July 2002, India placed a $200 million USD order for 12 AN/TPQ-37 Firefinder radars. Initially, only 8 were ordered for $140 million USD, but the order was later increased to 12. The radars were integrated on BEML-manufactured Tatra truck platforms. Delivery of all 12 radars was completed in May 2007. Concept design work on the WLR also accelerated in the aftermath of the Kargil War.

The WLR project was officially sanctioned in April 2002, with a sanctioned amount of Rs. 20 Crores and an estimated completion time of 40 months. The first working prototype was to be ready by April 2004. The final project cost was $49 million USD. In January 2003, an intent for procurement of 28 WLRs was placed with BEL.

Design

The WLR is similar to the AN/TPQ-37 radar in design and performance but is reportedly more user friendly. It is a passive phased array radar, derived from the Rajendra Radar (which is the fire control radar for the Akash missile system). During tests of the Akash missile at Chandipur, engineers noticed the Rajendra radar was able to detect and track artillery shells being test fired at a nearby range. Based on this observation, LRDE scientists were able to adapt the Rajendra Array into the WLR. The WLR Array is an electronically-steered radar, meaning the radar antenna does not move while in operation. The radar can electronically scan a +/-45° range of azimuths for incoming rocket, artillery and mortar fire. The radar antenna is slewable up to +/-135° within 30 seconds, which gives the WLR the ability to quickly change its scanning sector, and provides it 360 scan capability. The Coherent TWT based transmitter of the WLR emits 40 kW of power.

Tracking of the target is done with monopulse signals with Pulse compression, which improves the radar's LPI. The radar processors conduct real time signal processing of the received signals. The weapon locating algorithm is an adaptive algorithm based on a modified version of the Runge-Kutta method, and uses Constant false alarm rate (CFAR) techniques to detect the target accurately. The operator can choose the CFAR technique to be used to maximize the accuracy of information. The data is processed on a programmable digital signal processor using a modified extended Kalman filter, with two filters-one with 6 states, and another with 7 states. Clutter rejection is achieved through Moving target indication (MTI), Airborne MTI (AMTI) and Fast Fourier Transform (FFT).

Information is displayed on ruggedised power PCs on a high resolution multi-mode colour display. The data is displayed in real-time and can be overlayed on a 3D digital map. The WLR can store a 100 km x 100 km size digital map for display at any time. Other modes include Plan position indicator (PPI) display, RHI displays, etc. Up to 99 weapon locations can be stored and tracked at any time and can be transmitted to the command centre.

Operation

The WLR is designed to detect and track incoming artillery rounds, mortar and rockets and locate their launchers. In its secondary role, it can also track and observe the fall of shot from friendly guns and provide fire corrections to counter-battery fire. The detection range for large caliber artillery rounds is up to 30 km, and increases to 40 km for unguided rockets. The robust design of the radar array and algorithms allows the WLR to effectively operate even in a high density fire environment, in severe clutter and interference (jamming) conditions. Up to 7 targets can be tracked simultaneously. The radar can track rounds fired at both low and high angles, and at all aspect angles-from behind or towards the radar, or at an oblique angle to the array. The WLR features adaptive radar resource scheduling to increase efficiency and reliability.

At a given position, the radar can scan for targets in one quadrant, encompassing a 90 sector. The array can electronically scan up to +/-45 from its mean bearing. Additionally, for 360 coverage from a given position, the whole array can be rotated by 135° on either side within 30 seconds to quickly change the scanning sector in response to threats.

Upon detecting an incoming round, the automatically acquires and classifies the threat and initiates a track sequence, while continuing to search for new targets. The incoming round's trajectory is tracked, and a computer program analyzes the track data and then extrapolates the round's point of origin. This calculated point of origin is then reported to the radar operator, thus allowing friendly artillery to direct counter-battery fire towards the enemy artillery.

The WLR also allows for remote operation, and data-linking for better situational awareness at higher echelons of the command hierarchy. The data can be automatically transmitted to a command center, and can communicate with higher echelons. The radar data can also be displayed on a remote screen to protect operators from any targeted attacks on the radar. The operators can also remotely change the scanning sector. Many radars can be networked together to work in tandem and increase the accuracy and provide more information.

Platform

The WLR is configured on a wheeled Tatra 8x8 truck platform.

The trucks are manufactured by BEML in India under license. The WLR is designed to operate in a high-density fire environment and has all weather capability, high mobility and quick reaction time. The system is a two vehicle configuration, with the primary sensor, processors, displays and control unit on a single vehicle, and a separate power vehicle to power the radar. The radar data can also be displayed remotely.

The Radar is designed to operate in harsh environments ranging from-20 to +55 C, in hot and humid conditions, and can be safely stored from-40 to +70 C. It can operate at high altitudes up to 16,000 feet (4,900 m). Shock & vibration performance and resistance to EMI/EMC are according to international MIL standards. The WLR is designed for quick deployment and decamp, and can be ready for action within 30 minutes. In case of any incoming threats, the radar can be quickly moved out of the threat area.

Status

A basic prototype of the WLR was first unveiled at Aero India-2003. The WLR was showcased at the Republic Day Parade in 2007. User Trials of the WLR began in 2005. The Army also used WLRs to further their "shoot and scoot" doctrine using self-propelled guns and artillery to loosen up Defence before an offensive onslaught into hostile territory. By Mid-2006, the WLR was in advanced user acceptance trials and the radar was stated to be ready for production.

After user trials by the Indian Army in severe electronic clutter and "high density fire environment", in June 2008, the WLR was accepted by the Indian Army. 28 units are on order, and are being manufactured by BEL. A large number of components will be sourced from the private sector, including some Commercial off-the-shelf (COTS) components from the international market. The WLR will eventually service the Army's requirement for 40-50 systems. Further improved versions of the WLR are being planned and designed, including longer range versions, as well as more compact variants for better operation and navigation over mountainous terrains.

Central Acquisition Radar (3D-CAR)

The Central Acquisition Radar (3D-CAR) is a 3D radar developed by DRDO for use with Akash SAM. The 3D CAR was developed as part of a program between DRDO and Poland's PIT to develop a family of mobile, S-Band 3D radars. The areas of cooperation were in developing the Planar Array and general architecture. The Indian variant is the 3D CAR, a medium range surveillance radar for Akash at Group level, intended to provide high mobility and comprehensive high and low level coverage. The Polish versions, are the TRS series of S Band mobile radars such as the TRS-17 and TRS-19. The original Indian (3D CAR) and Polish (TRS 17) radars shared the basic architecture and antenna but differed in terms of purpose designed transmitter/receivers, and signal processing equipment. The TRS series for instance can track 120 targets, while the Indian radar tracks 150.

India has further developed its 3D CAR into all new locally produced ROHINI & REVATHI variants. The ROHINI is the Indian Air Force specific variant whereas the REVATHI is for the Indian Navy. These replace the original joint development items such as the planar array antenna with new locally developed ones which are more capable than the original design. A third variant, known as the 3D Tactical Control Radar has been developed for the Indian Army and has cleared trials.

Details

The Central Acquisition Radar (CAR) is a medium range high-resolution 3-dimensional surveillance radar. The Central Acquisition Radar has been designed by LRDE, a DRDO laboratory, and is produced by a joint venture between BEL, Larsen & Toubro and Astra Microwave. The radar employs a planar array antenna and provides simultaneous multi-beam coverage. It can handle 150 targets in track while scan mode.

Rohini

The Rohini radar is mounted on a modified TATRA heavy truck and supported by a mobile auxiliary power unit. The TATRA is license manufactured by Bharat Earth Movers Limited (BEML).

Features

These features relate to the 3D CAR radar. Specifications for the Rohini, 3D TCR and Revathi are available in the links below.

- Medium range 3D surveillance
- S band operation
- Surveillance Range up to 180 km
- Covers elevation of up to 18 km in height
- High altitude deployability
- Deployment in less than 20 minutes
- 150 Targets in TWS
- Array of ECCM features
- Integrated IFF
- Capable of detecting low altitude targets, and supersonic aircraft flying at up to Mach 3
- Frequency agility and jammer analysis

Current Status

BEL anticipates a requirement for 100 Rohini radars. BEL delivered the first ROHINI to the Indian Air Force on August 6, 2008. Around 20 radars can be manufactured annually.

The ROHINI has a new Indian-developed antenna which is more advanced than that on the original CAR terms of power handling and beam forming technology.

Seven Rohinis were initially ordered by the Indian Air Force for their radar modernization program. The IAF then ordered 30 more radars after evaluation, making total orders 37 of the type.

The IAF has ordered eight Akash SAM squadrons, and the ROHINIs act as the central early warning system for an Akash squadron deployment.

The Revathi adds two axis stabilization for operation in naval conditions, as well as extra naval modes.

Two REVATHI radars were ordered by the Indian Navy for their P-28 Corvette program. Given that the Indian Navy intends to have up to 4-6 P-28 Corvettes, further orders are likely from the Navy as well. A Revathi derivative is believed to be on the Shivalik frigate as well, which would translate to 3 additional radars as three ships of the Shivalik class are being made.

Additional orders are also expected from the Indian Army if they order the Akash SAM system.

The Indian Army is also expected to order another 3D CAR variant. The third Indian developed variant of the 3D CAR is known as the 3D TCR or tactical control radar, with a tracking range of 90 km. The radar has a lower antenna mount and is packaged in two vehicles instead of three for the Rohini. It can also feed data to a weapons station 20 km away. The radar cleared trials in 2008-09 and is expected to be ordered in numbers.

Overall, the 3D CAR program highlights India and DRDO's success in developing and manufacturing a modern 3D radar.

DRDO AEW&CS

The Airborne Early Warning and Control System (AEW&CS) is a project being undertaken by India's Defence Research & Development Organization to develop an AWACS for the Indian Air Force.

Program details

In 2003, the Indian Air Force and Defence Research and Development Organisation jointly carried out a study and evolved the system level requirements for an Airborne Early Warning and Control (AEW&C) system. Sanction was then given to DRDO to develop a suitable AEW&C system. Primary responsibility for the project was handed to DRDO's Bangalore-based Centre for Airborne Systems (CABS), which is responsible for design, system integration and testing of the system. LRDE is also involved in the design of the radar array.

The DRDO AEW & Control System program aims to deliver three radar equipped surveillance aircraft to the Indian Air Force. The aircraft platform will be the Embraer ERJ 145. Three ERJ 145 are to be procured at a cost of US $ 300 Million, for the project. The aim is to deploy these AEW & C aircraft by 2013.

The AEW & C project is in addition to the acquisition of larger and more capable Phalcon AWACS from Israel. Three Phalcons have been ordered, with follow on orders of 3 more likely to be placed.

Apart from providing the Indian Air Force with a cheaper and hence, more flexible AEW & C platform as a backup to its more capable Phalcon class systems, the local AEW & C project aims to develop the ability to locally design and operationalize airborne surveillance platforms. India's sole previous effort to develop an AEW & C system was the Airborne Surveillance Platform, but the program, codenamed Airavat was ended after the testbed crashed.

Capabilities

The AEW & C aircraft will have a locally developed AESA primary radar with IFF. The system will also have ESM (Electronic Support Measures), CSM (Communications Support Measures) ability. Datalinks to network the AEW & C with fighters, and ground based control systems will also be provided, as will be a SATCOM (Satellite Communication System). The aircraft will also have a comprehensive self defence suite. The entire avionics suite will be linked via a datahandling system, controlled by Mission computers.

Key Features

The DRDO has released an overview of the AEW & C aircraft.

- The Radar will have an extended range mode against fighter aircraft, and will consist of two back to back AESA arrays, with an additional dedicated IFF array.
- The ESM system will be able to track sources with a directional accuracy of 2 deg. RMS and a frequency accuracy of 1 MHz.
- The ESM system will have complete 360 degree coverage in azimuth and have a database of up to 3000 emitters against which threats will be scanned.
- Communication Support Measure system will analyse and record intercepted communications both inflight and post flight.

- Self Protection Suite will have a passive Missile Approach Warning System, a Radar Warning Receiver and countermeasures dispensers. The SPS will be integrated with the ESM & CSM suite.
- The aircraft will have Inflight refuelling.
- The aircraft will have SATCOM, and datalinks to pass on ESM, CSM and radar data to ground stations and datalinks to pass on target information to fighters. More than 40 other aircraft will be datalinked together by the AEW & C aircraft.

Work Partners

The responsibility between various DRDO laboratories is split as follows:

1. LRDE and DEAL-Primary radar, and IFF
2. DEAL-Communication Systems and Data Link
3. DARE-Self Protection suite, EW & CSM
4. DLRL-Self Protection suite (counter measures)
5. CABS-Overall Program Management, Integration & development of the data handling system, displays, mission computers et al.

Various Indian private sector firms are also supporting the program.

NAL, India is assisting in aerodynamic studies of the antenna array, and flight modelling of the entire AEW&C platform.

Indian Doppler Radar

The Indian Doppler Radar (INDRA) series of 2D radars were developed by India's DRDO for the Army and Air Force. The INDRA-I is a is a mobile surveillance radar for low level target detection while the INDRA-II is for ground controlled interception of targets.

INDRA-I

INDRA-I is a 2D mobile surveillance radar for low level target detection. The radar is housed in two wheeled vehicles. Some of the main features are automated Track While Scan (TWS), integrated IFF and high scan rate for high speed target detection. The radar is produced by Bharat Electronics Limited and inducted into service. The INDRA-I was a landmark project for the DRDO, as it was the first large radar system designed by the organization and produced in number for the defence forces. The Indian Air Force operates thirty INDRA-I's whereas the Indian Army also has several.

INDRA-II

It is a variant of INDRA radar for ground controlled interception of targets. The radar uses pulse compression for detection of low flying aircraft in heavy ground clutter with high range resolution and ECCM capabilities. The radar has been produced by Bharat Electronics Limited and is used by Indian Air Force and Army. Seven INDRA-IIs have been ordered by the Indian Air Force.

Features

- Fully coherent system
- Frequency agility
- Pulse compression
- Advanced signal processing using MTD and CFAR Techniques
- Track while scan for 2-D tracking
- Full tracking capabilities for manoeuvering targets
- Multicolour PPI Raster Scan Display, presenting both MTI and Synthetic Video
- Integral IFF
- Ease of transportation and fast deployment

System Characteristics

- Range up to 90 km (for small sized fighter aircraft)
- Height coverage 35m to 3000m subject to Radar horizon
- Probability of detection : 90% (Single scan)
- Probability of false alarm: 10E-6

- Track While Scan (TWS) for 2D tracking
- Capability to handle 200 tracks
- Association of primary and secondary targets
- Automatic target data transmission to a digital modem/ networking of radars
- Deployment time of about 60 minutes

Current Status

Indian Doppler Radars are in in production at BEL (Bharat Electronics Limited) and are being used by the Indian Armed Forces. A few systems have been exported to Sri Lanka and have been used to detect planes of the LTTE's air wing.

KALI (laser)

The KALI (Kilo Ampere Linear Injector) is a linear electron accelerator being developed in India, by the Defence Research Development Organization (DRDO) and the Bhabha Atomic Research Centre (BARC).

Overview

The KALI is not a laser weapon as commonly believed. It emits powerful pulses of electrons (Relativistic Electron Beams-REB). Other components in the machine down the line convert the electron energy into EM Radiation, which can be adjusted to x-ray (as Flash X-Rays) or microwave (High Power Microwave) frequencies.

This has fueled hopes that the KALI could, one day be used in a High-Power Microwave gun, which could destroy incoming missiles and aircraft through soft-kill (destroying the electronic circuitry on the missile). However, weaponising such a system has many obstacles to overcome.

History

The KALI project was first mooted in 1985 by the then Director of the BARC, Dr. R. Chidambaram. Work on the Project began in 1989, being developed by the Accelerators & Pulse Power Division of the BARC. (Dr. Chidambaram was also the Scientific advisor the Prime Minister, and the Chairman of the Atomic Energy Commission). DRDO is also involved with this project. It was initially developed for industrial applications, although defence applications became clearer later.

The first accelerators had a power of ~0.4GW, which increased as later versions were developed. These were the KALI 80, KALI 200, KALI 1000, KALI 5000 and KALI 10000.

The KALI-5000 was commissioned for use in late 2004.

Design

The KALI series (KALI 80, KALI 200, KALI 1000, KALI 5000 and KALI 10000) of accelerators are described as "Single Shot Pulsed Gigawatt Electron Accelerators". They are single shot devices, using water filled capacitors to build the charge energy. The discharge is in the range of 1GW. Initially starting with 0.4GW power, present accelerators are able to reach 40GW. Pulse time is about 60 ns.

The Microwave radiations emitted by the KALI-5000 are in the 3-5 GHz Range

The KALI-5000 is a pulsed accelerator of 1 MeV electron energy, 50-100 ns pulse time, 40kA Current and 40 GW Power level. The system is quite bulky as well, with the KALI-5000 weighing 10 tons, and the KALI-10000, weighing 26 tons. They are also very power hungry, and require a cooling tank of 12,000 liters of oil. Recharging time is also too long to make it a viable weapon in its present form.

Applications

The KALI has been put to various uses by the DRDO. The DRDO was involved in configuring the KALI for their use.

The X-rays emitted are being used in Ballistics research as an illuminator for ultrahigh speed photography by the Defence Ballistics Research Institute (DBRL) in Chandigarh. The Microwave emissions are used for EM Research.

The microwave-producing version of Kali has also been used by the DRDO scientists for testing the vulnerability of the electronic systems of the Light Combat Aircraft (LCA), which was then under development.

It has also helped in designing electrostatic shields to "harden" the LCA and missiles from microwave attack by the enemy as well as protecting satellites against deadly Electromagnetic Impulses (EMI) generated by nuclear weapons and other cosmic disturbances, which "fry" and destroy electronic circuits. Electronic components currently used in missiles can withstand fields of approx. 300 V/cm, while the fields in case of EMI attack reach thousands of V/cm.

As a Weapon

The KALI's potential for a military role as a beam weapon has made it, in the eyes of the people, "India's Star Wars". However, weaponisation of the KALI will take some time. The system is still under development, and efforts are being made to make it more compact, as well as improve its recharge time, which, at the present, makes it only a single use system.

There are also issues of creating a complete system, which would require development of many more components. There have also been reports of placing the weaponized KALI in an Il-76 aircraft as an airborne defence system. There is also speculation of using the KALI as an Anti-satellite weapon and as a space-based weapon system, although it is unlikely that they would be implemented, given India's stance on those issues.

If weaponized, it is quite likely that KALI would be integrated into India's Ballistic Missile Defence program.

DRDO Kapothaka

Kapothaka is a mini-UAV for reconnaissance. The Kapothaka (also spelled Kapothaha) which means "dove" is believed to be a preceder of Nishant UAV system.

History

Following the sussessful deployment of a remotely piloted vehicle by Israel during Lebanon war in 1982 Aeronautical Development Establishment (ADE) undertook the development of a remotely piloted piloted vehicle kapothaka in 1983 to develop the necessary technologies. During the next 4 years ADE developed a small RPV capable carring a nose mounted tv camera providing real time imagery intelligence.

This program enabled ADE to cut teeth on the intricacies of UAV design development and deployment. The endeavour culminated in successful demonstration of areal reconnaissance using an RPV during "operation Brass-tacks" in September 1987. Indian Army, impressed by the unique capability provided by an RPV, formulated a "qualitative requirement" for a tactical UAV system for artillery leading to the development of NishantUAV system.

DRDO Lakshya

The Lakshya is a remotely piloted high speed target drone system developed by the Aeronautical Development Establishment (ADE) of DRDO. The drone, remote piloted by a ground control station provides realistic towed aerial sub-targets for live fire training. The drone is ground or ship launched from a zero length launcher and recovery is by a two stage parachute system developed by ADRDE (DRDO), for land or sea based recovery. The drone has a crushable nose cone, which absorbs the impact of landing, minimizing damage. The flight path may be controlled or pre-programmed, based upon the type of mission.

Development

The requirement for a pilotless target aircraft (PTA) arose in 1976. Feasibility studies were carried out by ADE to provide for a target system that met the requirements of all 3 services of the armed forces. An Inter Services Qualitative Requirement (ISQR), common to the three Services, was formulated by a Working Group constituted by the Ministry of Defence in January 1977 and 35 ISQR points were identified. Subsequently, based on a feasibility study carried out by Aeronautical Development Establishment (ADE), the project for the design and development of Inter-Services PTA by ADE, satisfying the ISQR was sanctioned by Government in September 1980 at a cost of Rs. 170 million including a foreign exchange element of Rs. 80 million. The development activity was planned for completion within five years. In parallel, a development project for indigenous development of PTA Engine (PTAE-7) was also sanctioned at an estimated cost of Rs.45 million (Rs. One crore = 10 million) to Hindustan Aeronautics Limited (HAL) in September 1980, based on a feasibility study and project proposal submitted by HAL. The engine was to be developed by HAL by September 1985, concurrently with the PTA. HAL announced the successful trial of the indigenously-designed and developed remote-controlled PTAE-7 jet engine on 24 January 2001.

Between December 1985 and July 1986, four Lakshya PTA prototypes powered by Microturbo TRI-60-5 engines were launched for trials. While the first two launches were successful for planned flight times of 20 and 38 minutes respectively, the next two launches failed. By June 1994, 18 Lakshya PTA prototypes were fabricated by ADE itself and 43 trials were conducted, 24 of which were between December 1985 and February 1992. Due to rigorous evaluation and stringent quality control, a total of 10 prototypes were lost during the testing phase between 1985 and 1990. The project was formally closed on June 1994 and a final closure report was issued in April 1995 after incurring a total expenditure of Rs 218.2 million. The first 6 Lakshya drones were given to the Indian Air Force in 1998. Laskhya units are manufactured and overhauled at HAL's Aircraft division, Bangalore. The Lakshya was formally inducted into the services by CAS AY Tipnis, on 9 November 2000 at Interim test range (ITR) Chandipur. On May 9, 2002, an upgraded version of the Laskhya featuring the new engine from HAL was flown from ITR Chandipur, bringing user trials to a close. On 6 November 2002, HAL announced that they had received an initial order for 25 Lakshya drones and that limited series production to satisfy the order for all three services had already begun. By 16 January 2003, the drone had completed over 100 flights.

A modified reconnaissance version of the Lakshya is under development. This version was fitted with oblique cameras and a digital on board computer with a faster data-link enabling the drone to carry out completely autonomous operations. The development of this version was formally announced by Dr VK

Aatre, then Scientific Adviser to the Defence Minister, during his lecture on "Evolving Battlefields and Role of Technology" organized by Bangalore Science Forum on 5 July 2003.

Operational History

Indian Air Force had received the aircraft, ground systems and expendables in September 1999 and Indian Navy was scheduled to receive its first deliveries in November 2000. 23 Pilotless Target Aircraft Lakshya have been inducted into the defence services. The production cost of one aircraft is Rs. 293.75 lakh. Some countries, like Singapore, Malaysia and Israel have expressed interest for "paid demonstration" of the Lakshya aircraft as a target. A similar "paid demonstration" was conducted for Israel's Air Force during the year 2002. This information was given by the Defence Minister Shri AK Antony on 5 September 2007.

Nag missile

Nag is a third generation "Fire-and-forget" anti-tank missile developed in India. It is one of five missile systems developed by the Defence Research and Development Organisation (DRDO) under the Integrated Guided Missile Development Program (IGMDP). Nag has been developed at a cost of Rs 300 crore.

Technical Characteristics

As originally conceived, the Nag would have been available with three different types of guidance, These included a wire guided version, an infra-red version and a millimetric wave (mmW) version. The cumbersome nature of a wire guidance system had led to plans for this being dropped. Currently, guidance is based on an imaging infra-red (IIR) passive seeker that ensures a high-hit accuracy in both top-and front-attack modes.

The mmW seeker, on the other hand, is intended to operate as an optional system that can replace the IIR passive seeker as a module. Also incorporated into the guidance system, is a CCD camera. The missile has a weight of 42 kg and can engage targets at ranges 4-5 km. The Nag is claimed to be first anti-tank missile which has a complete fiberglass structure.

It has a flight speed of 230 metres per second, is armed with a 8kg tandem shaped-charge warhead, has a rocket motor using nitramine-based smokeless extruded double band sustainer propellant, has a single-shot hit probability of 0.77 and a CEP of 0.9 metres, and has a 10-year maintenance-free shelf-life.

The Nag will be produced in two main basic variants. The land version has been tested from a tracked vehicle known as NAMICA (Nag Missile Carrier). With the IR version of the missile, targets are acquired using a thermal sight, and are then assigned to the nose-mounted IIR seeker.

Missile guidance is initially by area correlation around the target, then by centroid tracking. Terminal homing is by area correlation around the centroid.

Nag is also configured to be used on the Advanced Light Helicopter (ALH). Eight missiles are carried in two quadruple launchers. Launchers mounted on either side are linked to a nose-mounted stabilized thermal sight and a laser range-finder package.

Advanced Variants

In addition to basic land and helicopter variants the DRDO is now developing number of advanced variants of the Nag missile:

- Helina, (HELIcopter launched NAg)with a range of 7-8 km, launched from twin-tube stub wing-mounted launchers on board the armed HAL Dhruv and HAL Light Combat Helicopter produced by state-owned Hindustan Aeronautics Ltd (HAL). It will be structurally different from the Nag. The Helina will make use of an IIR seeker for target engagement like the Nag.
- land version, will also have its range extended by development of a mast-mounted missile launcher that will be hydraulically raised out to a height of five metres to enable the Nag missile to acquire its targets out to a distance of 7-8 km.
- Air-launched, 10 km-range variant launched from tactical interdiction aircraft like the upgraded Jaguar IS. It will use a nose-mounted millimetric-wave active radar seeker.

- Man portable, DRDL will also start working on the 'Man Portable' Nag very soon. It would weigh less than 14 kg.

Namica

NAMICA (Nag Missile Carrier)is a tracked ICV built for the army. It is equipped with a thermal imager for target acquisition. NAMICA is a modified BMP-2 ICV produced as "Sarath" in India. The carrier weights 14.5 tonnes in full combat load and is capable of moving 7 km/h in water. The carriers are capable of carrying 12 missiles with 8 in ready-to-fire mode. The NAMICA carrier was put through transportation trials covering 155 km during summer trials.

Status

Nag was successfully test fired for the second day in a row on August 8, 2008 from the Test Range at Pokhran, Rajastan, marking the completion of the developmental tests. The DRDO and Indian Army plan to hold the user trial shortly. These trials will be the final trials to decide the induction of the missiles. The NAMICA carrier successfully completed its amphibious trials in the Indira Gandhi Canal at Rajastan on August 8, 2008.

The Indian Army has placed an order of 443 Nag missiles and 13 Namicas for introduction in the next 3 years. Nag will be the first weapon of such kind that will be inducted into the army by November-December of 2009. The Army urgently needs the more advanced Nag to improve kill probability as the missile using a high explosive warhead to penetrate the armor in modern tanks.

As part of the winter trial of the final user trials the Nag missile was tested successfully by the Indian Army on December 26, 2008. Before the induction of the missile into service and the summer trials will be carried out in June 2009.

During the winter trials the Nag missile zeroed in on the precise location of the target tank at a distance of 3.3 km, as required by the Indian Army. The Indian Army is also extremely satisfied with the performance of the warhead of the missile. The test conducted on 28th December 2008 was successfully completed by the Indian Army. During the test a moving target at 1.8 km was targeted in the top attack mode and a stationary target at a distance of 3.1 km. The two targets were completely destroyed. A total of five missiles were fired during day and night against stationary and moving targets. Summer trials were completed in the summer of 2009.

In July 2009 the Nag anti-tank guided missile (ATGM) was cleared for production. The production of the Nag missile was ordered after successful summer trials were carried out in the Rajasthan desert.

The latest trials of the missile were conducted using an advanced imaging infrared seeker head, as per Army's requirements. On 20 January 2000, field tests of the Nag's Thermal Sight system saw the system identify and lock on to a T-55 tank at a range of 5 km. The tank was then engaged and destroyed at a range of over 4 km thus the missile's fire-and-forget capability has been established using the day version of the IIR passive seeker.In its IIR form the Nag has limited all weather capability. This has given added impetus to develop the mmW seeker. Efforts are on to provide special embedded on-board hunters, that can hunt for targets using 'day seekers' and 'day-&-night seekers'.

The Nag will replace the existing Russian Konkours and European missile Milan, both of which are manufactured under license by Bharat Dynamics Limited.India's anti-tank guided missiles, which are competitively priced and had been bought by Tanzania, Botswana and Morocco. An Indian official said a country in the Middle East had shown keen interest in Nag anti-tank guided missiles during Abu Dhabi Defence Expo-2009.

Prithvi (missile)

Prithvi is a tactical surface-to-surface, short-range ballistic missile (SRBM) developed by DRDO of India under the Integrated Guided Missile Development Program.

Development and History

The Government of India launched the Integrated Guided Missile Development Program in 1983 to achieve self sufficiency in the development and production of wide range of Ballistic

Missiles, Surface to Air Missiles etc. Prithvi was the first missile to be developed under the Program.

DRDO earlier attempted to reverse engineer SA-2 Surface-to-air Missile under Project devil. The Prithvi is said to have its propulsion technology derived from the SA-2 surface-to-air missile. The dual liquid engine of Prithvi I might have been derived from scaling down of 30 ton Project Valiant Engine and scaling up of V-755 engine used by SA-2 surface-to-air missile.

Variants make use of either liquid or both liquid and solid fuels. Developed as a battlefield missile, it could carry a nuclear warhead in its role as a tactical nuclear weapon.

Variants

The Prithvi missile project encompassed developing 3 variants for use by the Indian Army, Indian Air Force and the Indian Navy. The initial project framework of the Integrated Guided Missile Development Program outlines the variants in the following manner.

- Prithvi I (SS-150)-Army Version (150 km range with a payload of 1,000 kg)
- Prithvi II (SS-250)-Air Force Version (250 km range with a payload of 500 kg)
- Prithvi III (SS-350)-Naval Version (350 km range with a payload of 500 kg)
- Dhanush-Dhanush is reportedly a naval version of Prithvi which can be launched from Ships.. Some sources claim that Dhanush is a System consisting of stabilization platform and missiles, which has the capability to launch both Prithvi II and Prithvi III from Ships while others report that Dhanush is a variant of Prithvi-II Ballistic Missile.

Over the years these specifications underwent a number of changes. While the *codename* Prithvi stands for any missile inducted by India into its armed forces in this category, the later developmental versions are codenamed as Prithvi II and Prithvi III.

Description

Prithvi I

Prithvi I class was a surface-to-surface missile having a maximum warhead mounting capability of 1000 kg, with a range of 150 km. It has an accuracy of 10-50 metres and can be launched from Transporter erector launchers. This class of Prithvi missile was inducted into the Indian Army in 1994.

Prithvi II

Prithvi II class is also a single stage liquid-fuelled missile having a maximum warhead mounting capability of 1000kg, but with an extended range of 250 kilometres. It was developed with the Indian Air Force being the primary user. It was first test-fired on January 27, 1996 and the development stages were completed in 2004. The Prithvi II class of missiles are in the process of induction by the Indian Airforce. In a recent test, the Missile was launched with an extended range of 350 kilometres and improved Aided Inertial Navigation. The missile has the features to deceive Anti Ballistic Missiles. According to news sources the range is now increased to 350kms.

Prithvi III

Prithvi III class (*codenamed* Dhanush *meaning* Bow) is a two-stage ship-to-surface missile. The first stage is solid fuelled with a 16 metric ton force (157 kN) thrust motor. The second stage is liquid fuelled. The missile can carry a 1000 kg warhead to a distance of 350 km and a 500 kg warhead to a distance of 600 kilometres and a 250 kilogram warhead up to a distance of 750 kilometres. Dhanush is a system consisting of a stabilization platform (Bow) and the Missile (Arrow). Supposedly it is a customised version of the Prithvi and that the additional customizations in missile configuration is to certify it for sea worthiness. Dhanush has to be launched from a hydraulically stabilized launch pad. Its low range acts against it and thus it is seen a weapons either to be used to destroy an aircraft carrier or an enemy port. The missile has been tested from the surface ships many times

Prithvi III was first tested in 2000 from INS Subhadra, a Sukanya class patrol craft. The missile was launched from an updated, reinforced helicopter deck of the vessel. The first flight test of the 250 km variant was only partially successful. The full operational testing was completed in 2004. The following year in December an enhanced 350 km version of the missile was tested from the INS Rajput and successfully hit a land based target.. The missile was again successfully tested-fired from INS Subhadra anchored about 35km offshore from the Integrated Test Range at Chandipur on December 13, 2009. It was the sixth test of the missile.

Rajendra Radar

Rajendra is a passive Phased Array Radar developed by the Indian DRDO. It is a multifunction radar, capable of surveillance, tracking and engaging low radar cross section targets. It is the heart of the Akash Surface-to-air missile system and is the primary fire control sensor for an Akash battery.

Current status

The Rajendra Multi-Function Phased Array radar system, designed at the Electronics and Radar Development Establishment (LRDE), part of DRDO, is currently in production at Bharat Electronics Limited. This is named after India's First president Dr. Rajendra Prasad. The LRDE is working on the Rajendra III radar for the Indian Army. Rajendra III is a slewable phased array radar based on the T-72 chassis. As of 2007, the BLR-III vehicle on T-72 chasis was ready for a track test. The Phased array antenna is fabricated at Bharat Electronics Limited (BEL), Ghaziabad. Collimated beam pattern and s/s cure for all 16 spot frequencies has been taken.

Current orders for the Rajendra and its derivatives are at least 32 units, considering the order for 2 Squadrons of the Akash system by the Indian Air force and the indent for 28 Weapon Locating Radars by the Indian Army.

Trials

By 2005, Rajendra II had participated in more than 15 flight trials at Balasore missile testing range. The flight trials have been spread over 4 missions in both group and autonomous mode. High altitude engagement, far boundary engagement, crossing and receding target engagement and multiple missions against multiple targets capabilities have been established. Consistency in performance of radar in guiding missiles as close as 15m has been established. During a mission, a Pilot less Target Aircraft (PTA) was neutralized while engaging crossing and receding target. In 2007, the Akash system cleared the Indian Air Force's user trials with the Rajendra tracking and engaging several targets with warhead equipped missiles. Prior to that, the Akash system elements, including the Rajendra underwent mobility trials at Pokhran and the radar successfully demonstrated its performance in an EW environment, and its ECCM features at the IAF Electronic warfare range at Gwalior.

Description

Rajendra is a slewable passive phased array radar used for 3-D target detection, multi target tracking and multiple missile guidance under extreme hostile EW environment. It makes use of a passive phased array to search a volume of space, distinguish between hostile and friendly targets, automatically track up to 64 targets and command one of several launchers to engage up to 4 targets simultaneously. Initially designed as a standalone system, Rajendra is now equipped with the ability to integrate with a network of sensors, including long and medium-range surveillance radars of foreign and indigenous origin.

Rajendra's multi-element antenna arrangement folds flat when the vehicle is in motion. The Radar consists of a surveillance antenna array with 4000 phase control modules (PCM's) operating in the G/H-Band (4-8 GHz), engagement antenna array with 1000 PCM's operating in the I/J-Band (8-20 GHz), a 16-element IFF array and steering units. A powerful high-end computer computes phases for all the elements of the array. Rajendra controls the beam positioning sequence through beam requests for each track at adaptive data rates and performs multifunctional roles like search –confirm –track-interrogate targets, assign and lock on launchers, and launch/acquire/ track/guide missiles. The RDP supplies track data to remote group control centre. Rajendra features a Dual channel radar receiver and a C band transmitter, although the complete transmitting and receiving features and bands are unknown.

Rajendra radar uses phase shifters integrated in large numbers for electronic beam steering. This allows Rajendra radar to simultaneously track multiple aircraft and also guide multiple missiles towards these targets. The phase shifter was designed and developed by Prof Bharati Bhat, a scientist from Centre for Applied Research in Electronics (CARE) of IIT, Delhi, and her team.

The phased array radar rotates 360 degrees on a rotating turnstile at a moderate speed. This allows it to perform 360 degree surveillance. The phased array itself has 45 degree scan limits to either side, giving a total scan coverage of 90 degrees, if the radar array is static.

During Multisensor Tracking a 2-D battery surveillance radar (BSR) with 360 degree coverage and a larger detection range provides track data to the multifunction, slewable, 3-D phased array radar. This is useful when a single battery of the Rajendra is detached from the group to fight alone, and early warning from the 3-D CAR is not available. The 2-D BSR data is then integrated by the Rajendra's radar vehicle. The multisensor direction finder in Rajendra processes the track data from the phased array radar and the BSR to identify the targets reported by both the sensors and maintains a common track database. For those BSR tracks, which are not being reported by Rajendra though under its coverage, target acquisition is initiated with elevation search in the designated direction. The antenna is skewed in the direction of threat to acquire the targets, which are outside the covered air space. The Rajendra's tracking range is 60 km against fighter aircraft flying at medium altitude.

The major functions of the Rajendra are:

- Surveillance of the assigned volume of space
- Acquisition of aircraft targets either independently or handed over from group control centre via the 3-D CAR or from the battery surveillance radar

- Tracking of targets (64)
- Tracking of assigned targets (up to 4) and missiles (up to 8) during engagement
- Command guidance of missiles (up to 8)
- Integrated IFF (Identification Friend or Foe) functions

Deployment

Each Akash battery has a single Rajendra radar which is linked to up to 4 Akash launchers, each with 3 missiles. Each Rajendra radar can guide up to 2 of these missiles against a single target, with 8 missiles in the air at the same time. 4 Akash batteries make up a group in the Indian Army configuration, with a central 3D CAR radar acting as the early warning sensor for the entire group. In 2007, the Indian Air Force ordered 2 Akash squadrons to begin with. Each squadron consists of a minimum of two batteries, and hence at least 4 Rajendra radars are on order. Many more orders are expected to come over time, as the Indian Air Force phases out its older Pechora systems. The IAF had 30 Pechora squadrons of which 9 were to be replaced by the DRDO-IAI LRSAM project. The rest were to be replaced by the Akash, over time. As of May 2008, the LRSAM project is on hold on account of Indian Government investigations over the earlier Barak SAM deal with the Indian Navy. This is expected to put more emphasis on orders for the Akash SAM, as the Indian Air Force moves towards revamping its SAM inventory.

Weapon Locating Radar

The Army intends to use a Rajendra radar derivative in the artillery locating role. During tests at Chandipur for the Akash missile system, engineers noticed the Rajendra radar was able to detect and track artillery shells being test fired at a nearby range. This led to the development of the indigenous Weapon Locating Radar, an item in high demand by the Indian Army's artillery units, especially after the Kargil War. 28 LRDE Rajendra based WLR's have been ordered by the Indian Army. In June 2008, the WLR was accepted for induction by the Army, and 28 units are being produced by Bharat Electronics Limited (BEL).

DRDO Rustom

Rustom (English: *Warrior*) is a Medium Altitude Long Endurance Unmanned Aerial Vehicle (UAV) being developed by DRDO for the three services, Indian Army, Indian Navy and the Indian Air Force of the Indian Armed Forces. Rustom is derived from the NAL's LCRA (Light Canard Research Aircraft) developed by a team under the leadership of late Prof. Rustom B. Damania in the 1980s. The UAV will have structural changes and a new engine. Rustom will replace/supplement the Heron UAVs in service with the Indian armed forces.. The first low speed taxi trials of the first prototype were carried out on September 22, 2008.

Design and Development

Rustom's basic design is derived from the NAL light canard research aircraft (LCRA). The aircraft has been named after Rustom Damania, a former professor of IISc, Bangalore who died in 2001. DRDO decided to name the UAV after him because it is derived from National Aeronautical Laboratories' light canard research aircraft (LCRA) developed under Rustom Damania's leadership in the 1980s. With the Rustom MALE UAV project, DRDO intends to move away from traditional ways of developing products whereby laboratories under DRDO, like the Aeronautical Development Establishment (ADE), which is involved in this project, develop and finalise the product and transfer technology to a production agency.

DRDO will follow a practice of concurrent engineering where initial design efforts also take into consideration production issues, with the production agency participating in the development of the system right from the design stage. The agency will also follow up issues related to infrastructure and expertise for the product and its support, thereby overcoming time delays in crucial projects.

Rustom which has a wingspan of 20 metres and weighs 1,800 kg, will be launched by the conventional method and not the launcher as in the case of the Lakshya and Nishant. Rustom will be able to see the enemy territory up to a distance of 250 km and carry a variety of cameras and radar for surveillance.

Current Status

The Indian government has allowed the development of the Rustom MALE UAV project in association with a production agency cum development partner (PADP).

The ADE officials indicated that the requests for proposals (RFP) would shortly be issued to four vendors which are the Tatas, Larsen and Toubro, Godrej and Hindustan Aeronautics Limited-Bharat Electronics (joint bid) who were chosen out of the 23 firms that responded.

Currently, negotiations are underway between these companies and the three Indian armed forces since the private majors are looking for support and commitment from them before they start executing any development and production plans. This is because of the fact that the chosen PADP will also have a financial stake in the Rustom project. The Armed Forces would also be asked to take up a financial stake and the Indian government may have to guarantee that a specific number of Rustom UAVs will be bought.

A prototype to validate the technology for the project has been built and the taxi trials has been completed.

First flight of Rustom-I took place on 16-11-2009 at the Taneja Aerospace Air Field near Hosur. The demonstration resulted as the prototype crashing to the ground. Stated by the DRDO, the taxiing and takeoff was exactly as planned. Due to misjudgment of altitude of the flight, the on-board engine was switched off through ground command which made the on-board thrust developed to go to zero. Despite the mishap, the state-owned Defence Research and Development Organisation stated: "The flight proved the functioning of a number of systems such as aerodynamics, redundant flight control, engine and datalink, which go a long way towards the development of a complex UAV."

At least 10 more test flights of the Rustom design are expected before the system can be taken up for production. The test work is being performed using a sub-scale version of the air vehicle (Rustom-I TD) with a 1.5 m (4.9 ft) wing span and an overall length of 3m.

5

Modernisation : Challenges for Indian Army

The 1 million-plus Indian Army, which is the second largest after China, is acclaimed to be one of the most professional and loyal land fighting forces in the world. But in view of the ever-changing roles of the battlefield soldier at the turn of the 21 century, it is beset with more challenges, than any Army has ever faced. In this era of global terrorism, revolution in military affairs with galloping and costly technology, the Indian Army is groping to reorient itself, with little or no political direction.

The Indian Army lacks a mission statement unlike the Navy and Air Force, which have crafted their own. The security affairs of India are guided through Cabinet Control and to add to the woes of the Army, India has a large coalition government with leaders of different hues, most of who have neither military training nor scholarship in strategic thought or modern management. The strength of some of the members is based on tradition and Indian scriptures, which may not be pertinent in the context of security today.

The Indian Armed Forces remain modeled on the archaic template bequeathed to India by the British and chiseled by its first Prime Minister Nehru to ensure the three Service Chiefs who are equal, are accorded minimal decision making capability for procurement and none for policy, for fear of "coup d'etats" that plagued West and South Asia in the late 50's. There is opportunity for the Army to now dispel this fear, as democracy is firmly rooted in India.

In a democracy, no Army, not even the best in the world, can deliver without the Government laying down military and political aims in clear terms, and attempting a holistic threat perception for weapon induction and joint operational planning for war, and to counter terrorism aggressively. This has not been attempted and no wonder cynics have dubbed the Indian Army "a meek reactive force", which reacts to Pakistan, when in fact, it has fangs, which, when sharpened, can be awesome in military terms.

Little initiative is left with the Army. Knee jerk reactions of the political leaders in all military operations (Op Pawan 1987–91 in Sri Lanka, Kargil war 1999 and Op Parakarm 2001–2002) and the four wars (1948, 1962, 1965 and 1971) the Army has fought, saw more decisions taken to placate the domestic and foreign audiences, to the detriment of the Army. With no CDS system, inter-service rivalry, which is a worldwide malady, has always reared its head higher in India, as each service attempts to get more of the 'defence pie'. The outgoing Chief of Integrated Staff Lt Gen Pankaj Joshi had shrilly articulated this in September. These challenges will persist, but they also pose opportunities for change, as India's defence budget is not so constrained, and as has been observed around the world, the mantra for success lies in jointness for procurement and operations.

Revolution In Military Affairs (RMA) And Terrorism

RMA on one hand, and unabated terrorism from Pakistan on the other, can be a heady mix for any professional Army as the US Army is learning only now in Iraq and Afghanistan. The QRs of soldiers inducted into the manpower intensive Indian Army are traditionally pegged low, and stress laid on brawn over brain, with the culture permeating even to the higher levels, where in India's poorer days, technology was feared and considered expensive for such a large Army. The soldier was cannon fodder for victory. Now with the arrival of nuclear weapons, sophisticated guns (155mm Bofors Howitzers), computers, WLRS ANTPQ 47s, advanced AA systems with associated radars (Strella, IGLA and Tangushka), anti tank missiles (Konkurs and Milan2) and ballistic missiles (Agni I and II and Prithvi), UAVs (Searchers) and surveillance and night vision equipment (from Israel and France), the current Army has had to suddenly change its philosophy, culture and mindset. India's foot soldier Army needs to convert to mechanized vehicles with protective armour and reduce manpower, to curtail revenue costs. The teeth to tail ratio needs change. With a shortage of 12,000 mid level officers alone, the Army is looking at net centric warfare, at a time when nearly half the fighting force is engaged in combating terrorism and border surveillance duties, leaving little time for reorientation and training of such a large Army for RMA.

India's Armed Forces are under bureaucratic control, which many claim is its biggest challenge. In times of peace the Army is required to combat terrorism unleashed by Pakistan, despite a 600,000 strong para-military force. The Army perforce has to coordinate Intelligence and almost every military action or operation with the police and para-military forces of the Central and State governments, which unfortunately for the Army are controlled by the powerful Home Ministry. The Army has little authority to chalk out field plans or employ pro-active tactics in any operation by itself, except restrictively along the LoC.

At most times, the secrecy of actions is lost, and human rights activists raise shrill voices. At the tactical level the initiative has therefore always been with Pakistan to dictate rates, methods and places of infiltration. The rules of engagement for the Army are therefore forever changing, and at most times, political considerations outweigh military objectives.

In times of peace, the cross border terrorism unleashed by Pakistan's ISI and other *Jehadi* forces in Kashmir, especially along the 740 km of the LoC, and through the Bangladesh border, has taken the lives of over one soldier per day at an average. The root cause lies in the camps established in Pakistan Occupied Kashmir where Pakistani, Afghani and foreign *Jehadis* are trained, motivated and armed before infiltration. The Army has always wanted to hit at the roots and decimate the camps in POK, but even in the Kargil war of 1999, the Army was restrained. More recently India leaned on the USA to restrain Pakistan, to no avail, and now opportunities exist, to call President Musharraf's bluff with pro-active operations.

The Army has excellent paratroop battalions. It has gleaned lessons from the recent Iraq war and after excelling in exercises with the US Special Forces, more recently in Ladakh in September, it has appreciated the importance of Special Forces. This poses great opportunities to equip and train, top-of-the-line Special Forces to carry out cross border punitive raids if Pakistan fails to contain the *Jehadis*. The Indian Army can achieve results and the Government must show resolve to support its Army.

Both in war, and in preparation for war, the Army is dependant on the Air Force for its air-land-battle concept to attack the enemy from the air. Though it is acquiring 36 units of SMERCH launchers, the MI 25/35 attack helicopters are flown by the Air Force, and perceptions differ on this too. The Indian Air Force has the philosophy to first achieve air superiority before interdiction, while the Army would like to open the battle with softening air strikes. The commanders try to resolve the Op plans locally, and the recent OP Parakram, when the Indian Armed forces were mobilized for war for almost one year 2001–02, witnessed a lot of coordination sector wise, but not as a policy.

The opportunity exists for the Army to take over the attack role helicopters in a phased manner. That is the way modern Armies are going. The 500 strong Army pilots are capable and are successfully carrying out arduous flying in the Siachen region.

DRDO and Force Modernisation

Since the 1970s the Defence and Research Development Organistion (DRDO) championed the cause of "Made in India" philosophy and assured the Armed Forces that by the turn of the century Indian Armed Forces would be 60% self sufficient for its hardware needs. It reinvented the wheel in large projects to the determent of the Army This was the story of socialism and non-alignment, and the greatest sufferer was the Indian Army. The main battle tank Arjun failed to appear despite 15 years in the making, the T-72 tank could not get night fighting capability, the basic rifle for the soldier remained the 7.62 mm and in EW and in night vision devices and weapon locating radars (the Cymbiline was attempted for upgrade), the Army found itself deficient and with unprotected vehicles. Russia bailed India out, by supply of essential hardware, and the Bofors 155mm Howitzer saved the day in the 1999 Kargil war.

The Indian Army leadership has only now understood that it needs to plug the chinks in its own armour both for fighting terrorism and to have an upper hand in war, as analysts claim India has only a slight edge over Pakistan in conventional capability. It has therefore, imported T-90s tanks (with poor night fighting capabilities) and a host of other equipment and gone to the private sector for vehicles and other programmes. The DRDO is now collaborating with NPO Mach of Russia to jointly build the Brahmos missile. The DRDO has expertise and facilities, hence opportunities now exist to collaborate with Western defence companies for most unfinished projects. Herein lies opportunity for the Army's modernization.

The IMF-led economic liberalization of India began in 1991 when its reserves fell to $1 billion. It resulted in neglect of the modernization needs of the Indian Army. As India's Defence allocation hovered around 2.4% of the GDP, deficiencies to the tune of $ 3 billion resulted in the Army by 1999. Gen VP Malik, who was the Army Chief during the 1999 Kargil war, stated, "The army's modernization programs are in a state of terminal illness. Our conventional combat edge over Pakistan has been eroding with every passing year. Unless additional funds are earmarked, future planning is not possible and the erosion in combat edge will soon become uncorrectable." In hindsight it is apparent that when the Indian armed forces were mobilized on 18 December 2001 in operation Parakram (Valour), the Army was the first to realize how woefully short it was of spares, night vision equipment and lethal punch.

However, as strategic thought and long-sighted planning in India has been lacking, it has now come to light that the Army never received any verbal or written directives on the aims of this massive mobilization, which lasted till 16th October 2002. Most training and peace-time activities suffered. The Government cloaked Op Parakarm as coercive diplomacy, but it tired the Army which lost 728 lives, some 130 first in laying over 1 million mines and then in clearing them. Malik's successor Gen S Padmanabhan had this to say on 9th November 2002. "Whenever there is a situation calling for (the) Army's help, the latter's role should be clearly defined to avoid confusion", hinting the Army was not clear why it was mobilised. It is providential that India did not go to war. India's political leadership was jolted out of its slumber in the stand off with Pakistan, which threatened to use nuclear weapons if its territorial integrity was transgressed. India realized that it had to honestly reexamine its nuclear weapon credibility.

The Nuclear and Air Defence Challenges

In May 1998, the strident BJP government took courage and exploded five nuclear devices including three fusion devices heralding India into the thermo nuclear club. India and Pakistan have been de facto accepted as nuclear powers. The scientists of BARC (Bhabha Atomic Research Centre) and DRDO rode piggy-back on the Army Engineer regiments deployed at the test site Pokhran, to ensure that their experiments were a success, but the 'top brass' of the Army were never brought into the loop to devise India's nuclear strategy or their deployment. This led to a woolly approach to chart India's plans for its nuclear deployment and a draft 'No First Use' policy was espoused for the first five years, which no one in uniform ever questioned. It will be the Armed Forces that would be hurt by a first strike and yet they were tasked to deploy the second strike, in a flawed theory. Only early this year an Air Marshal was appointed as the C in C Strategic Forces and a Nuclear Command Structure for decision-making announced. The first Nuclear Op Management course for mid level officers was conducted in November 2003.

The premise of command and control of nuclear assets remains diffused, as the Army believes in the principles of Artillery where Command means training, positioning and readiness of the gunnery forces, and control means "control of fire". Attempting to clarify SFC's position, the Chairman of the Chiefs of Staff Committee, Admiral Madhvendra Singh articulated three points and confirmed what this chapter is conveying. First, the training in nuclear weapons and servicing of delivery systems would be the responsibility of the individual services. Second, the utilization and use of nuclear weapons would be the prerogative of the newly formed SFC. And third, while the "control" of ballistic missiles will be transferred to the SFC initially, the Indian Air Force would soon decide on the transfer of its nuclear capable fighters to the SFC. So far this has not happened but the Army missile forces have just been nominated for raising.

Raising Of Missile Forces

The Cabinet Committee on Security (CCS) that stands in for the National Security Council has cleared the raising of India's ballistic missile force. The Pakistan-specific 700 to 800 km range Agni-I and 2,000 km plus Agni-II manufactured by DRDO and Bharat Dynamics are designated as 334 and 335 Missile groups and based at Secundrabad where they are manufactured. The scientists would help the Army in the deployment. Two new Prithvi (150-250km) units for the Army, which would be named 444 and 555 missiles groups will also be raised to augment the two Prithvi missile groups – the 222 and the 333, deployed in Central India, where the Command shelter for the top leadership is planned. The new missile groups would be operational by the beginning of 2005. This decision offers the Army its first opportunity to clarify the command and control structure by a revisit on all inter-services issues. The IAF-ARMY battle for nuclear assets and air defence has been simmering for long. India has received the first shipment of Green Pine AD radar and the plans for long range AD missiles including the Arrow and the Patriot and the Russian SU 300 series are in the melting pot. Aerostats are also due to be positioned soon by the IAF's Western Command.

India USA and International Cooperation

A defence review was attempted to take a holistic view of India's military threats and security challenges in 1998 by the National Security Advisory Board but the events of 9/11 and USA's lifting of sanctions and overtures has made the study redundant.

A new review is being attempted to look at the International World Order and how India can find a dominant position and voice its concerns. The Indian Army has close Infantry links with the British Army. An Indian Army Liaison Officer is stationed in HQ Infantry at Warminster in UK. More recently, USA is seeking cooperation and overseeing these interactions is the Defence Policy Group co-chaired by India's Defence secretary and the US Under Secretary of Defence for Policy. Under this is the Joint Technical Group between the two defence research establishments, the Military Cooperation Group between the US Joint Staff and the Indian Chief of Integrated Defence Staff, and the Executive Steering Groups of the Indian Army, Air Force and Navy, which interact with their counterparts.

The US Pacific Command is responsible for the region, which includes India. There is also a Joint Working Group on peacekeeping, a Security Cooperation Group formed after the 9/11 events to discuss counter-terrorism-related issues, and a regular exchange between the defence research and analysis communities in both countries. The Army is now exercising with US and other forces but it needs to take greater part in the International arena and opportunities now exist, with France too. Russian links are already strong. This will enable it to change its old mindset, and India can be a training hub to counter terrorism, as it already has facilities for training UN Peace Keepers.

Conclusion

In conclusion the challenges before the Indian Army are the unresolved issues of defining what exactly is expected of this huge professional military machine and how, in the next decade India will safe guard its borders and yet quell terrorism, which actually is the role of the Para military forces and the expanded Rashtriya Rifles (National Rifles). The policy direction and template for the Army has to be given by the government, which in the past has never guided the Army with ground realities in mind. Instead political realities have always dictated the Government's edicts to the India's Army. This has affected command, control and coordination and the culture in the Indian Army. However, as it is a loyal professional force at every level, it has never questioned the Government or asked it to clarify its role or to define the threat perception and ambitions of the Government. The Army has been content to have operational orders in place for its professional

Strike Corps to counter any threat from Pakistan and China. The arrival of nuclear weapons, ballistic missiles and most importantly better Reconnaissance, Surveillance and Target Acquisition (RSTA) capabilities has led to opportunities for the Indian Army to define the enemy's vulnerabilities and seek directions whether in the future the Pakistan Occupied Kashmir territory is to be gained, or offensive plans implemented, to ensure Pakistan does not dare to continue its policy of cross border terrorism, and China respects India. India's Army deserves a long overdue mission statement, and the recent cease fire is a good time for the Army to take advantage of the opportunities that lie ahead.

Army's Capability Accretion

The challenges that the army is expected to face in the next decade are not likely to be any less formidable. An appraisal of the emerging threats in fact indicates an increasing complexity of the missions that the army may be expected to execute.

The basic character of the Army's responsibilities is unlikely to witness significant changes. Till the boundary disputes with China and Pakistan remain unresolved, Army's most important role of ensuring the nation's territorial integrity will retain primacy. Concurrently, as in the past, the Army will continue to remain embroiled in combating militancy, insurgency and terrorism. With the prevailing instability in the immediate and near neighborhood, and the growing regional and global role of our country, the Army must also be prepared to undertake missions beyond our borders. It may be added that however much the Army may want to resist, it will continue to be drawn to tackle internal law and order situations and national manmade or natural calamities.

How has the Army fared in the last two decades in the discharge of its responsibilities? At considerable cost to itself it has barely managed to keep the lid on. Given the serious shortage of junior officers, and the indifferent and insufficient weaponry at its disposal, the Army it can be contended, has done exceedingly well. Regrettably the problems of the Army, and the stresses it is subjected to, are understood only by those who are in it. The MOD and the political leadership, or for that matter also the strategic community have a vague awareness, nowhere close to the ground realities. This explains the decades of inertia.

Exploiting the progressive decline of our conventional military capability all through the decade of the eighties, Pakistan launched a well orchestrated offensive through irregulars in Kashmir from about the beginning of 1990. When the momentum of this offensive seemed to be petering out Pakistan did not hesitate to gamble for higher stakes by resorting to Kargil. The Kargil fiasco and the growing domestic instability, however, did not dampen Pakistan's appetite for fomenting trouble for us. The terror attack on our Parliament in 2001 and 26 Nov 2008-Mumbai is still fresh in our memory.

Over the last few years China too has begun to demonstrate bellicosity, tinged with arrogance, against us. Border intrusions with the purpose of intimidation coupled with force accretions in Tibet and along the LAC, portend problems for us. Its aggressive posturing on other fronts compounds the basket of our concerns.

Viewed from the national security perspective it emerges that our concept of military deterrence has failed or is failing. Clearly then, the Army's conventional war fighting capabilities must be brought to levels that promise if not absolute, sufficient deterrence.

So how do we go about building a credible dissuasive conventional military deterrence? For the past two to three decades the three services have been unsuccessfully trying to drive the process. It would be mindless to persist with the same approach. The responsibility must shift to the PM and his Cabinet Committee on Security. This is not going to happen without some precipitate action. How this is to be brought about is a matter that the services must address?

The Army could do with a totally fresh appraisal to cover its overall strength, its structure and equipment profile, the quality of its man power, its leadership and its training. Such a review could perhaps be relevant and necessary for the Navy and the Air Force as well.

Technological advancements are taking place rapidly. Correspondingly the rate of obsolescence is also increasing. It is therefore imperative that we manage change with much greater sophistication so as to ensure available funds are utilized optimally. It follows that individuals charged with formulating qualitative requirements, induction plans and evaluation of systems must be competent and have the requisite grooming and experience. Even though this issue has been debated before no concrete remedial steps have yet been taken.

Infantry

The Infantry is the largest arm of our Army and the only arm which has perhaps never had a respite from combat from the time the Naga insurgency began in the fifties. Matters worsened when we sent the expeditionary force to Sri Lanka for Operation Pawan. Ever since, the Infantry has continued, without break, to climb the stress ladder.

Considering the Infantry's constant engagement, aware that all Army Chiefs from the early nineties have sought to give the Infantry the highest priority in terms of equipping and modernizing it. But if we were to carry out a critical appraisal of the Infantry in 2010 the report card of twenty years effort would be quite dismal. How ironical, especially when costs are lower and the systems involved are relatively not so complex? The story is eloquent testimony to the manner in which the country's higher Defence management works.

Almost everything that a soldier needs, from the clothes and boots to the weapon he carries, is at present well below par.

Consider the 5.56 family of weapons that the Army is currently equipped. The Army was virtually bulldozed into accepting these weapons. It was told that indigenous R&D must be encouraged. Promises were made that in the production models the user will get a much improved and more reliable version and that a superior Mark 2 will follow. The DRDO also hinted that high volume orders from many foreign customers would be placed soon after the Indian Army accepted the induction and placed orders for delivery. The Army had no choice but to accept though none of the commitments materialized. It has lived with these weapons for more than a decade and paid an incalculable price. A good and reliable personal weapon we know does wonders to a soldier's confidence and morale. But we have failed in giving him such a weapon. Shouldn't there be review and people held accountable?

Conceptually the start point of capability-building and modernization has to be the individual soldier. So we must begin by giving him the best we can. Essentially what the soldier needs is a good and reliable personal weapon, comfortable clothing with stealth and concealment features designed to ergonomically accommodate everything he has to carry, the best protection (body armor) that portable weight permits, stabilized helmet mounted computer screens, sensors and night vision devices for observation and using his weapons, effective communications and position locating/ situational awareness systems.

In addition he requires a host of sundry items like eye protection goggles, contemporary light bag pack equipment etc. The approach should be to look at the tactical vest and the helmet (protective gear) as a platform on which the future soldier systems are embedded so that weight reduction and mobility improvements issues are optimally addressed.

The resolve to modernize the infantry soldier has been there for long, but the process has been painfully slow. Ways have to be found to accelerate the process and do it comprehensively. We must therefore begin as of yesterday.

When considering assault rifles we have quite a few options available; each having its unique features. Let us briefly look at the 21st century trends in assault rifles. Essentially they are refinements to the systems developed in the previous decades. Some exciting options that could be considered are:-

- *Heckler & Koch HK 416 firing the 5.56x 45 or the HK 417 firing the 7.62×51 NATO rounds.* Both these weapons have updated features with Picatinny rails, a drop free magazine release, and some other smart features.
- *Israel's IMI Tavor TAR-21.* It has a compact bull pup design and uses the NATO 5.56x 45 cartridges. It can easily be set up for right or left handed shooters and has several modular variants that come with a standard reflex sight.

- *XM 8 from the US*. This has quite a few modular variants with inbuilt electronics such as a laser sight, round counter and integral infra red and visible sights.
- *South Korea's XK11*. This is an interesting new rifle that has a ballistic computer, a laser range finder and a digital scope that provides the soldier with combat data and enables night firing through thermal imaging sights. The product is still at a prototype stage but has considerable promise.
- *The AK Series*. The Kalashnikovs family of assault rifles is much too well known.

An important trend in small arms in the 21st century is that sophisticated electronics is now being built into the design of these weapons. There could be some justification for the approach we have now adopted. A few years ago we had considered integration of night sights in our tender for assault rifles. At that time there weren't many who were offering such embedded systems. To my mind the idea was right though the timing was wrong. But now, with most weapon manufacturers developing weapons with built in electronics.

Given the current employment of the Army and looking at the two vital needs of the infantry soldier i.e. his personal weapon and his body armor, it is difficult to decide which merits greater priority. What is but evident that on both counts the establishment has been found wanting.

Today we have all of the Rashtriya Rifles and a significant proportion of the Army deployed in combating militancy, terrorism and insurgencies. Of these how many of their personnel, are equipped with suitable body armor? And what are the constraints to procuring body armor? On both counts we will get answers that are far from convincing, particularly when today we have a host of companies in India manufacturing body armor and combat helmets. With a dynamic and inclusive approach we can harness the capabilities of these companies to give us quality protection suits and helmets at competitive prices. As a matter of fact with some support in terms of investment in R&D and inducements of assured orders, our companies can well become global leaders in protective solutions. Assessments suggest that in the development of 'small arms protective inserts' (SAPI), technology today is at only the 40 percent level. Both in the case of X SAPI-silicon carbide and ceramic and E SAPI, and high molecular weight polyethylene (HMW-PE) and aramid fibers, there are possibilities that by improving the quality of resins and making the weave more unidirectional, weight to protection ratios can be substantially improved.

The infantry also needs to acquire better surveillance and target acquisition capabilities as well as more potent fire power at the section level and above. A mission, terrain and adversary based analysis may suggest the induction of special weapons and surveillance systems on a regional basis. It can be assumed that such an exercise would have been undertaken.

Artillery

In my reckoning Artillery modernization has not made any headway because of two reasons. The first is that-blinded by the labels of 'support' and 'supported', the Army has not yet grasped the full import of the modern artillery on tomorrow's battlefield. The second can best be described by just one word: jinxed.

However like the Infantry, modernization of the artillery has also been a matter of concern in the last decade or so. In these years much has apparently been done but unfortunately without any headway. Actually the process began in the early eighties. But other than 400 Bofors guns procured in the mid eighties we have nothing else to show.

The exercise to procure new towed and mounted self propelled tracked and wheeled 155 mm 52 caliber guns are on. We are also planning to induct a specified number of light weight 155 mm guns for certain areas and missions. It is important at this juncture to focus on ensuring that the process of evaluation and induction moves without any hiccups and delays.

As we induct these guns the space of the contact battle at the tactical level will increase to a 30 km envelop thus enhancing our ability to destroy, maneuver, and defeat. Similarly we need to pay more attention to the requirements of the Artillery at the operational and strategic level. In this context even though we have been inducting the Prithvi, the BrahMos and the Agni series, the process has been based on the developmental projects of the DRDO and not on the basis of a well thought through conceptual framework. The subject of rocket and missile artillery thus merits deeper examination. We require more systems that can provide coverage between the 30 to 100 Km ranges. Besides, the liquid propellant based Prithvi imposes certain operational limitations. Admittedly the Smerch rocket system has filled this gap to some extent but much more needs to be done.

Firing platforms like the guns and rocket and missile launchers are just one of the four pillars upon which comprehensive artillery capability is structured. The other pillars are communications to include artillery command and control systems, surveillance systems and the ammunition systems. In the Kargil war our communications and surveillance systems were not adequate. Thus the guns could be exploited to only 30 percent of their potential.

In principle surveillance and target acquisition capabilities must exceed our delivery systems ranges by at least 30 percent. The ideal would be 50 percent. We have been working on this for a while but more needs to be done. We should be able to establish a comprehensive surveillance and target acquisition grid by using a mix of ground and air/ space based sensors to include satellites, aircraft, drones, helicopters and tethered balloons. On the ground besides, electro optical devices and thermal cameras we will also require a sufficient number of weapon locating radars some of which should be employable in the mountains. The surveillance grid must allow for transmission and exchange of data to all shooters and decision makers in real time. The problems of surveillance in the mountains merit special attention.

Advancements in ammunition technology have led to a dramatic enhancement in the lethality and destructiveness of the artillery. With improved conventional munitions (ICM) the kill capacity of the ordinary shell has gone up in multiples. Smart and intelligent munitions now permit pinpoint accuracy enabling the artillery to engage and destroy fortifications and tanks from long ranges. We must induct such sophisticated ammunition speedily. However while doing so the challenge lies in getting the mix right since sensor/seeker based munitions are relatively very expensive.

Armor and Mechanized Infantry

The Armor is the only arm of the Indian Army whose upgradation and modernization has by and large been on track. With the induction of the T 90 tanks our armor is as good as any in the world even though some upgrade programs on the T 72 are a bit behind schedule. With the planned induction of TI based fire control systems and active protection systems our armor is likely to remain contemporary for the foreseeable future.

The BMP 2 inventory merits attention. It is understood that comprehensive plans have been drawn up to improve its fire power mobility and night fighting capabilities. Once implemented the BMP units will have the requisite level of compatibility with our tank fleet.

Supporting Arms

AD Artillery. Traditionally the Army's approach to air Defence has been to look at a family of guns and missiles to provide a tiered air Defence umbrella to the tactical battle area (TBA). With the advancements in missile technology there is a case to review this approach. Contemporary medium and short range surface-to-air missiles have hit probabilities that are close to 0.9 and 1 (90 to 100 percent). If backed by sound surveillance, acquisition and tracking systems, the air Defence umbrella provided can be reasonably effective. It is for this reason that not many countries/weapon manufacturers are today in the business of making air Defence guns. To my mind the focus should be on procuring adequate numbers of both the short range and the medium range missiles and have them backed up by effective surveillance coverage of the air space impacting the TBA. In this, field coordination with the air force has been lacking in the past. Hopefully the problem has now been addressed.

Engineers. With battle field transparency progressively improving there is a case to review our concepts of laying defensive and tactical minefields. We should instead graduate to the concept of laying reactive/impromptu minefields using mechanical systems to lay mines or have them remotely delivered. Based on the conclusions arrived appropriate capabilities would have to be built up.

Signals. Communications are getting cheaper and better by the day. Advancements are extremely rapid. We must radically change our approach to remain in step. Gone are the days of plans like the AREN and the ASCON. The attitude required is that of the average mobile phone user who changes his phone without much ado. Rapidity of decision making and implementation will now be vital.

Other than the requirements of the arms there are two areas that deserve much greater attention in the future. The first is a subject that we have been grappling with for a while, made some progress, but not enough, and that is simulators. Virtual reality and graphics can today bring enormous realism to training. Most of our section and platoon/troop training should be based on contemporary simulation systems. Again at the unit and formation level we should depend much more on war gaming and simulation to train our officers and commanders.

The second is robots. These are futuristic platforms that will be performing a variety of missions in the battlefields of tomorrow. Some have already been deployed, many more will follow. An executive of a company engaged in the development of robots asked me recently as to why the Indian Defence forces were not interested in this subject. My cryptic response was that we have not yet learnt to value human lives sufficiently. However the topic goes beyond lives. It is about doing certain missions more effectively. Besides other things a robot can perform quite a few human tasks without experiencing stress and fear.

The preceding analysis of the possible requirements of the Army is by no means exhaustive. It is just a cursory survey from a given perspective. There could be other differing views on some of the suggestions made. But what perhaps is beyond debate is the imperative of substantive capability accretion if the Army is expected to successfully face the challenges of the coming decades.

More importantly, is that the plans for induction of new weapons and equipment and force multipliers must not follow the pattern that we have witnessed in the past two or three decades. Acquisitions have to be urgently undertaken. Following the rigid rigor of the DPP is a prescription for inaction or interminable delays. Important acquisitions must therefore be brought under some fast track procedures. Surely, we have the genius to conceive a policy and a structure that can ensure that within the framework of fiscal and procedural prudence, sound procurement decisions are taken within the desired time frames.

We do not need astrologers to tell us that the security climate for us over the next decade or so is unlikely to be benign. If we do not then prepare to face the potential threats it is possible that we may face humiliation similar to what happened to us in 1962.

6

Modernisation Armed Forces

The Armed Forces of India are responsible for defending the country against external aggression and safeguarding the territorial integrity of the nation. The Indian Army has to be extremely vigilant at all times to meet various challenges along the borders of the country encompassing different geographical and climatic conditions. Keeping in view the threat perceptions, advances in technology and geo-political environment, the Indian Army is suitably structured, equipped and trained to effectively perform its tasks. Efforts are always continued to modernise and upgrade the weapons and weapon systems of the Army to prepare it to address the requirements of modern day warfare, and enhance its combat efficiency. Following are some of the notable efforts:-

Armoured Corps: As a part of the effort to equip the Armoured Corps with night fighting capabilities. Thermal Imager Based Stand Alone Sight and Thermal Imager Fire Control System for the T-72 Tanks are under process for procurement. Image Intensification Based Sights for the drivers of T-72 Tanks and Image Intensification Based Sights for the commanders, gunners and drivers of T-55 Tanks are undergoing trials and evaluation as part of the procurement process. Armoured Recovery Vehicle have also been contracted for procurement.

Mechanised Infantry: To enhance the combat efficiency, Konkurs-M Anti-Tank Guided Missiles have been acquired along with transfer of technology. Anti-tank Guided Missile Launchers of the Infantry Combat vehicle BMP-II are being equipped with the Thermal Imaging sights to enhance night-fighting capability.

Image Intensification based Night Vision Devices for the drivers of BMPs are also in the process of procurement.

Artillery: To enhance the fire-power of the Army, efforts are being made of equip them with 155 mm Artillery Gun, for employment in various types of terrain. Besides, trials have been successfully completed for the Multi-barrel Rocket Launchers. Trial Evaluation of the latest Artillery Ammunition System for induction viz Terminally Guided Munitions, Velocity Enhanced Long Range Artillery Projectiles and anti-radiation Ammunition is also in progress. Moreover, to enhance the Surveillance Capability of the Army, considerable progress has been made in the direction of acquisition of Long Range Reconnaissance and Observation System, Weapon Locating Radar and Unmanned Aerial Vehicle.

Air Defence Artillery: The negotiations for induction of improved version of Tunguska M1 Weapon system in Air Defence Artillery units of strike/ mechanised formations are going on. Air Target System 'Lakshya', developed by Aeronautical Development Establishment (ADE) of DRDO has also been recently evaluated by the Army and will be used for practice firing of Air Defence Weapon Systems. In conjunction with the IAF, a revamp of the existing Control and Reporting System of Air Defence Artillery is being carried out. The thrust is towards automation of various warning and control systems and processes. A review of the requirement of modern Air Defence Weapon System has been carried out to replace the obsolescent equipment in a phased manner to enable it to meet emerging air threats.

Infantry: The combat potential, surveillance and counter-insurgency capability of the Infantry is being significantly improved by acquisition of following equipment and weapon systems:-

Fire Power: 20 mm Calibre and 14.5 mm Calibre Anti Material Rifles, Automatic Grenade Launcher-30, Multiple Grenade Launcher, 84 mm MM Rocket Launcher MK II and Kornet –E Anti-Tank Guided Missile are under procurement.

Surveillance Devices: Battle field Surveillance Radars (BFRS), Hand-Held Thermal Imagers (HHTI) and various types of Unattended Ground Sensors (UGS) have been procured for surveillance in conventional and counter-insurgency roles and to monitor the intrusion across the Line of Control/ Actual Ground Position Line.

Mobility: A family of High-Mobility Vehicles, Bullet-Proof Vehicles and Anti-Tank Guided-Missile Vehicle are being procured to improve the mobility of the infantry.

Signals: Procurement of state-of-the-art communication equipment and system has brought about substantial qualitative improvements in the communications capability of the Army. Some of the major procurements are: RS HX long-range frequncy-hopping high-frequency radio sets, Hand-Held Walkie-Talkie Radio Sets, Interception Receiver AR 5000, Radio Set 5 Watt/ 20 Watt VHF, and Radio Set 5 Watt/ 20 Watt VHF for Armoured Fighting Vehicles. A country wide – secured value-added backbone data network is also being established connecting the important Formation headquarters of the Army.

Engineers: After withdrawal of forces from the border, equipment to assist de-mining operations, have been procured to minimise the causalities. Trials and procurement of various equipment's is also underway which will improve capability for disaster-management during a nuclear, chemical and biological warfare scenario. Army's capability to fight against insurgency/ terrorism has been considerably bolstered by equipping them with more equipment.

In written reply to a clarification sought by the Committee in regard to the functioning and performance of recently inducted Arjun Tank, the Ministry have furnished the following details:-

The project on development of MBT Arjun was initially sanctioned in May 1974 at a cost of Rs. 15.50 Cr with a PDC of 10 years. Time and cost have undergone revision on 3 occasions (in 1980, 1987 and 2000).

The reason for revision in cost and time are-major changes in qualitative requirements, delay in import of sub-systems due to import embargoes, increase in number of prototypes, manufacture of pre-production series tanks, long and extended user trials, difficulties in organising for field evaluation, general inflation and devaluation of rupee etc. MBT Arjun has been indigenously designed and developed as per the General Staff Qualitative Requirement (GSQR) given by the Army. It has been tested and evaluated exhaustively by the Army (user) in all types of terrains and weather conditions for more than a decade.

Various modifications suggested by the user, during pre-induction trials, have been systematically attended to and the performance of the tank improved as laid down in the GSQR.

The confidence of the Users in MBT Arjun is reflected very well, as they have already placed an order on DGOF for manufacture of 124 Nos. of ARJUN tanks.

During the presentation on the modernisation plans of the Indian Army, a representative of the Ministry of Defence provided detailed information as outlined below : "Modernisation is an ongoing process and sometimes mid-course corrections may become necessary to be undertaken because of the availability of various kinds of technologies or even changes in the overall geo-strategic perceptions and requirements of relevant force structures, the thrust we have given in the Tenth Plan is primarily to modernise the infantry battalions and the special forces. Our infantry battalions and special forces, for a long time since the 60's, had no major modernisation of their equipment and structures. So, this was given the highest priority by the Chief of the Army Staff.

Thereafter, we wanted our mechanised forces to be able to fight at night. Fighting by night has become a norm today in modern warfare and the removal of night blindness was given the next kind of priority. Then there is the refurbishment of our medium artillery. As you would be aware, a bulk of our artillery comprises of very vintage 130 millimetre guns which were there from the 60's other than the Bofors of 155 millimetre calibre. So, a refurbishment of medium artillery will continue to mark our efforts right up to the end of Twelfth Plan and beyond. Balanced modernisation of other arms and services and making up of deficiencies is what we call a hollowness in our structure".

As regard the capability being looked for each arms, representative of the Ministry deposed as under: "I will take this up arm by arm and indicate to the Hon. Standing Committee as to what is the capability that we are looking for each of the arms. What are the kind of equipment we are providing to them?

The Committee note that modernisation of Armed Forces is a continuous process which requires long term planning and huge investments. The Ministry of Defence have undertaken a plan to modernise the Indian Army and to equip with the latest machine and equipment so that it can meet the security requirements of the country. The Committee note that during the three years of the Tenth Plan period, the stress primarily was on the modernisation of the infantry battalions and the special forces. The Committee further note that as far as special forces are concerned, 40 items of various kinds have been identified for modernisation. Efforts are being made to modernise and upgrade the weapons and weapon systems of the Army to prepare it to address the requirements of modern day warfare. These efforts cover the ability to exercise surveillance up to a distance of three kilometres of infantry battalion detection of infiltration by troops or vehicles in areas not physically held, destroying targets like vehicles, stores dumps and troop clusters, neutralise enemy commanders, various kinds of equipment, Battle Field Surveillance Radars, High Resolution Binoculars, Night Vision Devices, Thermal Imaging Sight for ATGM Launch, Mechanised Forces and their equipments, induction of T-90 and Arjun Tanks and T-72 Tanks.

From the presentation made by the Army before the Committee, it is observed that the number and type of weapons available with the Army are much less as compared to their requirements. The Committee, therefore, keeping in view the threat perceptions, advances in technology with special emphasis on Information Technology and geo-political environment, strongly recommend that there is an imperative need to prepare a long term policy to modernise the Indian Army and upgrade their weapon systems in areas identified by the Army and desire that a time bound programme should be drawn to acquire those weapons etc. and also ensure proper financial allocations for the purpose. The Committee desire that the quality of the equipment etc. should be the best available in the market which can enhance the combat efficiency of the soldiers in an effective manner. The Committee feel that our priority should be to equip the infantry man with superior light weight weapons and equipment & clothing.

The Committee are of the opinion that there needs to be a more focused thrust on development, production of indigenous equipment into the Army, with particular reference to the Arjun Main Battle Tank. It is understood that though a limited order for 124 number of these tanks have been placed, the first production models are being further subjected to additional performance trials by the Army. This is primarily due to the unstated concern over quality control at the Ordnance Factory, Avadi at time of issue, which must be ensured by the Ordnance Factory Board to the satisfaction of the user. The Committee are surprised to note that instead of giving firm order for sufficient number of Arjun Tanks by indigenous production, only a very small order has been placed and the Government has decided to acquire tanks from a foreign country to meet its requirement. 461-1-

Having incurred an expenditure of approximately Rs. 3,300 crores on the development and productionisation of the MBT Arjun, the Committee are of the firm opinion that the Arjun must be inducted into the Army in large numbers, for which an initial production order for 50 tanks must be placed on Heavy Vehicles Factory, Avadi. This does not absolve DRDO (AHSP for Arjun Tank) and the Ordnance Factory Board of their prime responsibility to ensure that the production model of the tank meets the user requirement in every respect. The procurement plan of the Army must be structured (or re-structured if necessary) to provide for induction of increased numbers of Ajrun Tanks by the 11th, 12th Army Plans, as a replacement for T-72 Tanks.

Procurement of Guns for Indian Artillery

Upgradation of the weapon system is a continuous process based on threat perception and technological development. Accordingly, upgradation of the existing stock of artillery and procurement of advanced guns based on modern technology for the modernisation of Indian Artillery are being planned. In written reply to a question on the acquisition of different types of Guns for the Indian Artillery, the Ministry of Defence have furnished the details as given below : Wheeled SP Gun-Request for Proposals (RFP) for procurement of 155 mm/52 Calibre Wheeled Self Propelled (SP) Guns was issued to 11 vendors. Only 5 vendors responded. Of these, 4 were rejected in Technical Evaluation as they did not meet the required parameters. Since only one SP Gun met all the qualitative requirements, it has since been decided to explore if there are any additional vendors currently producing Wheeled SP Guns so that a competitive situation can be developed.

Tracked SP Gun-Tracked SP Gun is a project developed by Defence Research and Development Organization (DRDO). It involves mating a suitable imported 155 mm /52 Calibre turret with indigenously developed BHIM chassis. Process of identification of a suitable turret was completed after global tendering and successful trial evaluation. Commercial negotiations were completed in December, 2003. The case is being processed for approval of the competent authority.

Towed Guns-Global RFP was in December, 2001. Three vendors responded. Trial evaluation of all three guns was carried out in May/July, 2002 and June/July, 2003. Validation firing of all three guns were held in November, 2004. Currently, environmental tests are in progress.

About the upgradation plan of Guns in Indian Artillery a representative of the Ministry of Defence stated as under: "We are upgrading 130-mm guns to 155-mm guns, 45 calibre. Ten regiments are being done with imported kits, and the ordnance factories would do for another 14 regiments. We are planning to introduce 155 mm 52 calibre guns, which are presently at trial stage as propelled guns. For self propelled guns, we are determined that Bhim T 6 gun will cater for the requirements of target as propelled guns, and in future, we will continue to look for wheeled self propelled guns. The upgradation of existing 155-mm guns, that is, Bofors Guns is also on the anvil. We are planning to introduce a long-range rocket artillery, the Pinaka System, which is an effort of DRDO. For this system, two major firms, L & T and Tata, have collaborated. For a multi-barrel launcher system, capable of sending rockets up to a depth of 90 kms., negotiations are currently under way. We hope that they will be contracted some time in the current year."

In regard to the acquisition programmes of guns the representative further stated: "We have 155 mm SP Guns for the artillery. We were to acquire in two versions. One was wheeled version and the other was tracked version. Track is like a tank and it was mounted on tracked chassis and you have got a turreted gun on top. Both planned to be the same. One between the wheels and one would be on tracks. What we have now sent up to the CCS or will be sending for the CCS for approval will be high breed gun as was mentioned, used the Arjun chassis, which is a heavy chassis and used the South African gun to be mounted on top of it. That has been on trial and evaluated and it is found to be in order. South African gun mounted on Arjun chassis. This will not impede production of Arjun tanks because they will be manufactured by Bharat Earth Movers Limited, an alternative production line for the chassis. As far as wheeled guns are concerned, we are not yet ready for it. We are going to have or invite vendors and check out with out trials and identify the suitable wheeled gun. So, that is the present situation.

As far as Towed Guns are concerned we had carried out trials earlier. Now we want fresh trials and more competitors to come in. Hopefully, in the next year, we will be going for GSQR evaluation. It will be ready for contracting. There were three vendors in this trial evaluation as a user trial has been carried out. Three rounds of trials have been carried out and now maintenance and evaluation and other aspects are going on. All three will be processed for all stages of the trials. User trial is just one stage of the trials. Then, there are maintenance and environmental trials and DGQA trials".

The Committee note that the Indian Army is facing critical shortage of wheeled Self Propelled (SP) guns of the required standard. The Ministry have informed that though the request for proposals for its procurement was issued to 11 vendors in response to which 5 bids were received and one gun has been finally found to be matching the qualitative requirements. The Committee are, however, surprised to note that no fields trials were held to decide the suitability or otherwise of the bids received which is the normal procedure. The Committee also note that trials are still continuing for the procurement of tracked SP Guns and towed

Guns. The delay in the procurement of such crucial weaponry has adversely affected the modernisation of schemes of the defence sources resulting in wastage of a lot of time. The Committee feel that global RFP should have been issued in the first instance to avoid the single vendor situation.

The Committee now want immediate decision to be taken to procure the guns at the earliest. The Committee further recommend that R & D efforts for their indigenous production should go simultaneously with the acquisition programme of the Ministry so that Artillery is not made to face the shortage of critical components of the weapons system. 501-1-

Phasing out of Cheetah /Chetak Helicopters

Presently, Indian Army depends on Cheetah and Chetak helicopters for surveillance system in the high altitude regions. The design of these helicopters is 40 to 45 years old due to which the emerging requirements of the Army in the high altitude terrains are inadequately addressed. In reply to a question on the replacement of ageing Cheetah/Chetak Helicopters the Ministry have stated in a written reply that the Army is looking for alternative options for replacement of Cheetah with the state-of-the-art technology helicopters available in the global market. Salient technical specifications of the replacement helicopter of Cheetah are as under:-

a) Integrated Doppler Global Positioning System (GPS) Navigation System;

b) Auto Pilot in all three axis;

c) Service ceiling not below 6500 m (desirable 7000m) pressure altitude;

d) The helicopter must be cleared for full night and inclement weather operations; and

e) The helicopter must be capable of being fitted with :-

- Suitable Sighting System comprising of Forward Looking Infra Red Radar, Laser Range Finder and a designator.
- Data Link System

- Flare / Chaff dispenser with suitable defence mechanism.

The Advanced Light Helicopter (ALH) Dhruv, is in the category of 5.5 Ton class. It can operate in high altitude, but due to its larger class than that of the Cheetah, it requires bigger landing ground/helipads.

A representative of the Ministry of Defence, during oral evidence stated: "As far as Army Aviation is concerned, what we are looking at is superior reliability and endurance in high altitude areas; rapid response to emerging situations in combating terrorism; enhancement of capabilities in the utility role and armed helicopter capability. This being the benchmark requirements, the present acquisitions which are planned are that we are planning to upgrade our existing Cheetah / Chetak fleets. Two squadrons we have already inducted and in a couple of months it will be finished and the third squadron the order for which has already been placed. We are also going ahead with weaponising the Dhruv helicopters for six squadrons of them eventually and we are also planning a replacement of the Cheetah and Chetak fleet for which the trials are presently on. Utility Helicopters in the 10-12 class to enable the Army to move at core and divisional level, a certain body of men to quickly and rapidly react to report about infiltration being undertaken by the terrorists as also for various other operations in conventional wars and helicopters mounted surveillance systems".

The Committee note that the Army is looking for alternative options for replacement of Cheetah Helicopters with state-of-the-art helicopters available in the global market. The Committee, keeping in view the requirement of superior reliability and endurance in high altitude areas, rapid response to emerging situations in combating terrorism, desire that the Ministry should also examine the feasibility to upgrade existing Cheetah/ Chetak fleets before inducting the new helicopters. The Committee also desire that efforts should be made to modify the configuration of Dhruv Helicopters so as to make it operate at high altitude regions. The Committee also desire that a time bound road map for indigenous manufacturing of helicopters should also be drown up at the earliest. The Committee hope and trust that sufficient financial allocations are made available to make the new purchases in a time-bound manner.

System of Delivery of justice under Military Law

In the Army, justice is administered by the Commanders at various levels. Minor offences can be disposed of summarily by powers vested in them under the provisions of the Army Act. For grave offences, Courts Martial are assembled on the orders of superior commanders. Commanding Officers are empowered to hold summary Courts Martial, decision of these Tribunals are not appealable. It is, therefore, essential to judiciously exercise these powers and adhere to the laid down procedures. With this background, the Institute of Military Law was established at Shimla. On August 26, 1989, the institute was shifted to Kamptee. The Charter of Duties of the School is to cater for a comprehensive system of legal education for Officers of all Arms and Services of the Army and to undertake wide ranging research, development and dissemination work in the field of Military and allied laws.

The Committee on Defence, in their 20th report on "Welfare of Serviceman and ex-Servicemen" have recommend that a special court of appeal in the line countries like France, Germany, Russia, Sweden, and United Kingdom, be constituted for redressal of grievances of the service personnel where aggrieved personnel may appeal against the judgement of Military Court.

The Ministry of Defence, in their Action Taken reply submitted as under; "As recommended in 169th Report of the Law Commission, a proposal for setting up of an Armed Forces Tribunal for adjucating service matters and appeals arising out of the verdict of Court martials is under active consideration of the Government. The modalities are being worked out in consultation with Ministry of Law, Ministry of Finance and Department of Personnel and Training".

The Committee, keeping in view the Law Commission recommendations and increase in number of court cases arising out of personnel matters feel that Government should create separate mechanism to resolve them for the settling of Armed Forces court cases. The Committee, therefore, earnestly desire that the modalities for the setting up of new mechanism may be worked out expeditiously to deal with all personnel court cases. The Committee would like to be apprised of the progress made by the Ministry in this regard within 3 months after presentation of this report.

Modernisation of Ordnance Factories

The Ordnance Factories form a strategic and dedicated production base for both lethal and non-lethal defence stores. They form an integrated base for the indigenous production of defence hardware and equipment that include highly specialized, complex and large variety of ammunition and explosives, weapons vehicles and equipments, materials and components, armoured vehicles and ordnance equipment. They also produce rockets, grenades, mines, transport vehicles, optical and fire control systems, bridges, parachutes, clothing and personal equipment for the armed forces.

Products for the Defence Forces have to be safe, reliable, consistent and capable of operating under varying terrains as well as under extreme climatic conditions. Accordingly, the required technologies cover a wide spectrum of engineering, metallurgy, chemical, textile, leather and optical areas, they must ensure high quality and productivity, apart from meeting the important objective of self-reliance. The Ordnance Factories also fulfil certain requirements of the paramilitary and police forces for arms, ammunition, clothing and equipment thereby ensuring that their capacity is optimally utilized, not only by securing work from the defence forces, but also by diversification into non-defence customers and by exports.

A modernization plan for all Ordnance Factories has been finalized. The plan envisages upgrading technology, augmenting capacities and replacement of old/obsolete plant and machinery with those having state-of-the-art technology. Modernisation and automation of the infrastructure in the Ordnance Factories is being done to meet the Quantitative and qualitative demands of the end products. The product technology, as well as the process requirements and capabilities, are kept in mind during the process of modernisation. The technologies and machines being planned are flexible so as to cater to a wide range of products.

In a written note the Ministry of Defence have further stated that the Ordnance Factory Board draws up an annual action plan for taking up modernisation works in the factories. For the year 2005-2006, an amount of Rs. 250 crores has been projected in the Budget Estimates for modernisation involving replacement of old & unserviceable plant and machinery. Apart from this a significant amount sanctioned under the Head "New Capital " would also be spent on modernisation works in the existing factories. Some of the major plant and machinery being procured are Computerized Numerical Control (CNC) cold Swaging Machine, CNC Rifling Machine, Barrel Straightening Press, CNC Alignment Lathe, 3-D Coordinate Measuring Machine, CNC Chamber Boring Machine, Magnaform Machine, Luminosity Testing Machine, High Vacuum Thin Film Coating Machine, Jersey knitting Machine, Auto Side & Heal Lasting Machine, Automation of Assembly Line for Vehicle, Furnaces, X-ray Machine, Nosing Press, Horizontal Machining Centres, Vertical Machining Centres, Turning Centres etc.

In a written reply to a question on the involvement of Private Enterprises in Defence Production, the Ministry of Defence have stated that a Committee headed by Dr. Vijay L. Kelkar was set up by the Government in April 2004 to, inter alia, examine the current procedures and recommend changes required in order to modify acquisition process on an approach based on a "Product Strategy", modalities of integration of the user, Ministry of Defence and the Indian Industry including both private and public in the acquisition process of equipment required by the Armed Forces. The Report of the Committee is expected shortly. A proposal is under consideration of the Government to provide a level playing field between Indian Private companies vis-à-vis foreign suppliers and Defence Public Sector Undertakings/Ordnance Factories for evaluation of bids by off loading various taxes/duties payable by private companies and to provide similar payment terms.

In accordance with the policy decision taken by the Government in May 2001, the Defence Industry sector is opened upto 100% for Indian Private Sector participation with FDI permissible upto 26% both subject to licensing. In regard to increasing production capacity of ordnance factories the representatives of the Ministry, during the evidence held on 2nd April,2005 stated as under: "About the increase of production capacity which is concurrently being done, by 2006-07, the capacities would have been increased to 40 tanks a year; and by 207-08, it will be 45 tanks.

The Committee note that a modernisation plan which envisages upgrading technology, augmenting capacities and replacement of old/obsolete plant and machinery with those having state-of-the-art Technology has been prepared. Further Modernisation and automation of the infrastructure in the Ordnance Factories is also being done to meet the quantitative and qualitative demand of the end products. The Committee further note that in addition to significant amounts sanctioned under the Head "New Capital" an amount of Rs. 250 Crores has been projected by the Ministry in the Budget Estimates 2005-06 for modernisation involving replacement of old and serviceable plant and machinery.

The Committee are given to understand that the basic problems of the Ordnance Factories are how to augment the revenue resources and their capacity to increase the annual rate of production.

From the foregoing, the Committee are of the view that for augmenting revenue resources and production capacities of the Ordnance Factories, there is a need to significantly change the character and nature of working of these Factories by conferring on them status of Public Sector undertakings and running them on commercial lines like the PSUs. This change of the ordnance factories would enable them to raise funds from market, private banks and through Public Issue. Thus Ordnance Factories would gradually become not only financially viable but also strong enough to increase their production capacity, as envisaged. The Committee, also desire that these Ordnance Factories should take upon themselves the task of peripheral development and social work responsibilities in area of their operation like other PSUs. The Ordnance Factories can involve private sector in product upgradation and value addition wherever feasible.

The Committee desire that an in-depth study of the modernisation requirements of each ordnance factory, based on its future requirements, should be carried out and a time-bound programme should be chalked out to modernise the ordnance factories. There is also an unstated perception in the Defence Forces regarding unsatisfactory quality control of equipment produced by the Ordnance Factories. They establish their credibility with their main customers, the Armed Forces. The Committee desire that a vigorous quality maintenance drive be carried out in the Ordnance Factories, so that the Armed Forces are not hesitant about the quality of equipment and stores supplied to them from Ordnance Factories. The Committee also desire that Quality Control Organisation may be reviewed and re-structured including transferability of HRD posts. Supplier-Quality Control and user Committee should be established and Quality Control Authority be responsible to the user.

It has been brought out that outdated ammunition is either put on fire or sometime fire takes place of obsolete ammunition. In all parts of the world, there is a complete service which is available for re-cycling of ammunition. The process consists of dismantling the shell and removal of explosives. The entire machinery is self contained and consists of a Mobile Modular Complex with sub-modules with the help of electric generators can be operated by virtue of which the obsolete ammunition is re-cycled by the state of art technology over other methods of destroying or otherwise disposing outdated ammunition. All types of ammunition can be de-militarised from small arms i.e. grenades of bigger Missiles. The Committee are of the opinion that steps should be taken immediately to have the complete services for re-cycling of the obsolete ammunition so as to yield substantial quantities of usable explosives, ferrous/non-ferrous metals. Besides, it saves the lives of lot of people.

India's Military Preparedness

India has a penchant for blacklisting foreign arms producers without considering negative effects it has on India's military preparedness. This is the reason why recent reports of irregularities in the procurement of seven Barak anti-missile defence systems and 200 missiles from Israel Aircraft Industries Ltd (IAI) have caused serious concern to the Indian Armed Forces. They fear that the Government may get forced to blacklist IAI as per the provisions of defence procurement procedure. Should that happen, India's defence modernisation plan would suffer irretrievable damage.

Having seen the adverse effects of banning Bofors, HDW and Denel, they dread a similar fate for a large number of ambitious plans under implementation. IAI is deeply involved in most of the major modernisation plans of the three services. In addition to the upgradation of fighter aircraft (Jaguar, MIG-21, MIG-29 and Mirage-2000), transport aircraft (AN-32) and all helicopters of MI series, it is supplying three Airborne Early Warning and Control System (AWACS) systems to India. It is also the prime supplier of unmanned aerial vehicles to the three services. Most importantly, IAI is involved in a number of developmental projects. India simply cannot afford to cut off all dealings with it. The saga of banning Bofors, HDW and Denel cannot be repeated.

Bofors

After carrying out trials of various guns on offer, India opted for Bofors 155 mm FH-77B towed artillery system. A contract for 410 systems was signed with the Swedish firm in 1986 for Rs1437.72 crore. The contract included transfer of technology for subsequent manufacture of guns in India. India had planned to produce 1,840 pieces within the country to equip 92 artillery regiments. However, with the exposure of kickbacks, the Government banned Bofors for all future dealings. It had the following effect:-

- Although India had paid for transfer of technology, it failed to utilise it. India lost an opportunity to create a base for further development of artillery weapon systems. As a result, indigenous competence to manufacture and maintain guns remained stunted.
- As spares could not be procured from Bofors, middlemen thrived making huge profits. In the absence of adequate spares, the Army had to cannibalise parts from some guns to keep other guns functional. Essential maintenance also suffered.

- Without help from Bofors, India is struggling to carry out overhauling of guns in the stipulated time frame. It is feared that delay in overhaul will adversely affect extension of useful life of the gun systems. Indigenous capacity installed with a Base Repair Workshop is far too less and it will take unacceptably long to overhaul the complete inventory.
- The Navy was already using Bofors guns on some ships and they faced difficulties in ensuring regular supply of spares.
- Indian inventory of 84 mm Carl Gustav Rocket Launchers suffered as Carl Gustav subsequently became a subsidiary of Bofors and thus, came under the ban.

Denel

Discussions were in final stages with Denel of South Africa for 155 mm howitzers (both towed and self-propelled) when it emerged that Denel had employed unacceptable means to grab contract for the supply of NTW-20 Anti-Material Rifle. It was alleged that Denel had engaged middlemen to offer bribes to obtain sensitive information about the internal proceedings of the Commercial Negotiation Committee. The Government decided to blacklist Denel in 2005 and cancel all orders placed on it. The development was highly unfortunate. Bhim project was almost concluded with Denel's T-6 155mm turret from the G-6 being mounted on Arjun hull.

An initial order had also been placed on a public sector undertaking. With the blacklisting of Denel, Indian Army's Field Artillery Rationalisation Plan suffered a crippling blow. The total requirement envisaged by 2025 is 3600 artillery guns of 155mm/52 calibre. The current inventory is of 410 Bofors guns only. Therefore, India desperately wants to procure 400 additional gun systems (220 wheeled and 180 tracked) on priority to meet inescapable minimum requirement.

Field trials in respect of wheeled systems were carried out in 2003 to ascertain compliance of Services Qualitative Requirements. Three competitors participated-Denel, Soltam Atmos 2000 and

FH77 of SWS Defence. All the three systems failed to meet specified standards. Retrials of duly improved versions were held in 2004. With the blacklisting of Denel, the choice got limited to Soltam and FH77. As per the press reports, FH77 emerged far superior to Soltam and was the choice of the Army. However, due to politically sensitive reasons, the Government incorrectly termed the case as a single vendor situation and decided to float fresh tender enquiries with reformulated Qualitative Requirements. Tender for wheeled guns was floated in March 2007 and the second tender for tracked guns followed soon thereafter. It is learnt that 12 producers of guns have been invited.

Nearly 20 years have passed since the induction of Bofor guns; no new gun system has been procured. Due to ban on Bofors and Denel, India has shut doors on two major producers of guns and thereby limited its choice. Continued shortage of suitable 155mm/52 calibre gun systems implies major gaps in India's defence preparedness. Additionally, India's quest for indigenous production of 155 mm ammunition also suffered a major blow. Work on a new ordnance factory in Nalanda to manufacture 155mm ammunition for Bofors guns has got stalled, as Denel was to provide technical know-how. Hundreds of crores of rupees have also gone down the drain.

HDW

The case of HDW makes instructive reading. A contract was signed with the German firm in December 1981. India was to get two HDW 209 class fully built submarines and sub-assemblies and components for assembling two other submarines in India. HDW was also to provide required training to Indian personnel.

HDW delivered two submarines in 1987 and two more were assembled in India in due course. As allegations of bribery and kickbacks became public, the Government decided to blacklist the company. It was also decided not to build any more submarines of the same class. Marlog, a company jointly owned by HDW and Ferrostal, took over the responsibility to fulfil all contractual obligations.

There are just a handful of competent submarine manufacturers in the world. By blacklisting HDW, India antagonized one of the leading producers and thereby deprived itself of the benefits of latest technological advancements. HDW is the world leader with the most advanced air-independent propulsion system. Continued collaboration would have given a boost to indigenous submarine building competence. Additionally, India would have acquired wherewithal as regards maintenance, overhaul and repair support.

As India had not received the complete drawings and NATO identification numbers for all spare parts of the submarines, it faced immense problems in procuring them from other sources. Middlemen made huge profits. The Navy wanted to increase the offensive punch of the submarines by mounting Exocet missiles on it. As HDW could not be engaged, others laid unacceptably harsh conditions. Indian plans for the upgradation of the submarine entailed an increase in their length and that could be done only by HDW. To sum up, by blacklisting HDW India deprived itself of maintenance support, upgradation opportunities and development of indigenous skills.

Defence Procurement Procedure

Defence Procurement Procedure-2008 (DPP-2008) has laid down clear guidelines for all foreign vendors. They are warned not to resort to any unethical practice to influence the decision makers. A 'Pre-Contract Integrity Pact' has been made mandatory for all schemes exceeding Rupees 100 crores. The vendors are required to sign and submit it separately along with the technical and commercial offers.

It is a binding agreement in which the procurement agency promises that it will not accept bribes during the procurement process and bidders promise that they will not offer bribes. It also includes an undertaking by each bidder to disclose all payments made in connection with the contract in question to anybody (including agents and other middlemen as well as family members of officials).

The Government can enforce the following sanctions for any violation by a bidder of its commitments or undertakings:-

- Denial or loss of contract.
- Forfeiture of bid security and performance bond.

- Liability for damages to the principal and the competing bidders.
- Finally, debarment of the violator by the principal for an appropriate period of time.

While signing the final contract, every vendor (irrespective of the contract value) is required to give an undertaking that he has not given, offered or promised to give, directly or indirectly any gift, consideration, reward, commission, fees, brokerage or inducement to procure the contract. Any breach of the aforesaid undertaking by the seller or any one employed by him shall entitle the buyer to cancel the contract and all or any other contracts with the seller and recover the loss arising from such cancellation. Should the Government desire to ascertain if any unauthorized payments have been made, a vendor has to allow inspection of his account books. It will be seen that debarment of a vendor is the last resort and has to be taken only in extreme cases.

Appraisal of the Issue

Before initiating any action against a company, the Government must weigh pros and cons of all alternatives open to it. While punishing a defaulting vendor, own interests must be fully safeguarded. India must consider the following points while taking decision on blacklisting foreign vendors:-

- There are limited manufacturers of major high-tech defence systems in the world. Additionally, world defence trade is circumscribed by embargoes on technology export. Thus, there are very few manufacturers who possess and are willing to offer advanced weaponry to India.
- To develop indigenous defence industry, India needs imported technology and reliable foreign partners with long term commitment. Blacklisting nullifies all transfer of technology agreements, even if paid for.
- India needs to modernize its armed forces expeditiously and its shopping list spans a vast canvas, including all major systems. As most major defence companies produce a large array of equipment, blacklisting in one contract will have a ripple effect on all other purchases as well.

- India possesses a huge inventory of weapon platforms which are in need of immediate upgradation to increase their useful life. This task can be undertaken by a handful of companies. Banning any will reduce own options.
- No company produces a complete defence system. Most major producers are in fact mere integrators. They outsource major assemblies from varied sources. Blacklisting of an assembly supplier can also jeopardize major acquisition proposals.
- One of the stated aims of DPP-2008 is to 'demonstrate the highest degree of probity and public accountability, transparency in operations, free competition and impartiality'. Blacklisting of vendors reduces competition and forces the Government to resort to single vendor procurements with related cost penalty. This is also contrary to Government's declared policy.
- Every time a finalised contract is suspended, the earmarked funds remain unexpended resulting in their surrender.
- Most importantly, the services get deprived of the essential equipment. It may have critical effect on nation's war preparedness. Fresh floating of tenders entails major delays and cost overruns.

In every irregular transaction, there are always two parties- the bribe giver and the bribe taker. Action must be taken against both and in equal proportion. It is unfair to apportion the entire blame to bribe givers and take no action against those who demand and extract bribes. It conveys an impression that the Government is reconciled to the fact that procurement functionaries are bound to fall prey to temptations, if offered to them.

It amounts to a tacit admission by the Government of its inability to find officials with unimpeachable integrity and to exercise control over them. The Government thus, feels that the onus of keeping all transactions clean is entirely on the vendors- they should decline to pay bribes even if demanded by the decision makers. This is a strange logic. Instead of putting its own house in order, India holds foreign vendors accountable for all wrong-doings.

The Way Forward

The Government must have conclusive proof that a major breach of probity provisions has taken place. Media reports and rumours cannot be the sole basis. As has been seen, a majority of media reports are subjective, biased and even planted to sabotage a deal. This could be done either by a losing vendor or even by entities inimical to India's interests. As has been seen earlier, every blacklisting of a foreign vendor puts back India's defence modernisation plans by decades. Undoubtedly, it is the most cost effective option available to adversaries to impede India's defence preparedness.

Retaliatory action must always be well considered and commensurate with the degree of misdemeanor. It does not have to be blacklisting at the outset. It is prudent to follow a phased and graduated approach for two reasons. One, the defaulting vendor gets unambiguous message that the Government means business and the vendor should exercise due caution in further dealings. Secondly, should blacklisting become inescapable, the Government can time it to suit own requirements. In the case of HDW, hasty action to ban the company deprived India of catalogues and drawings. India could have easily waited for a few months.

India must also remember that banning a major foreign vendor mav have little effect on his business and India mav suffer more. Thus the whole exercise of punishing a foreign vendor for his alleged misdemeanor may become counter productive and end up boomeranging on India. In fact this is exactly what has happened in all cases. We have ended up shooting in our own foot. There cannot be another example of immature and reckless decision making. While trying to fix a vendor for his misconduct, we put our own defence modernisation plans in disarray, with consequent critical capability gaps and cost overruns.

The Government seems to have realised the foolhardiness of its policy. It has decided to tread cautiously. Blacklisting of Bofors has been revoked as the company is now owned by SWS Defence with considerable equity being held by a US based company. The Government should similarly allow HDW to do business with

India. Nearly 20 years have lapsed and India has not been able to collate conclusive proof of wrong-doings. It is time to close the old chapter and start afresh. Although Denel has been proscribed recently, the Government should offer a way out by asking it to make good financial loss with stiff penal deduction. For generating maximum competition to obtain best deals, the Government has to show maturity, practicality and adroit handling. Outright blacklisting is the easiest and the most imprudent way of managing a delicate and highly critical issue.

A sustained and inspired media campaign was carried out by a small section of press to sabotage Scorpene submarine deal. It is to the credit of the Government that it resisted all demands to reopen the case. It is similarly hoped that the current reports against IAI would be looked into judiciously and an objective view taken. In case any misdemeanor is proved, appropriate and balanced action should be taken against both the vendor and the functionaries involved. Blacklisting, however, must remain the last resort. Cutting off your nose to spite your face can never be considered a prudent policy.

7

Indian Army during World War II

The Indian Army during World War II in 1939, numbered just under 200,000 men. By the end of the war it would become the largest volunteer army in history, rising to over 2.5 million men in August 1945. Serving in divisions of infantry, armour and a fledgling airborne force, they fought on three continents in Africa, Europe and Asia.

The Indian Army fought in Ethiopia against the Italian Army, in Egypt, Libya and Tunisia against both the Italian and German Army, and, after the Italian surrender, the German Army in Italy. However the bulk of the Indian Army was committed to the fighting the Japanese Army, first during the defeat in Malaya and the retreat from Burma to the Indian border. Then after resting and refitting the victorious advance back into Burma, part of the largest British Empire army ever formed. These campaigns cost the lives of over 36,000 Indian servicemen, another 34,354 more were wounded, and 67,340 became prisoners of war. Their valour was recognised with the award of 4,000 decorations and 38 members of the Indian Army were recipients of the Victoria Cross or the George Cross.

The Indian Army was an experienced force, having fought in the Third Afghan War and two major campaigns in Waziristan, during 1919–1920 and 1936–1939 and in smaller disputes on the North West Frontier since World War I. There was no shortage of manpower to call upon, but they did suffer from a shortage of skilled technical personnel. The conversion of the cavalry force to a mechanized tank force had only just began, and was hampered by the inability to supply adequate numbers of tanks and armoured vehicles.

Organization

The Indian Army of 1939, was different from the Indian Army during World War I, it had been reformed in 1922, moving away from single battalion regiments to multi-battalion regiments. Overall the army was reduced to 21 cavalry regiments and 107 infantry battalions. The field army now consisted of four infantry divisions and five cavalry brigades. There was a covering force of 12 infantry brigades to protect the North West Frontier from incursions and one third of the infantry, 43 battalions, were allocated to internal security and to aid the civil power. In the 1930s, the Indian Army began a programme of modernization, they now had their own artillery—the Indian Artillery Regiment—and the cavalry had started to mechanise. By 1936, the Indian Army had committed to supplying in wartime a brigade each for Singapore, the Persian Gulf, the Red Sea, Burma and two for Egypt. But by 1939, further reductions had reduced the Indian Army to 18 cavalry regiments and 96 infantry battalions, in total 194,373 men including 34,155 non-combatants. They could also call upon 15,000 men from the Frontier Irregular Force, 22,000 men from the Auxiliary Force (India), consisting of European and Anglo-Indian volunteers, 19,000 from the Indian Territorial Force, and 53,000 from the Indian State forces.

The Indian Army started World War II underprepared and short of modern weapons and equipment. It had not expected to be involved in any hostilities and had been advised after the outbreak of war in Europe, by the British government that it was unlikely to be required at all. So it was with some surprise when the 4th Infantry and 5th Infantry divisions were requested to serve in the North African and East African Campaigns and four mule companies to join the British Expeditionary Force in France.

1940

In May 1940, agreement was reached between the British and Indian governments over the formation of another five infantry and one armoured divisions, which became the 6th, 7th, 8th, 9th,

10th infantry and the 31st Indian Armoured Divisions. These new divisions were intended to be used in the defence of Malaya (9th Division) and Iraq (6th, 8th and 10th Divisions). The 3rd Indian Motor Brigade, from the armoured division, was to go to Egypt but the formation of the rest of the armoured division was put on hold, because of the shortage of armoured vehicles.

1941

In March 1941, the Indian government revised the defence plan for India. Concerned with what the Japanese were planning and the requirement to replace the divisions sent overseas, seven new armoured regiments and 50 new infantry battalions were needed for five new infantry divisions that were formed: the 14th, 17th,19th, 20th, 34th and the two armoured formations 32nd Indian Armoured Division and 50th Indian Tank Brigade.

1942

With the previously formed divisions mostly committed overseas in 1942, the army formed another four infantry divisions (23rd, 25th, 28th, 36th) and the 43rd Indian Armoured Division. However events during 1942, and the Japanese conquests meant the 28th division was not formed and the units earmarked for it were used elsewhere. The 36th division uniquely, was created as a British Indian Army formation, but was formed from British brigades that had reached India from the Madagascar campaign and from Britain. The final division formed in 1942 was the 26th Indian Infantry Division, which was hastily formed from the various units in training or stationed near Calcutta.

After the perceived poor performance in battles in Malaya and Burma in 1942, it was decided that the existing infantry divisions were over–mechanized. To counter this the 17th and 39th divisions were selected to become light divisions, of only two brigades which would rely more on animal and four-wheel-drive transport. By December 1942, agreement was reached that India should become the base for offensive operations. Support should be in place for 34 divisions, which would include two British, one West African, one East African and eleven Indian divisions, and what was left of the Burma Army.

1943

The plans for 1943 included the formation of another infantry division, an airborne division and a heavy armoured brigade. Only the 44th Indian Armoured Division was formed, by amalgamating the 33rd and 43rd armoured divisions. There was a change to the infantry division formation, when they received two extra infantry battalions as divisional troops.

A committee was set up in 1943 to report on the readiness of the army and suggest improvements. Its recommendations were:

1. The infantry should have first claims on cadet officers and educated recruits, the quality of officers and non commissioned officers (NCO) should be improved and there should be an increase in pay.
2. Basic training should be increased to nine months followed by two months' specialised jungle training.
3. The reinforcement system should be improved and drafts should include experienced NCO's
4. Infantry brigades should include a British, an Indian and a Gurkha battalion.

To assist in the jungle training of the infantry from July 1943, the 14th and 39th divisions were converted to training divisions. The 116th Indian Infantry Brigade, part of 39th Division, provided the specialised jungle conversion training. An infantry battalion would spend from four to six months with the brigade, before being sent to the front to replace a tired battalion in one of the fighting divisions. The brigades and units of the 14th Division provided jungle training for drafts of reinforcements for the Indian battalions already serving on the Burma front.

1944

The planned 44th Indian Airborne Division was finally formed from the 44th Armoured Division, leaving the 31st Armoured as the only armoured division in the army. The infantry division formation was changed again; they were now standardised with three infantry brigades each and three infantry battalions assigned as divisional troops.

The success of the 116th brigade in training for jungle warfare was recognised. From in May 1944, 116th Brigade trained units destined for the Fourteenth Army and 150th Brigade, which was converted from the Risalpur Training Brigade, trained units destined for the Southern Army. The 155th Indian Infantry Brigade was formed to provide training for units destined for the western theatres of war.

Infantry Divisions

Infantry divisions consisted of three infantry brigades, of three infantry battalions (one British and two Indian). The divisional units were a reconnaissance unit provided by a mechanised cavalry regiment, and a heavy machine gun battalion armed with the Vickers machine gun. The divisional artillery consisted of three field artillery regiments, one anti tank and one anti aircraft regiment. There were three engineer field companies and one engineer field park company, plus signals, medical and transport units.

There were variations on the infantry formation, depending on role. The light divisions (17th and 39th) as formed in 1942 had only two brigades and lacked much heavy equipment. Transport was provided by six mule and four Jeep companies. This type of division was later dropped. The Animal and Mechanised transport divisions (A & MT) (7th, 20th and 23rd) had a mixture of animal and vehicle transport, as the name suggests. In particular, one of the vehicle-drawn field artillery regiments was replaced by a mountain artillery regiment, carried on mules. The divisional reconnaissance unit was replaced by a lightly equipped infantry battalion, and another standard infantry battalion provided the HQ Defence unit. On 27 May 1944, General George Giffard (the commander of 11th Army Group) ordered that all Indian divisions fighting in Burma should adopt the standard A & MT establishment. Late that year however, Lieutenant General William Slim (commanding Fourteenth Army) converted two divisions (the 5th and 17th) to a mixed establishment of two motorised brigades and one airportable brigade, in anticipation of mechanised operations in the comparatively open terrain of central Burma. In April 1945, the 20th Division was also converted to a partially motorised establishment by acquiring the vehicles from a British division whose personnel were being withdrawn from Burma.

Armoured Divisions

It was intended to form an armoured division in the plans for 1940, 1941 and 1942. However, the Indian armoured formations suffered from a lack of equipment. The shortage of tanks in 1940 was reflected in the organisation of 31st Armoured Division, which first had one armoured and two motor brigades. At the end of 1940, this was changed to two armoured and one motor brigade. When the 3rd Indian Motor Brigade was sent to Egypt, the British armoured division organisation of two armoured brigades and a Support group was adopted.

In June 1942, the division's establishment was fixed as one armoured and one infantry brigade. The surplus armoured brigades (50th, 254th, 255th and the 267th) became independent brigades and served in the Burma campaign. In March 1943, the shortage of technical staff forced another review of the armoured force and the 32nd and 43rd armoured divisions were amalgamated to become the 44th Indian Armoured Division. In March 1944, a further review reduced the armoured force to one division (the 31st Armoured Division serving in the Middle East) and three tank brigades (the 50th, 254th and 255th) serving in Burma.

Airborne Troops

The Indian 50th Independent Parachute Brigade was formed on 29 October 1941, with the British 151st Parachute Battalion, 152nd Indian Parachute Battalion and 153rd Gurkha Parachute Battalion, a medium machine gun company and a medium mortar detachment. The 151st Battalion was later renumbered as the 156th Battalion and returned to Britain and another Gurkha battalion (154th) was formed, but had not joined the brigade when it was heavily involved in the Battle of Sangshak in March 1944.

The headquarters of the 44th Indian Armoured Division was converted in April 1944, to 9th Indian Airborne Division, which was renamed the 44th Airborne Division a few weeks later. After a delay caused by the Japanese invasion of India, the division resumed forming in July. It absorbed the 50th Parachute Brigade, and later two brigades from the disbanding Chindit force The division now consisted of the 50th, 77th Parachute Brigades and 14th Airlanding Brigade, two field artillery regiments, two anti-aircraft regiments and a joint anti-aircraft and anti-tank regiment.

Artillery

The Royal Artillery still provided some of the artillery required for Indian Army formations, but the Indian Regiment of Artillery had been formed in 1935, initially consisting of four horse–drawn batteries. The regiment was expanded during the war and by 1945, had formed 10 field artillery regiments, 13 mountain artillery regiments, 10 anti–tank artillery regiments. Three anti–aircraft brigades were formed from the four heavy anti–aircraft artillery regiments and five light anti–aircraft artillery regiments created. For the regiments service during the war it was granted the title *Royal Indian Artillery* in 1945.

Engineers

The Indian Engineers were a part of every division in the army. The engineers corps started the war with two army troops companies, 11 Field Companies and one field park company. Expansion during the war took the totals of engineers to; five army troops companies, 67 Field companies, six independent field squadrons, 20 field park companies and two independent field park squadrons.

Women's Auxiliary Corps

The Women's Auxiliary Corps was formed in May 1942, recruits had to be a minimum age of 18 years and their duties were clerical or domestic. In December 1942, the minimum age was reduced to 17 years and 11,500 women had enlisted by the end of the war. Volunteers could enlist on Local service of General service terms, those on General service could be sent to serve anywhere in India. Compared to over two million men a corps of 11,500 women does not seem many, but recruitment was always hampered by caste and communal inhibitions. Indian women at the time did not mix socially or at work with men and a large part of the corps was formed from the Anglo–Asian community.

Indian States Forces

The Indian States or Princely states provided 250,000 men during the war. They contributed five cavalry regiments and 36 infantry battalions, and between them had 16 infantry battalions plus signal, transport and pioneers companies on active service. One of their men Captain Mahmood Khan Durrani was awarded the George Cross while in Japanese captivity.

Chindits

The Chindits (named after a mythical beast, statues of which guarded Burmese temples) were the brainchild of Brigadier Orde Wingate, who intended that long-range penetration raids behind enemy lines would become the main effort against the Japanese in Burma. In 1943, he mounted Operation *Longcloth* by the 77th Indian Infantry Brigade. In 1944, they staged a much larger operation which involved disbanding the 70th British Infantry Division, Its three brigades together with three more brigades were grouped as *Special Force* and referred to for cover purposes as 3rd Indian Infantry Division. Chindits were in fact ordinary infantry units arbitrarily selected for the mission on the basis of their availability. There was no commando, airborne or other selection procedure, although there was some "weeding out" of less fit personnel during training for operations.

The Chindits were disbanded in February 1945. Several of the brigade headquarters and many of the veterans of the Chindit operations were reformed and merged into 44th Airborne Division, while the force headquarters and signals units formed the core of XXXIV Indian Corps.

Armies

The Indian Army supplied formations for the following Allied armies:

Eighth

The Eighth Army was formed from the Western Desert Force in September 1941, under the command of Lieutenant General Sir Alan Cunningham. Over time Eighth Army would be commanded by Generals Neil Ritchie, Claude Auchinleck and Bernard

Montgomery. In the early years of the war Eighth Army suffered from poor leadership and repeated reversals of fortune until the Second Battle of El Alamein when it advanced across Libya into Tunisia.

Ninth

The Ninth Army was formed on 1 November 1941 with the re designation of the Headquarters of the British Troops in Palestine and Transjordan. It controlled British and Commonwealth land forces stationed in the eastern Mediterranean. Its commanders were General Sir Henry Maitland Wilson and Lieutenant-General Sir William George Holmes.

Tenth

The Tenth Army was formed in Iraq and from the major part of Paiforce after the Anglo-Iraqi War. It was active in 1942–1943, under the command of Lieutenant-General Sir Edward Quinan and consisted of the III Corps and the XXI Indian Corps. Its main task was the maintenance of the lines of communication to the Soviet Union from the Persian Gulf to the Caspian and the protection of the South Persian and Iraqi oilfields which supplied Britain with all its non American sourced oil.

Twelfth

The Twelfth Army was reformed in May 1945, to take control of operations in Burma from the Fourteenth Army. The army Headquarters was created by re designating the Headquarters of the XXXIII Indian Corps, under Lieutenant-General Sir Montagu Stopford.

Fourteenth

The Fourteenth Army was a multinational force comprising units from Commonwealth countries, many of its units were from the Indian Army as well as British units and there were also significant contributions from 81st, 82nd and 11th African divisions. It was often referred to as the "Forgotten Army" because its operations in the Burma Campaign were overlooked by the contemporary press, and remained more obscure than those of the corresponding formations in Europe for long after the war. It was formed in 1943, under the command of Lieutenant General William Slim. The Fourteenth Army was the largest Commonwealth Army during the war, with nearly a million men by late 1944. At various times, four corps were assigned to the army: IV Corps, XV Indian Corps, XXXIII Indian Corps and the XXXIV Indian Corps.

Southern

The Southern Army was formed from Southern Command in 1942, and disbanded in August 1945. Mostly a British formation used on internal security and for units out of the front line. The 19th Indian Infantry Division was one of its units from 1942 to 1944.

North Western

The North Western Army was formed from North Western Command in April 1942, formed to guard the North West Frontier it controlled the Kohat, Peshawar, Rawalpindi, Baluchistan and Waziristan Districts.

Middle East and Africa

North Africa

Just before the declaration of war one Indian infantry brigade was sent to reinforce the British garrison in Egypt. In October 1939, a second brigade was sent and both were grouped together as the 4th Indian Infantry Division. By March 1940, two additional brigades and a divisional headquarters were sent to Egypt which became the 5th Indian Infantry Division.

Operation Compass (4th Indian and 7th Armoured Division) was the first major Allied military operation of the Western Desert Campaign during the Second World War. It resulted in British and Commonwealth forces pushing across a great stretch of Libya and capturing almost all of Cyrenaica, 115,000 Italian soldiers, hundreds of tanks and artillery pieces and more than 1,100 aircraft with very few casualties of their own.

The Allies success against the Italians forced the Germans to reinforce North Africa. The Afrika Corps commanded by Erwin

Rommel attacked in March 1941. The 3rd Indian Motor Brigade, fought a delaying battle at Meikili on 6 April, which allowed the 9th Australian Division to safely withdraw to Tobruk.

Operation Battleaxe (4th Indian and 7th Armoured) in June 1941 had the goal of clearing eastern Cyrenaica of German and Italian forces; one of the main benefits of this would be the lifting of the Siege of Tobruk. The operation did not succeed losing over half of their tanks on the first day and only achieved victory at one out of three thrusts. On the second day, they achieved mixed results, being pushed back on their western flank but repelled a significant German counter-attack in their centre. On the third day, the British narrowly avoided outright disaster by successfully withdrawing just prior to a German encircling movement which would have cut them off from retreat.

Operation Crusader (4th Indian, 7th Armoured, 1st South African, 2nd New Zealand and 70th British divisions) between 18 November–30 December 1941. The initial plan was to destroy the Axis armoured force before advancing its infantry. 7th Armoured were heavily defeated by the Afrika Korps at Sidi Rezegh. Rommel's subsequent advance of his armoured divisions to the Axis fortress positions on the Egyptian border failed to find the main body of the Allied infantry, which had bypassed the fortresses and headed for Tobruk, so Rommel had to withdraw his armoured units to support the fighting at Tobruk. Despite achieving some tactical successes at Tobruk, the need to preserve his remaining forces prompted Rommel to withdraw his army to the defensive line at Gazala, west of Tobruk, and then all the way back to El Agheila.

4th Division left the desert for Cyprus and Syria in April 1942. By May 1942, their 11th Brigade had returned attached to the 5th Indian fighting south of Tobruk.. Their 5th Brigade returned in June 1942, and fought at Mersa Matruh. The 10th Indian Infantry Division arrived from Syria, in time to take part in the Battle of Gazala May–June 1942, then held the Axis forces for 72 hours, in the First Battle of El Alamein permitting Eighth Army to safely withdraw. HQ 4th Division returned for the Second Battle of El Alamein, holding Ruweisat Ridge at the centre of the Eighth

Army's line, made a mock attack and two small raids intended to deflect attention to the centre of the front.

Operation Pugilist (4th Indian, 2nd New Zealand and 50th Northumbrian divisions) was an operation in the Tunisian Campaign The object of was to destroy the Axis forces in the Mareth Line, and to capture Sfax. Pugilist itself was indecisive and failed to make a decisive breakthrough. It did, however, establish an alternative route of attack and thus laid the ground for Supercharge II, an outflanking manoeuvre via the Tebaga Gap.

East Africa

The Italian conquest of British Somaliland started on the 3 August 1940, the 3/15th Punjab Regiment were amongst the forces on hand and the were quickly reinforced from Aden by the 1/2nd Punjab Regiment on the 7 August. After the battle of Tug Argan the British force were forced to withdraw, the 3/15th Punjab forming part of the rearguard. By the 19 August the British and Indian battalions were evacuated to Aden. British ground losses were 38 killed, 102 wounded, and 120 missing, compared to Italian casualties of 465 killed, 1,530 wounded, and 34 missing.

In December 1940, the 4th Indian Infantry Division was rushed from Egypt to join the 5th Indian Infantry Division in the Sudan. From February to April 1941, the Indian 4th and 5th Infantry Divisions took part in the Battle of Keren, By the end of the campaign the Italian forces had been cleared from Eritrea and Abyssinia 220,000 of them becoming prisoners of war.

Iraq and Persia

In 1941, forces were required to participate in the Anglo-Iraqi War, to safeguard the overland supply route to the Soviet Union. In April the 8th Indian Infantry Division landed at Basra and marched on Baghdad securing Iraq for the Allied cause from the pro German Rashid Ali Operation Barbarossa the German invasion of the Soviet Union in June 1941, placed the Persian oil fields in danger from the advancing German Army. In August 1941, the Indian 8th and 10th Infantry Divisions invaded southern Persia to secure the oil installations.

The 8th and 10th Indian Infantry Divisions, 2nd Indian Armoured Brigade and the British 4th Cavalry Brigade. Were all involved in the Anglo-Soviet invasion of Iran (August–September 1941), which was rapid and conducted with ease. From the south two battalions from 8th Divisions 24th Indian Brigade making an amphibious crossing of the Shatt al-Arab, captured the petroleum installations at Abadan. The 8th Division then advanced from Basra towards Qasr Shiekh and by 28 August had reached Ahvaz when the Shah ordered hostilities to cease. Further north, eight battalions of British and Indian troops under Major-General William Slim advanced from Khanaqin into the Naft-i-Shah oilfield and on towards the Pai Tak Pass, leading towards Kermanshah and Hamadan. The Pai Tak position was taken on 27 August after the defenders had withdrawn in the night and the planned assault on Kermanshah on 29 August was aborted when the defenders called a truce to negotiate surrender terms.

After hostilities had ended the 2nd Indian Infantry Division, 6th Indian Infantry Division and 12th Indian Infantry Division all remained in the region on internal security duties.

Syria and Lebanon

The Indian Army supplied the 5th brigade, 4th Indian Infantry Division which attacked from the south with the Australian I Corps and the 10th Indian Infantry Division which also had the 17th Indian Infantry Brigade, 8th Indian Infantry Division under command was part of Iraqforce attack northern and central Syria from the east. 5th Brigade took part in the Battle of Kissoué and the Battle of Damascus, June 1941, and 10th Division the Battle of Deir ez-Zor in July.

South-East Asia

Hong Kong

The Japanese Army attacked Hong Kong on the 8 December 1941, less than eight hours after their attack on Pearl Harbor, among the defenders were the 5/7th Rajput Regiment and the 2/14th Punjab Regiment. The garrison held out for 18 days before being forced to surrender.

Malaya

As in Egypt, the Indian Army dispatched one infantry brigade to Malaya just before the start of the war. By 1941, all training and equipment was geared to fight in North Africa and the Middle East and the forces in Burma and Malaya had been depleted to supply reinforcements to the forces in the west. So in the spring of 1941, the 9th Indian Infantry Division was sent to Malaya,

On 8 December, the Japanese Army attacked the Malayan peninsula, the defenders now included the Indian 9th and the 11th Indian Infantry Divisions, the 12th Indian Infantry Brigade and a number of independent battalions and units of Imperial Service Troops, in the III Indian Corps. The 11th Indian division fought the Battle of Jitra 11–13 December, the Battle of Kampar 30 December–2 January, the Battle of Slim River 6–8 January 1942. The 44th Indian Infantry Brigade and the 45th Indian Infantry Brigade had arrived as reinforcement in January 1942. The 45th Brigade fought the Battle of Muar 14–22 January, of the 4,00 men in the brigade only 800 survived the battle.

Singapore

The Battle of Singapore 31 January–15 February ended with the capture of 9th and 11th Indian Divisions and the 12th, 44th and 45th brigades and 55,000 Indian servicemen were made prisoners of war.. During the battle for Singapore Indian units fought in the Battle of Bukit Timah and the Battle of Pasir Panjang.

Burma

At the same time the 9th Division was sent to reinforce Malaya, in the spring of 1941, an infantry brigade was sent to reinforce Burma followed by a second brigade later in the year. On 8 December the Japanese Army invaded Burma from Siam. Withdrawing to India the last British and Indian escaped from Burma in July 1942.

Japanese conquest of Burma

The Battle of Bilin River was fought in February 1942, by the 17th Indian Infantry Division. The 17th Division held the Japanese at the Bilin River for two days of close-quarters jungle fighting. The Japanese tactics were to outflank, and eventually with encirclement imminent, they were given permission to fall back. The division disengaged under cover of darkness and began a 30 miles (48 km) retreat along the dusty track to the Sittang bridge. The Battle of Sittang Bridge followed after which 17th Division lost most of its artillery, vehicles and other heavy equipment. Its infantry manpower was 3,484 just over 40% of its establishment, though it was already well under-strength before the battle started. The Battle of Pegu in March was carried out by the surviving elements of 17th Division and the 7th British Armoured Brigade which had just arrived from the Middle East. In April the Battle of Yenangyaung was fought between the 7th Armoured Brigade, 48th Indian Infantry Brigade and 1st Burma Division for control of the Yenangyaung oil fields. The Japanese suffered heavy casualties during the battle, but the Allied forces were too weak to hold the oil fields and had to retreat to the north. The fighting retreat to India, was successfully completed in May just before the monsoons would have cut them off..Approximately 12,000 of the 40,000 Indian prisoners of war who were captured either during the Malayan campaign or surrendered at Singapore were led by Mohan Singh as the First Indian National Army which was dissolved in December 1942.

Burma Campaign 1943

The Arakan Campaign which began in December 1942, conducted by what at the time was an improvised formation 14th Indian Infantry Division was a failure. The average British and Indian soldier was not properly trained for fighting in jungle, which together with repeated defeats adversely affected morale. This was exacerbated by poor administration in the rear areas. Drafts of reinforcements sent to replace casualties were found in some cases to have not even completed basic training. There were also question asked about the ability of the Indian Army's high command, which led to the creation of the position of Supreme Allied Commander South East Asia Command, leaving the army high command to concentrate on internal security and administration. There was continual patrol activity and low-key fighting south of Imphal, but neither army possessed the resources to mount decisive operations. 17th Division held positions around the town of Tiddim 100 miles (160 km) south of Imphal, and skirmished with units of the 33rd Japanese Division. The Japanese had a shorter and easier supply line from the port of Kalewa on the Chindwin River and had the upper hand for most of 1942 and 1943.

Burma Campaign 1944

The Battle of the Admin Box (5th, 7th and 26th Indian, 81st (West Africa) Division, 36th British Infantry Division) in February, came after a limited allied offensive. The Japanese had infiltrated the widely dispersed lines of the 7th Division, and moved north undetected crossed the Kalapanzin River and swung west and south, and attacked the HQ of 7th Division. The forward divisions were ordered to dig in and hold their positions rather than retreat, while the reserve divisions advanced to their relief. On the ground, the fighting for the Admin Box was severe and Japanese fire caused heavy casualties in the crowded defences and twice set ammunition dumps on fire. However, all attempts to overrun the defenders were thwarted by the tanks of the 25th Dragoons. Although Allied casualties were higher than the Japanese, the Japanese had been forced to abandon many of their wounded to die. For the first time in the Burma Campaign, the Japanese tactics had been countered and turned against them and British and Indian soldiers had held and defeated a major Japanese attack.

The Battle of Imphal and the Battle of Sangshak (17th, 20th, 23rd Indian Divisions, 50th Indian Parachute Brigade and 254th Indian Tank Brigade) took place in the region around the city of Imphal, the capital of the state of Manipur in North-East India from March until July 1944. Japanese armies attempted to destroy the Allied forces at Imphal and invade India, but were driven back into Burma with heavy losses.

The Battle of Kohima (50th Indian Parachute Brigade 5th, 7th Indian and 2nd British Division) was the turning point of the Japanese U Go offensive. The Japanese attempted to capture Kohima ridge, a feature which dominated the road by which the major British and Indian troops at Imphal were supplied. British and Indian reinforcements counter-attacked to drive the Japanese from the positions they had captured. The Japanese abandoned the ridge But continued to block the Kohima-Imphal road. From May 16 to 22 June, the British and Indian troops pursued the retreating Japanese and reopened the road. The battle ended on 22 June when British and Indian troops from Kohima and Imphal met at Milestone 109,

Burma Campaign 1945

The Battle of Meiktila and Mandalay (5th 7th, 17th, 19th, 20th Indian, 2nd British Divisions and 254th and 255th Indian Tank Brigades) between January and March 1945, were decisive battles near the end of the Burma Campaign. Despite logistical difficulties, the Allies were able to deploy large armoured and mechanised forces in Central Burma, and also possessed air supremacy. Most of the Japanese forces in Burma were destroyed during the battles, allowing the Allies to later recapture the capital, Rangoon, and reoccupy most of the country with little organised opposition.

The Battle of Ramree Island (26th Indian Infantry Division was fought for six weeks during January and February 1945, as part of the XV Indian Corps 1944–45 offensive on the Southern Front of the Burma Campaign. Ramree Island lies off the Burma coast and was captured along with the rest of Southern Burma, during the early stages of the Campaign, by the rapidly advancing Imperial Japanese Army in 1942. In January 1945 the Allies were able to launch attacks to retake Ramree and its neighbour Cheduba, with the intention of building sea-supplied airbases on them.

Operation Dracula and the Battle of Elephant Point (5th, 17th Infantry, and 44th Indian Airborne Division 2nd, 36th British Division and 255th Tank Brigade) was the name given to an airborne and amphibious attack on Rangoon by British and Indian forces. When it was launched, the Imperial Japanese Army had already abandoned the city.

Return to Malaya and Singapore

25th Indian Infantry Division with 3 Commando Brigade, in January 1945 the Division took part in the first large scale Amphibious Operations in South East Asia, They were ferried across the Four Mile wide Mayu Estuary to land on the Northern beaches of Akyab Island, in the course of the following weeks they occupied Myrbaw and Ruywa. In April 1945.

The division was withdrawn to South India to prepare for Operation Zipper the invasion of Malaya, having been chosen for the assault landing role. Although hostilities then ceased, the operation proceeded as planned, 23rd and 25th Divisions was the first formations to land in Malaya 9 September, and then accepting the surrender of the Japanese Army.

Operation Tiderace (5th Indian Infantry Division) commenced when troops set sail from Trincomalee and Rangoon on August 21 for Singapore. The fleet arrived in Singapore on September 4, 1945, and Japanese forces in Singapore officially surrendered to Admiral Lord Louis Mountbatten, Supreme Allied Commander South East Asia Command on 12 September 1945.

Mopping up

After the Japanese surrender some divisions were sent to disarm the Japanese and assist the local governments. 7th Division moved to Thailand, where it disarmed the Japanese occupying army, and liberated and repatriated Allied prisoners of war. 20th Division was sent to Indo China occupying the southern part of the country.

There were several battles with the Viet Minh who were intent on achieving independence. 23rd Division was sent to Java, where the end of the war had brought widespread disorder and conflict between the Dutch colonial regime and pro-independence movements.

Europe

France

Probably the most unusual posting of any unit of the Indian Army during World War II was in 1940, when four mule companies of the Indian Army Service Corps joined the British Expeditionary Force (BEF) in France, and were evacuated from Dunkirk with the rest of the BEF in May 1940, and were still stationed in England in July 1942.

Italy

The Allies landed in Italy 9 September 1943, the 4th, 8th 10th Divisions and the 43rd Independent Gurkha Infantry Brigade were all involved during the campaign In October 1943, the 8th Indian Division fighting on the Adriatic front reached the Barbara Line which was breached in early November.

The 8th Division lead the assault on the German defensive Bernhardt Line, crossed the Sangro River and advanced to just short of Pescara where Eighth Army halted to wait for better weather in the spring.

The 4th Indian Division took part in the second battle of Monte Cassino, In the final fourth battle of Monte Cassino 11 May on the Eighth Army front, XIII Corps had made two strongly opposed crossings of the Rapido by the 4th British Infantry Division and 8th Indian Division. By 18 May the Germans had withdrawn to their next line.

The Gothic Line formed the last major line of defence in the final stages of the war along the summits of the Apennines The Gothic Line was breached on both the Adriatic and the central Apennine fronts during the Battle of Gemmano in August (4th Indian Divisions last battle before moving to Greece).

On 5th Army's far right wing, on the right of the XIII Corps front, 8th Indian Division fighting across trackless ground had captured the heights of Femina Morta, and 6th British Armoured Division had taken the San Godenzo Pass on Route 67 to Forlì, both on 18 September. On 5 October 10 Indian Division, switched from British X Corps to British V Corps, had crossed the Fiumicino river high in the hills and turned the German defensive line on the river forcing the German Tenth Army units downstream to pull back towards Bologna.

In the 1945 spring offensive the critical role of getting across the Senio, honeycombed with defensive tunnels and bunkers front and rear, was given to 8th Indian Division, reprising the role they played crossing the Rapido in the final Battle of Monte Cassino. On 29 April 1945, the Germans signed an instrument of surrender, and hostilities in Italy formally ceased on 2 May.

Greece

On 24 October 1944, the 4th Indian Infantry Division were shipped to Greece, to help stabilise the country after the German withdrawal. The plan called for 4th Division to be dispersed in three widely scattered areas.

7th Indian Brigade with Divisional troops were allocated Greek Macedonia, Thrace and Thessaly, with instructions to keep watch on the borders of Yugoslavia and Bulgaria. 11th Indian Brigade would garrison the towns of Western Greece and the Ionian islands. 5th Indian Brigade would take over the Agean area and the Cyclades, and would move into Crete when the enemy garrisons in that island capitulated.

On 3 December the ELAS members of the Greek Government resigned. A general strike was declared, and police opened fire on demonstrators. In Italy 4th British Infantry Division and 46th British Infantry Divisions were ordered to leave for Greece. On 15 January a truce had been concluded in Athens, by the terms of which ELAS undertook to withdraw from the capital and Salonika and to occupy rural concentration areas. Except for isolated incidents this truce ended operations in Greece.

India

The 14th Indian Infantry Division and the 39th Indian Infantry Division were converted to training formations in 1943, and remained in India till the end of the war. Other units that only served in India include the 32nd Indian Armoured Division and the 43rd Indian Armoured Division which never completed forming before being converted to the 44th Indian Airborne Division in 1943. The Assam based 21st Indian Infantry Division was also broken up to form 44th Airborne in 1944. The 34th Indian Infantry Division provided the garrison for Ceylon, and remained there during the war, they were disbanded in 1945, never having seen active service.

Victoria Cross

Indian personnel received 4,000 awards for gallantry, and 31 Victoria Crosses. The Victoria Cross (VC) is the highest military decoration which is, or has been, awarded for valour "in the face of the enemy" to members of the armed forces of the Commonwealth countries, and previous British Empire territories. The Victoria Cross is awarded for... most conspicuous bravery, or some daring or pre-eminent act of valour or self-sacrifice, or extreme devotion to duty in the presence of the enemy.

The following members of the Indian Army were recipients of the Victoria Cross in World War II;

East African Campaign Awards

- Second-Lieutenant Premindra Singh Bhagat, Corps of Indian Engineers

  During the pursuit of the enemy following the capture of Metemma on the night 31 January – 1 February 1941, for his persistence (over a period of 96 hours working from dawn to dusk) and gallantry, in personally supervising the clearing of 15 minefields.

- Subadar Richhpal Ram, 6th Rajputana Rifles (posthumous award)

  On 7 February 1941 at Keren, Eritrea, Richhpal Ram led a successful attack on the enemy and subsequently repelled six counter-attacks and then, without a shot left, brought the few survivors of his company back. Five days later, when leading another attack, his right foot was blown off, but he continued to encourage his men until he died.

Malayan Campaign Awards

On 3 January 1942 near Kuantan, Malaya, the Japanese made a furious attack on the battalion and a strong enemy force penetrated the position. Cumming, with a small party of men, immediately led a counter-attack and although all his men became casualties and he, himself, had two bayonet wounds in the stomach he managed to restore the situation sufficiently for the major portion of the battalion and its vehicles to be withdrawn.

Later he drove in a carrier, under very heavy fire, collecting isolated detachments of his men and was again wounded. His gallant actions helped the brigade to withdraw safely.

Tunisian Campaign Awards

On the night of 19–20 April 1943 at Djebel Garci, Tunisia, despite being wounded took command of the company, leading them in hand-to-hand fighting. Wounded again, he continued rallying his men until he died.

On 5–6 April 1943 during the silent attack on Rass-es-Zouai, Tunisia, Lalbahadur Thapa, commanding two sections, made his first contact with the enemy at the foot of a pathway winding up a narrow cleft which was thickly studded with enemy posts. The garrison of the out-posts were all killed by the subadar and his men, by kukri or bayonet and the next machine-gun posts were dealt with similarly. This officer then continued to fight his way up the bullet-swept approaches to the crest where he and the riflemen with him killed four-the rest fled. This made advance by the whole division was made possible.

Burma Campaign Awards

On 11 June, 1944, when his platoon come within twenty yards of the Pin Hmi Road Bridge, the enemy opened heavy and accurate fire, inflicting severe casualties and forcing the men to seek cover. Captain Allmand, however, with the utmost gallantry charged on by himself, hurling grenades into the enemy gun positions and killing three Japanese himself with his kukrie. Inspired by the splendid example of their platoon commander the surviving men followed him and captured their objective. Two days later Captain Allmand, owing to casualties among the officers, took over command of the Company and, dashing thirty yards ahead of it through long grass and marshy ground, swept by machine gun fire, personally killed a number of enemy machine gunners and successfully led his men onto the ridge of high ground that they had been ordered to seize. Once again on June 23 in the final attack on the Railway Bridge at Mogaung, Captain Allmand, although suffering from trench-foot, which made it difficult for him to walk, moved forward alone through deep mud and shell-holes and charged a Japanese machine gun nest single-handed, but he was mortally wounded and died shortly afterwards.

On 9 July 1944, Major Blaker was commanding a company

which was held up during an important advance by close-range firing from medium and light machine-guns. The major went ahead of his men through very heavy fire and despite being severely wounded in the arm, located the machine-guns and charged the position alone. Even when mortally wounded he continued to cheer on his men whilst lying on the ground. His fearless leadership inspired his men to storm and capture the objective.

On 2 March 1945, during an attack, Naik Fazal Din's section was held up by fire from the enemy bunkers, whereupon he personally attacked the nearest bunker and silenced it, then led his men against the other. Suddenly six Japanese, led by two officers wielding swords rushed out and Naik Fazal Din was run through the chest by one of them. As the sword was withdrawn, the naik wrested it from the hands of its owner and killed him with it. Having killed another Japanese with the sword he waved it aloft, continuing to encourage his men before staggering back to make his report and collapsing.

During the period 24–27 May 1943, Havildar Gaje Ghale was in charge of a platoon of young soldiers engaged in attacking a strong Japanese position. Wounded in the arm, chest and leg he nevertheless continued to lead assault after assault, encouraging his men by shouting the Gurkha's battle-cry. Spurred on by the irresistible will of their leader, the platoon stormed and captured the position which the havildar then held and consolidated under heavy fire, refusing to go to the Regimental Aid post until ordered to do so.

On 5 March 1945 his company became pinned down by an enemy sniper and were suffering casualties. As this sniper was inflicting casualties on the section, Rifleman Bhanbhagta Gurung, being unable to fire from the lying position, stood up fully exposed to the heavy fire and calmly killed the enemy sniper with his rifle, thus saving his section from suffering further casualties.The section advanced again but came under heavy fire once again. Without waiting for orders, Gurung dashed out to attack the first enemy fox-hole. Throwing two grenades, he killed the two occupants and without any hesitation rushed on to the next enemy fox-hole and killed the Japanese in it with his bayonet. He cleared two further fox-holes with bayonet and grenade. "During his single-handed attacks on these four enemy fox-holes, Rifleman Bhanbhagta Gurung was subjected to almost continuous and point-blank Light Machine Gun fire from a bunker on the North tip of the objective." For the fifth time, Gurung "went forward alone in the face of heavy enemy fire to knock out this position. He doubled forward and leapt on to the roof of the bunker from where, his hand grenades being finished, he flung two No. 77 smoke grenades into the bunker slit." Gurung killed two Japanese soldiers who ran out of the bunker with his Kukri, and then advanced into the cramped bunker and killed the remaining Japanese soldier. Gurung ordered three others to take up positions in the bunker. "The enemy counter-attack followed soon after, but under Rifleman Bhanbhagta Gurung's command the small party inside the bunker repelled it with heavy loss to the-enemy. Rifleman Bhanbhagta Gurung showed outstanding bravery and a complete disregard for his own safety. His courageous clearing of five enemy positions single-handed was in itself decisive in capturing the objective and his inspiring example to the rest of the Company contributed to the speedy consolidation of this success.

On 12–13 May 1945, Rifleman Lachhiman Gurung was manning the most forward post of his platoon which bore the brunt of an attack by at least 200 of the enemy. Twice he hurled back grenades which had fallen on his trench, but the third exploded in his right hand, blowing off his fingers, shattering his arm and severely wounding him in the face, body and right leg. His two comrades were also badly wounded but the rifleman, now alone and disregarding his wounds, loaded and fired his rifle with his left hand for four hours, calmly waiting for each attack which he met with fire at point blank range. Afterwards, when the casualties were counted, it is reported that there were 31 dead Japanese around his position which he had killed, with only one arm.

On 6 April 1944, Jemadar Abdul Hafiz was ordered to attack with his platoon a prominent position held by the enemy, the only approach to which was across a bare slope and then up a very steep cliff. The Jemadar led the assault, killing several of the enemy himself and then pressed on regardless of machine-gun fire from another feature. He received two wounds, the second of which was fatal, but he had succeeded in routing an enemy vastly superior in numbers and had captured a most important position.

On 18 March 1945, Lieutenant Karamjeet Singh Judge, a platoon commander of a company ordered to capture a cotton mill, dominated the battlefield by his numerous acts of gallantry. After eliminating ten enemy bunkers he directed one tank to within 20 yards of another and asked the tank commander to cease fire while he went in to mop up. While doing so he was mortally wounded.

On 12 June 1944,'B' Company was attempting to stem the enemy's advance when it came under heavy machine-gun and tank machine-gun fire. Rifleman Ganju Lama, with complete disregard for his own safety, took his PIAT gun and, crawling forward, succeeded in bringing the gun into action within 30 yards of the enemy tanks, knocking out two of them. Despite a broken wrist and two other serious wounds to his right and left hands he then moved forward and engaged the tank crew who were trying to escape. Not until he had accounted for all of them did he consent to have his wounds dressed.

On 23 June 1944, during an attack on the railway bridge, a section of one of the platoons was wiped out with the exception of Rifleman Tul Bahadur Pun, his section commander and one other. The section commander immediately led a charge on the enemy position but was at once badly wounded, as was the third man. Rifleman Pun, with a Bren gun continued the charge alone in the face of shattering fire and reaching the position, killed three of the occupants and put five more to flight, capturing two light machine-guns and much ammunition. He then gave accurate supporting fire, enabling the rest of his platoon to reach their objective.

on 26 June 1944, under withering fire Agansing Rai and his party charged a machine-gun. Agansing Rai himself killed three of the crew. When the first position had been taken, he then led a dash on a machine-gun firing from the jungle, where he killed three of the crew, his men accounting for the rest. He subsequently tackled an isolated bunker single-handed, killing all four occupants. The enemy were now so demoralised that they fled and the second post was recaptured.

On 22 November 1944, Sepoy Bhandari Ram's platoon was pinned down by machine-gun fire. Although wounded he crawled up to a Japanese light machine-gun in full view of the enemy and was wounded again, but continued crawling to within 5 yards of his objective. He then threw a grenade into the position, killing the gunner and two others. This action inspired his platoon to rush and capture the enemy position. Only then did he allow his wounds to be dressed.

On 19–20 January 1945, Lance Naik Sher Shah was commanding a left forward section of his platoon when it was attacked by overwhelming numbers of Japanese. He broke up two attacks by crawling right in among the enemy and shooting at point-blank range. On the second occasion he was hit and his leg shattered, but he maintained that his injury was only slight and when the third attack came, he again crawled forward engaging the enemy until he was shot through the head and killed.

On 2 March 1945, Naik Gian Singh who was in charge of the leading section of his platoon, went on alone firing his tommy gun, and rushed the enemy foxholes. In spite of being wounded in the arm he went on, hurling grenades. He attacked and killed the crew of a cleverly concealed anti-tank gun, and then led his men down a lane clearing all enemy positions. He went on leading his section until the action had been satisfactorily completed.

On 11–12 March 1944, Naik Nand Singh, commanding a leading section of the attack, was ordered to recapture a position gained by the enemy. He led his section up a very steep knife-edged ridge under very heavy machine-gun and rifle fire and although wounded in the thigh, captured the first trench. He then crawled forward alone and, wounded again in the face and shoulder, nevertheless captured the second and third trenches.

On 6 January 1943, Havildar Parkash Singh drove his own carrier forward and rescued the crews of two disabled carriers under very heavy fire. Again on 19 January in the same area he rescued two more carriers which had been put out of action by an enemy anti-tank gun. He then went out yet again and brought to safety another disabled carrier containing two wounded men.

On 16/17 February 1945, Jemadar Prakash Singh was commanding a platoon which took the main weight of fierce enemy attacks. He was wounded in both ankles and relieved of his command, but when his second-in-command was also wounded, he crawled back and took command of his unit again, directing operations and encouraging his men. He was wounded in both legs a second time but he continued to direct the Defence, dragging himself from place to place by his hands. When wounded a third time and final time, he lay shouting the Dogra war-cry as he died, inspiring his company that finally drove off the enemy.

On 15–16 December 1944,Havildar Umrao Singh was a field gun detachment commander in an advanced section of the 30th Mountain Regiment, Indian Artillery, attached to the 81st West African Division. Singh's gun was in an advanced position, supporting the 8th Gold Coast Regiment. After a 90 minute sustained bombardment from 75 mm guns and mortars, Singh's gun position was attacked by at least two companies of Japanese infantry. Using a Bren light machine gun he directed the rifle fire of the gunners, holding off the assault, and was wounded by two grenades. A second wave of attackers killed all but Singh and two other gunners, but was also beaten off. The three soldiers had only a few bullets remaining, and these were rapidly exhausted in the initial stages of the assault by a third wave of attackers. Undaunted, Singh picked up a "gun bearer" (a heavy iron rod, similar to a crow bar) and used that as a weapon in hand to hand fighting. He was seen to strike down three infantrymen, before succumbing to a rain of blows. Six hours later, after a counter attack, he was found alive but unconscious near to his artillery piece, almost unrecognisable from a head injury, still clutching his gun bearer. Ten Japanese soldiers lay dead nearby. His field gun was back in action later that day.

On 25 October 1944, two platoons were ordered to attack a particularly strong enemy position. The platoon commanded by Subadar Ram Sarup Singh attained its objective, completely routing the enemy, and although the subadar was wounded in both legs he insisted on carrying on. Later, the enemy's fierce counter-attack was only halted by Subadar Ram Sarup Singh's dashing counter-charge in which he killed four of the enemy himself. He was again wounded, in the thigh, but continued to lead his men, killing two more of the enemy, until he was mortally wounded.

On 25–26 June 1944, Acting Subedar Thapa was in command of a small isolated hill post at Bishenpur, Burma when the Japanese army attacked in force. The men, inspired by their leader's example, held their ground and the enemy were beaten off, but casualties were very heavy and reinforcements were requested. When these arrived some hours later they also suffered heavy casualties. Thapa retrieved the reinforcements' ammunition himself and mounted an offensive with grenades and kukris, until he was killed.

Italian Campaign Awards

On 10 July 1944, a rifle section commanded by Naik Yeshwant Ghadge came under heavy machine-gun fire at close range which killed or wounded all members of the section except the commander. Without hesitation Naik Yeshwant Ghadge rushed the machine-gun position, first throwing a grenade which knocked out the machine-gun and firer and then he shot one of the gun crew. Finally, having no time to change his magazine, he clubbed to death the two remaining members of the crew. He fell mortally wounded, shot by an enemy sniper.

On 10 November 1944, Rifleman Thaman Gurung was acting as a scout to a fighting patrol. It was undoubtedly due to his superb gallantry that his platoon was able to withdraw from an extremely difficult position without many more casualties than were in fact incurred and that some very valuable information was obtained which resulted in the capture of the feature three days later. The rifleman's bravery cost him his life.

On 9 April 1945, during the crossing of the Senio River, only Sepoy Ali Haidar and the two other men of his section managed to get across under heavy machine-gun fire. Then, while the other two covered him, the sepoy attacked the nearest strong point and, in spite of being wounded, put it out of action. In attacking a second strong-point he was again severely wounded but managed to crawl closer, throw a grenade and charge the post; two of the enemy were wounded, the remaining two surrendered. The rest of the company were than able to cross the river and establish a bridgehead.

On 9 April 1945, Italy, when a small party were almost wiped out in an assault on the east floodbank of the river, Sepoy Namdeo Jadav carried two wounded men under heavy fire through deep water, up a steep bank and through a mine belt to safety. Then, determined to avenge his dead comrades, he eliminated three enemy machine-gun posts. Finally, climbing on top of the bank he shouted the Maratha war cry and waved the remaining companies across. He not only saved many lives but enabled the battalion to secure the bridgehead and ultimately to crush all enemy resistance in the area.

On 12 May 1944, the company advance was held up by heavy machine-gun fire from four posts on the front and flanks. The capture of the position was essential and Sepoy Kamal Ram volunteered to get round the rear of the right post and silence it. He attacked the first two posts single-handed, killing or taking prisoner the occupants and together with a Havildar he then went on to complete the destruction of a third. His outstanding bravery unquestionably saved a difficult situation at a critical period of the battle.

On 18–19 September 1944, when a company of the 9th Gurkha Rifles encountered bitter opposition from a German prepared position, Rifleman Sher Bahadur Thapa and his section commander, who was afterwards badly wounded, charged and silenced an enemy machine-gun. The rifleman then went on alone to the exposed part of a ridge where, ignoring a hail of bullets, he silenced more machine-guns, covered a withdrawal and rescued two wounded men before he was killed.

George Cross

The George Cross (GC) is the counterpart of the Victoria Cross and the highest gallantry award for civilians as well as for military personnel in actions which are not in the face of the enemy, or for which purely military honours would not normally be granted.

The following members of the Indian Army were recipients of the George Cross in World War II;

He was taken prisoner by the Japanese after they invaded Hong Kong in December 1941. After the Japanese discovered that he was related to the ruler of one of the Princely States they demanded that he renounce his allegiance to the British and foment discontent in the ranks of Indian prisoners in the prison camps. He refused and was thrown into the notorious Stanley Jail in May 1942 where he was starved and brutalised. When he remained firm in his allegiance to the British on his return to the prison camps he was again incarcerated in Stanley Jail where he was starved and tortured for five months. He was then returned to the original camp, where he continued in his allegiance to the British, and even helped to organise escape attempts by other prisoners. He was sentenced to death, with over thirty other British, Chinese and Indian prisoners and beheaded on 20 October 1943.

Sowar Ditto Ram was posthumously awarded the George Cross for his gallantry in helping a wounded comrade on 23 July 1944 at Monte Cassino in Italy.

At the time of his capture, he was attached to the 1st Bahawalpur Infantry of the Indian State Forces. During the retreat in Malaya in 1942, he and small party of soldiers managed to evade capture for three months before their location was betrayed to the Japanese sponsored Indian Nationalist Army. He refused to co-operate with the INA and worked to counter their attempts to infiltrate agents into India. In May 1944 he was arrested and systematically starved and tortured by the Japanese but refused to betray his comrades. He was then handed over by the Japanese to the INA where he was again brutally tortured and, at one point, sentenced to death. He stood firm throughout his ordeal.

12 April 1945 in Pyawbwe, Central Burma when he sacrificed his own life to save others.

During a field firing exercise at a rest camp in Bangalore a rifle grenade misfired and fell only 8 yards from his section. The twenty eight year old soldier rushed forward, shouting at the men to take cover and attempted to throw it to a safe distance. It exploded in his hand, wounding him fatally, but his self sacrifice saved his comrades from harm.

He was awarded the decoration for the gallantry he showed in attempting an air crash rescue on the 22nd of February, 1945 in Kletek in Java.

Sacrificd his own life on 24 June 1944 by throwing himself over a mine to protect others from the blast.

Aftermath

World War II cost the lives of over 36,000 Indian servicemen and another 34,354 more were wounded, and 67,340 became prisoners of war. World War II, would be the last time the Indian Army fought as the British Indian Army, as independence and partition followed in 1947. After partition the British Indian Army was divided between the new Indian Army and the Pakistan Army. On 3 June 1947, the British Government announced the plan for the partition of the sub–continent between India and Pakistan. On 30 June 1947, the procedure for the division of the armed forces was agreed upon. Field Marshal Claude Auchinleck, then Commander-in-Chief, India, was appointed Supreme Commander to ensure smooth division of units, stores and so on. It was announced on 1 July 1947, that both countries would have operational control of their respective armed forces by 15 August 1947. Assessment of the Indian Army's Cold Start Strategy

The Failure of the Sundarji Doctrine in Operation Parakram

Following the successful operational innovations displayed during the 1971 war, the Indian Army underwent a reorganization in the 1980s that was principally directed by Chief of the Army Staff (COAS) General Krishnaswamy Sundarrajan. Under Sundarji's strategy, the international border was protected by seven defensive "holding corps," which consisted of infantry divisions for static Defence, mobile mechanized divisions that could respond to enemy penetrations, and a small number of armored units. Although possessing limited offensive power, as their name implies, the primary role of the holding corps during a war was to check an enemy advance by manning the extensive defensive obstacles constructed in the border region.

Sundarji concentrated the army's offensive power into three mobile armored columns that were capable of striking deep into Pakistan. Each "strike corps" was built around an armored division with mechanized infantry and extensive artillery support. In a war, after the holding corps halted a Pakistani attack, the strike corps would counterattack from their bases in central India (I Corps in Mathura, II Corps in Ambala, and XXI Corps in Bhopal) and penetrate deep into Pakistani territory to destroy the Pakistan Army's own two strike corps (known as Army Reserve North and Army Reserve South) through "deep sledgehammer blows" in a high-intensity battle of attrition. The strike corps would operate under the protection of the Indian Air Force, which would be expected to first gain air superiority over Pakistan and then provide close air support to ground operations.

Although innovative, the Sundarji's doctrine proved poorly suited to respond to the challenges posed by Pakistan's proxy war in Kashmir. Following the December 13, 2001 attack on the Indian Parliament building in New Delhi by suspected Kashmiri militants, India attempted to compel Pakistan to ban the Lashkar-e-Taiyyaba and Jaish-e-Mohammad, extradite twenty named individuals accused of terrorism in India, and prevent militants from crossing the line-of-control into Kashmir by launching Operation Parakram (Operation Valor) on December 18, the largest activation of Indian forces since the 1971 Bangladesh war. Although uncertainty still surrounds the actual objectives of Operation Parakram, at a minimum, India clearly intended to signal to Pakistan that, nuclear weapons or not, it was willing to go to war to end Pakistani support for militants in Kashmir. After the attack on the heart of its government, "something concrete needed to be done to show people at home and in the international community that India meant business." Unfortunately for India's efforts, the decisiveness of its message was undercut by the inability of the Indian Army to present a timely threat to Pakistan.

The armored columns of the strike corps took nearly three weeks to make their way to the international border area after the mobilization order was given. In this intervening period, the

Pakistan Army was able to countermobilize on the border, and more important, major powers became increasingly concerned by the extent of India's military mobilization and counselled New Delhi to exercise restraint. Although initially sympathetic to India in the wake of the December 13 attack, the United Kingdom and the United States, which was conducting military operations in Afghanistan from support bases in Pakistan, were troubled by Delhi's increasing forcefulness as well as the subsequent diversion of Pakistani forces away from operations along the Afghan border that occurred in response to Parakram.

Senior British and American officials urged the Indian government to refrain from military action until Pakistani President Pervez Musharraf delivered his "about turn" speech on January 12, 2002. In a nationwide address Musharraf denounced terrorism in the name of Kashmir and pledged a renewed crackdown on militant groups in Pakistan.

By the time the strike corps had reached the border region, India's political justification for military action was significantly reduced as a result of Musharraf's declaration, and Operation Parakram quickly lost momentum. The result was a ten-month standoff, which cost an estimated $2 billion and ended with India's quiet withdrawal rather than a military clash.

Assessment of Operation Parakram's outcome within India was mixed. Senior government officials, including the Prime Minister, the Defence Minister and the National Security Advisor have all claimed that the mobilization was a successful exercise in coercive diplomacy as it pressured Washington and Islamabad to take action against Islamic militant groups based in Pakistan. In contrast, a number of independent observers believe that Operation Parakram was a less successful endeavor.

For example, former COAS Shankar Roychoudhry called the mass mobilization a "pointless gesture" that had harmed India's credibility while journalist Praveen Swami went further in denouncing Operation Parakram as "arguably the most ill-conceived maneuver in Indian military history," which "ended as an ignominious retreat after having failed to secure even its minimum objectives." Bolstering the critics' case is the fact that

India had failed to achieve either the extradition of the wanted criminals or, despite Musharraf's public statements, a permanent end to Pakistani support for terrorism within India. This latter failure was made clear in the years following Operation Parakram as the death toll from terrorist attacks in Kashmir continued to rise.

Pressure for a New Operational Concept

The Indian Army's postmortem analyses of Operation Parakram identified three principal failings with the performance of the Sundarji doctrine:

1. The enormous size of the strike corps made them difficult to deploy and maneuver. By the time the strike corps had reached their forward concentration areas, President Musharraf had given his "about turn" speech, and the international community was putting significant pressure on India to restrain its response. In the eyes of many senior Indian officers, this allowed Pakistan to inflict a high-profile attack on the Indian capital via its proxies and then exploit the Indian Army's long deployment time to internationalize the crisis in a manner that allowed Pakistan to escape retribution. Even those in the Indian government who claim that Operation Parakram was never intended to be anything more than an exercise in coercive diplomacy had to be disappointed in the long delay between policy decisions and military action.
2. The strike corps lacked strategic surprise. Pakistan had its intelligence agencies focused on the three strike corps, so that any action on their part would be quickly noticed—particularly given their large, lumbering composition. Furthermore, once the strike corps mobilized, their progress and destination could be easily deduced by Pakistani forces, which could move to counter any intended attack. 3. The holding corps' lack of offensive power was a cause for concern. Although these units were forward deployed in the border regions, they could carry out only limited offensive tasks. In the eyes of senior Indian Army officers,

the total dependence on the strike corps for offensive power hindered India's rapid response to the December 13 attacks.

Part of the blame for Operation Parakram's failure to achieve significant political aims fell on the Indian political leadership, which failed to define any strategic objectives for the mobilization. As Sawhney and Sood note, "Operation Parakram was ordered without giving any political direction to the armed forces about the target to be achieved." However, there were a number of additional factors that motivated the demand for a new operational concept capable of responding promptly to contingencies requiring limited military force in a nuclear environment:

Military Utility. A war-fighting strategy that called for massive armored thrusts to dismember Pakistan was too crude and inflexible a tool to respond to terrorist attacks and other indirect challenges. Furthermore, it was recognized that mobilizing the entire military was not an appropriate policy to pursue limited aims.

Desire to Avoid External Intervention. The long delay between the mobilization order and the actual deployment of the strike corps allowed outside powers, particularly the United States, to intervene before India could bring military force to bear. Rapid mobilization would be necessary to achieve a decisive outcome in a future crisis before Pakistan could internationalize the dispute.

Military Autonomy. It has been argued that the delay between the mobilization order and the commencement of military operations created a gap which allowed India's political leadership to lose its nerve. For its part, the army was reportedly "furious" when it was told that there would be no war with Pakistan. It is believed that the ability to rapidly mobilize and commence offensive operations will oblige the political leadership to define strategic goals ahead of a mobilization and prevent interference once military operations are underway. ? *Interservice Rivalry*. The past decade has seen the Indian Air Force and Navy enhance their relative share of the Defence budget at the army's expense. Moreover, Defence analysts suggest that airpower and sea power will play an increasingly important role in India's national security, while the army finds itself increasingly relegated to internal security missions. A new limited war doctrine that makes conventional force relevant to India's national security could justify the army's own modernization program vis-à-vis the air force and navy.

Cold Start

The Chief of Army Staff unveiled the new Cold Start concept in April 2004. The goal of this limited war strategy is to launch a retaliatory conventional strike against Pakistan before the international community could intercede, one that would inflict significant harm on the Pakistan Army while denying Islamabad a justification to escalate the clash to the nuclear level.

Cold Start seeks to leverage India's considerable conventional strength to respond to Pakistan's continued provocation. This concept requires a reorganization of the Indian Army's offensive power from the three large strike corps into eight smaller division-sized "integrated battle groups" (IBGs) that combine mechanized infantry, artillery, and armor in a manner reminiscent of the Soviet Union's operational maneuver groups. The eight battle groups would be prepared to launch multiple strikes into Pakistan along different axes of advance.

The ground operations of the IBGs require integration with close air support from the Indian Air Force and naval aviation assets to provide highly mobile fire support. According to Gurmeet Kanwal, director of the Army's Center for Land Warfare Studies, India is seeking to "mass firepower rather than forces." In addition, the holding corps are redesignated as "pivot corps" and would be bolstered by additional armor and artillery. This would allow them to concurrently man defensive positions and undertake limited offensive operations as necessary. Under the Cold Start concept, all elements of the Indian military would engage in continuous operations, day and night, until their military objectives were achieved. Rather than deliver a catastrophic blow to Pakistan (i.e., cutting the country in two), the goal of Cold Start would be to make shallow territorial gains, 50-80 kilometers deep, that could be used in post-conflict negotiations to extract concessions from Islamabad. Some commentators have emphasized the ability to quickly mass ground and air firepower to deliver a punishing blow to the Pakistan Army, perceived to be the source of much of Pakistan's aggressive foreign policy, while not harming civilian centres. Although the operational details of Cold Start remain classified, it appears that the goal would be to have three to five IBGs entering Pakistani territory within seventy-two to ninety-six hours from the time the order to mobilize is issued. As Kanwal argues, "[the IBGs] should be launching their break-in operations and crossing the 'start line' even as the holding (defensive) divisions are completing their deployment on the forward obstacles. Only such simultaneity of operations will unhinge the enemy, break his cohesion, and paralyze him into making mistakes from which he will not be able to recover."

A major emphasis of Cold Start is on the speed of both deployment and operations. By moving forces into unpredictable locations at high speeds and making decisions faster than their opponents can, the IBGs would seek to defeat Pakistani forces in the field by disrupting their cohesion in line with the tenants of maneuver warfare. The Indian Army would also seek to take advantage of surprise at both the strategic and the operational levels to achieve a decision before outside powers such as the United States or China could intervene on Pakistan's behalf. There also appears to be an unspoken assumption that rapid operations would prevent India's civilian leadership from halting military operations in progress, lest it have second thoughts or possess insufficient resolve.

The perceived advantages of the Cold Start doctrine over its predecessor are six fold:

1. Forward-deployed division-sized units can be alerted and mobilized more quickly than larger formations. If the battle groups and the pivot corps start closer to the international border, their logistics requirements are significantly reduced, enhancing their maneuverability and the ability to surprise.
2. Even though division-sized formations can "bite and hold" territory, they lack the power to deliver a knockout blow. In the minds of Indian military planners, this denies

Pakistan the "regime survival" justification for employing nuclear weapons in response to India's conventional attack.

3. Under Cold Start, the Indian Army can undertake a range of responses to a given provocation rather than the all-or-nothing approach of the Sundarji doctrine. This has the potential to enhance India's ability to deter Pakistan, as Cold Start presents a significantly more credible threat of retaliation which can create uncertainty in the minds of Pakistani decision-makers about the level of impunity their nuclear deterrent provides.
4. Multiple divisions, operating independently, have the potential to disrupt or incapacitate the Pakistani leadership's decision-making cycle, as happened to the French high command in the face of the German blitzkrieg of 1940.31 Indian planners believe that when faced with offensive thrusts in as many as eight different sectors, the Pakistani military would be hard-pressed to determine where to concentrate its forces and which lines of advance to oppose.
5. Having eight units capable of offensive action rather than three significantly increases the challenge for Pakistani intelligence's limited reconnaissance assets to monitor the status of all the IBGs, improving the chance of achieving surprise. In a limited war, India's overall goals would be less predictable than in a total war, where the intent would almost certainly be to destroy Pakistan as a state. As a result, Pakistan's Defence against Indian attacks would be more difficult because the military objectives would be less obvious.
6. If Pakistan were to use nuclear weapons against Indian forces, divisions would present a significantly smaller target than would corps. The dispersed operations by highly mobile units envisioned by Cold Start are the kind that would be required on a nuclear battlefield.

From a tactical and operational standpoint, Cold Start is a creative attempt to formulate a military solution to the security challenges on India's western border. However, the problems

India faces are both political and military in nature. As a result, it is not clear that limited war can enhance India's ability to achieve its strategic goals. This issue, along with several others is explored in the subsequent section. Five Questions About Cold Start

As of mid-2008, Cold Start is in the experimental stage of development, having moved beyond mere speculation, but still more than a decade away from achieving full implementation. As a result, there are a number of outstanding questions about the employment of Cold Start that remain to be answered. This section explores five of the most pertinent issues surrounding the limited war concept.

1. Does the Indian army possess the resources necessary to execute Cold Start?
2. There is significant disagreement as to whether India possesses sufficient conventional superiority over Pakistan to warrant discussion of a limited war strategy. Fighting on the defensive, Pakistan would have the advantage of shorter lines of communication as well as a network of linear obstacles and prepared fighting positions designed to blunt India's advance.

In these circumstances, some analysts point to the conventional wisdom of a 3 to 1 superiority in offensive strength at the tactical level as a requirement for successful breakthrough operations and note that India's deployed forces in the West achieve only parity with their Pakistani counterparts. Others suggest that a 1.5 to 1 superiority in forces at the theatre level, which India possesses, would "guarantee" an advantage in combat power ranging from 5 to 1 to 6 to 1 "on 3 or 4 decisive strike axes." As Stephen Biddle has noted, however, "Even outnumbered invaders can create a large local advantage on a chosen frontage" by differentially concentrating forces against a small section of the battle line and deploying fewer troops elsewhere. Turning to the quality of the forces on the two sides, some experts have argued that the Pakistanis are qualitatively superior to the Indians, which could make up for their numerical inferiority. Others observers believe that when quality and sophistication of weapons systems are taken into account, India's relative superiority in military forces is increased. Yet, still others contend that "neither side can undertake a major conventional attack with a high degree of confidence in its success." It is beyond the scope of this section to render a definitive judgment on the matter, rather it simply seeks to highlight the considerable uncertainty surrounding the existing conventional balance.

Looking within the Indian Army, at present there appear to be significant material shortfalls that call into question its ability to execute Cold Start in the near-term. The army's tank corps suffers from a low operational readiness rate because much of its equipment is at the end of its service life. Although several hundred T-90 tanks recently acquired from Russia possess significant battlefield capabilities, they are at best a "silver bullet" force. Similarly, the integrated battle groups will require organic self-propelled artillery to have the mobility and firepower necessary to accomplish their mission. Yet, by one estimate, the army possesses only 10% of the self-propelled guns it needs. In addition, there are serious questions as to whether the army possesses the mobility and logistical capability to implement Cold Start.

It is estimated that only thirty-five percent of the army is equipped to move about India, and an even smaller portion possesses the mobility to mount cross-border operations. Similarly, one recent assessment suggests that the armed forces possess less than 15% of the helicopter airlift capability Cold Start would require to move men and material. Limited supplies of spare parts, primitive logistical networks, and inadequate maintenance facilities will also hinder offensive operations. The army is attempting to gain the necessary funds to address these issues as part of its modernization program, however, India's Defence budget is limited, and both the air force and the navy are pressing their own competing claims. 45 Even more deficient than the Indian Army's material shortfall is its lack of officers capable of executing Cold Start operations. A Cold Start-style maneuver doctrine requires high-quality junior officers who possess the initiative and flexibility to react to changing circumstances on the battlefield without explicit instructions from their superiors.

This poses a significant challenge for the army which, as an institution, has demonstrated an unwillingness to entrust authority to junior officers and NCOs. Furthermore it faces a shortage of more than 11,000 junior officers, while those it does have are the product of a military education system that emphasizes rote learning and the careful implementation of "schoolhouse solutions" rather than free thinking. A conservative institutional culture that is resistant to change with subordinate units tightly controlled by higher command does not foster the initiative and creativity demanded by maneuver warfare.

As an army concept for warfare on land, Cold Start places the other two services in a subordinate combat role. This is particularly true of the air force. Cold Start employs airpower according to the army's own vision of joint warfare, where elements of all three services are under the control of a unified (presumably army) commander. As Y.I. Patel notes, this plan runs counter to the Indian Air Force's own concept of joint operations, which involves the services fighting wars separately but according to a coordinated plan. Furthermore, the air force believes that attaching aircraft to specific ground units in a defined geographic space, as the integrated battle group concept requires, is a fundamental misuse of airpower that fails to leverage the air force's numerical superiority over its Pakistani counterparts. Given the army's previously mentioned shortages of self-propelled artillery, close air support takes on an ever more vital role in Cold Start as the IBGs will require highly mobile firepower of the type provided by attack helicopters and ground attack aircraft.

This issue is unlikely to be resolved quickly, as the air force continues to focus its efforts on air-to-air combat and strategic bombing while downplaying the importance of close air support as a core mission. This can be seen in the IAFs recent acquisition pattern which has focused on air superiority platforms such as advanced fighter aircraft and airborne early warning systems. Moreover, the focus on the IAF's own new doctrine, which reportedly emphasizes deep attack and strategic reach, appears to be moving further away from the types of missions Cold Start would require. An operational Cold Start capability would, therefore, require the air force to support the strategy at a level at which it has heretofore been unwilling to do. In the absence of the appointment of a chief of the Integrated Defence Staff, India's three services function largely autonomously. Strong joint leadership would be required to force the army and the air force to integrate their wartime strategies and plans and overcome inter-service rivalries. Such leadership is unlikely to be forthcoming in the near term, suggesting that service-specific rather than joint warfighting strategies will continue to proliferate within the Indian military.

Does India posses the civil-military structures necessary to manage limited war in a nuclear environment?

Policymakers contemplating limited war must craft a strategy and related objectives that are achievable by the use of military force yet sufficiently limited to ensure that the conflict does not escalate to the nuclear threshold. Clear policy objectives are of utmost importance in limited wars because they must overcome both internal and external pressures to expand the scope of a conflict. Wars have a way of taking on a life of their own: Once lives have been lost, money has been spent, and territory has changed hands, leaders could face tremendous pressure to expand the scope or objectives of a conflict. In theory, clearly defined strategic objectives with a properly developed correlation between means and ends could be an effective way to prevent the escalation of a conflict.

In practice, the selection of ways and means to conduct a limited campaign can be challenging for a national security bureaucracy such as India's, which is characterized by a high degree of disconnection between civil and military authorities. In peacetime, the country's elected leadership is often disengaged from security matters and provides the military with only vague planning guidance. Within India's Defence community, civilian bureaucrats at the Ministry of Defence dominate decisionmaking, while the uniformed military is largely excluded from the security policymaking process. The impact of this disconnect between politicians and the military is apparent when evaluating Operation Parakram, which lacked clear objectives and terminated with inconclusive results. This raises questions about the ability of

India's civilian leaders to set the kind of concrete objectives and associated military tasks that would be necessary to successfully engage in limited warfare between two nuclear powers.

Where would Cold Start be employed?

At present, it is not necessarily clear where a Cold Start-style limited military operation would be directed: Against jihadi training camps in Kashmir or their support bases in Punjab and Sindh?

In pursuit of militants crossing the line-of-control?

Against vulnerable parts of Pakistan as part of a response to a terrorist attack within India?

There is an implicit assumption behind Cold Start that punishment inflicted by limited conventional strikes can persuade Pakistan to halt its support for Kashmiri militants. Theorists of both limited war and coercion have suggested that an asymmetry of interests in the particular issue being contested is an important pre-condition for the successful use of limited force to change an opponent's behaviour. Yet, the issue of Kashmir is not a peripheral one for either India or Pakistan.

As Paul Kapur notes, the disposition of the disputed territory has both important symbolic and strategic implications for the two countries. As a result, it is not necessarily clear that a sufficient level of punishment can be inflicted on Pakistan to change its behaviour without crossing its nuclear threshold.

Can India undertake limited conventional operations against Pakistan without triggering a nuclear response?

Preventing escalation in limited war requires clear signaling of intentions by both sides. However, by its very purpose, maneuver warfare seeks to surprise, confuse and disorient the adversary's decision-makers. Furthermore, it is not necessarily clear that politicalmilitary objectives that are considered limited in New Delhi will be viewed the same way in Islamabad or Rawalpindi. Cold Start envisions "limited" thrusts into Pakistan to a depth of 50-80 km. Yet as Raja Mohan notes, "in no past war [between India and Pakistan] has there been a penetration of the territory of the other side beyond 15-20 kilometers." Given that a number of important Pakistani cities, as well as transport networks and lines of communication, lie close to the international border, it is easy to see how these limited offensives could be perceived to be quite unlimited. Moreover, it is not at all clear that in a future conflict Pakistan would play by India's rules. As one Indian official has noted, "The idea that Pakistan will cooperate in a conflict and comply with India's wishes to fight a limited war is ridiculous.

It will be naturally in [Pakistan's] interest to keep any conflagration as unlimited as possible." Although the exact conditions under which Pakistan would use its nuclear weapons remain ambiguous, it has not ruled out employing them in response to a conventional attack. The clearest articulation of Pakistan's "red lines" comes from Lt. Gen. Khalid Kidwai, who, while head of the Strategic Plans Division, outlined the general conditions under which nuclear weapons could be used: India attacks Pakistan and conquers a large part of its territory; India destroys a large part of Pakistan's land or air forces; India blockades Pakistan in an effort to strangle it economically; or India pushes Pakistan into political destabilization or creates large-scale internal subversion in Pakistan.

The development of the Cold Start doctrine and associated improvements in the army's conventional war fighting capabilities has significant implications for stability on the subcontinent. Analysts such as Ashley Tellis have argued that the cornerstone of the "ugly stability" that has persisted between India and Pakistan is a product of the incapacity of either side to gain its political objectives through conventional war. As the asymmetry between India and Pakistan's conventional military power grows, Pakistan will come under increasing pressure to rely on its nuclear arsenal for selfDefence.

An operational Cold Start capability could lead Pakistan to lower its nuclear red line, put its nuclear weapons on a higher state of readiness, develop tactical nuclear weapons, or undertake some equally destabilizing course of action. As the five questions explored in this section indicate, there is still a considerable need to think through the implications of Cold Start for India's national security goals. Fostering public discussion of these types of national security matters can help ensure that India's military doctrines are well aligned with the country's grand strategy. That issue is explored in the subsequent section.

Cold Start and India's Grand Strategy

India's national security establishment faces significant difficulty in linking its grand strategy to the development of its military doctrines and plans. As a result of the grand bargain struck at independence, Indian civil-military relations appear to conform to the Huntingtonian model of separate political and military spheres: Indian service chiefs have been granted operational autonomy in return for extremely limited input into national security policy-making at the highest levels. Barry Posen has argued that the intervention of civilian leadership is necessary to ensure that a state's military doctrine is well integrated with its grand strategy, a situation that does not appear to be the case with Cold Start.

Within India, few politicians are well versed in military affairs, and the actual expertise in Defence matters possessed by civil servants in the Ministry of Defence is "patchy" at best. Moreover, following Nehru's blundering political interference in the 1962 war, Indian politicians have been wary of intervening in the details of military matters. As a result, the armed services are often left to develop their strategies and plans without significant civilian direction, a practice that is unlikely to result in the fusion of strategic and military goals.

While this structural-bureaucratic problem is unlikely to be resolved in the near term, the Indian Army can take steps to address many of the issues raised in this chapter by adopting a more transparent stance on Cold Start. The available evidence indicates that the Indian army developed Cold Start with minimal guidance from the country's political leadership. Refusal to engage in broader-based discussions of the Cold Start concept on the grounds that it is a warfighting strategy is myopic. If Cold Start is indeed a real concept for limited war rather than just a bureaucratic justification for army modernization programs, its strategic and policy implications deserve to be assessed by both India's political establishment and its strategic community. In particular, there needs to be a rigorous examination of the impact the development of an organizational Cold Start capability would have on India's strategic goals vis-à-vis Pakistan. Active pursuit of a limited war strategy runs the risk of upsetting favourable trends within Pakistan, most notably improved bilateral relations between India and Pakistan and the Pakistan Army's fight against domestic militancy.

Indo-Pak relations have improved considerably since the Composite Dialogue was initiated in February 2004. Although progress has been slow, the effort to promote a normalization of bilateral relations has resulted in the establishment of direct bus services across the line of control in Kashmir as well as confidence-building measures such as a ban on nuclear testing and a notification regime for ballistic missile tests. The new civilian Pakistani government, elected in February 2008, has signalled a more pragmatic approach to relations with India, which suggests that it may be possible for both sides to make progress on Kashmir and other outstanding territorial disputes. As Pakistan's first civilian government in years, the present coalition retains an unstable position, albeit one that has been helped by the Pakistan Army's decision to take a step backward from its visible intrusion into the country's governance. The perception of a renewed conventional threat from India could have the pernicious effect of reversing gains that have been made in the Composite Dialogue and encouraging the Pakistan army to reassert itself in the domestic political sphere.

The spread of Islamism and militancy from Pashtun tribal areas in eastern Pakistan has been a continual source of instability in Afghanistan and one that increasingly poses a threat to Pakistan itself. Over the past four years, the Pakistan Army has been focusing its attention on the Afghan border region and the associated challenge posed by domestic terrorists/insurgents in the Federally Administered Tribal Areas and North-West Frontier Province. While some Indian observers may gleefully welcome the sight of suicide bombers attacking the Pakistan Army as well-deserved "blowback" from Pakistan's past sponsorship of Jihadis in South

Asia, the fact remains that it is in New Delhi's long-term interest to see Pakistan succeed in containing the spread of Islamic militancy. As a result, any action on India's part that leads the Pakistani government to concentrate its forces on a future Indo-Pak conflict rather than domestic counterinsurgency will be self-defeating. As the analysis above indicates, the Indian Army's leaders must broaden their vision beyond the narrow military imperatives of responding to proxy war and consider the degree to which Cold Start fits in with India's broader strategic goals. At the same time, India's political leadership needs to engage with the Cold Start concept and think through the political and strategic implications of such a warfighting strategy.

It is a well-worn military axiom that no plan survives contact with the enemy. Cold Start is an example of creative military problem-solving in response to Pakistan's support for terrorism and stated rejection of a no-first-use nuclear doctrine. By moving away from the Sundarji doctrine, the Indian Army believes that it is developing the ability to respond to a Pakistani proxy war with conventional force, while remaining below the nuclear threshold. While Cold Start represents a significant advance in India's conventional capabilities, it is a concept that is poorly aligned with India's broader strategic goals. In the near term, active pursuit of Cold Start could have a pernicious impact on India's burgeoning relations with Pakistan. In the longer-term, if Cold Start were operationalized, it could risk provoking or escalating a crisis on the subcontinent that could breach the nuclear threshold.

8

Indian Peace Keeping Force and Mass Destruction

Indian Peace Keeping Force was the Indian military contingent performing a peacekeeping operation in Sri Lanka between 1987 and 1990. It was formed under the mandate of the Indo-Sri Lankan Accord signed between India and Sri Lanka in 1987 that aimed to end the Sri Lankan Civil War between militant Sri Lankan Tamil nationalists such as the Liberation Tigers of Tamil Eelam (LTTE) and the Sri Lankan military.

The main task of the IPKF was to disarm the different militant groups, not just the LTTE. It was to be quickly followed by the formation of an Interim Administrative Council. These were the as per the terms of the accord signed between India and Sri Lanka, at the behest of Rajiv Gandhi, then Prime Minister of India. Given the escalating level of the conflict in Sri Lanka, and with the pouring of refugees into India, Rajiv Gandhi, took the decisive step to push this accord through. The IPKF was inducted into Sri Lanka on the request of then-Sri Lankan president J. R. Jayewardene under the terms of the Indo-Sri Lanka Accord. Currently LTTE is proscribed as a terrorist organization by the United States and European Union.

The force was initially not expected to be involved in any significant combat by the Indian High Command. However, within a few months, the IPKF became embroiled in battle with the LTTE to enforce peace. The differences started with LTTE trying to dominate the Interim Administrative Council, and also refusing to disarm, which was a pre-condition to enforce peace in the island. Soon, these differences led to the LTTE attacking the IPKF, at which point the IPKF decided to disarm the LTTE militants, by force if required. In the two years it was in northern Sri Lanka, the IPKF launched a number of combat operations aimed at destroying the LTTE-led insurgency. Given LTTE's tactics in guerrilla warfare and using women and child soldiers to fight battles, it soon escalated into repeated skirmishes between the IPKF and LTTE.

The IPKF began withdrawing from Sri Lanka in 1989, following the election of the Vishwanath Pratap Singh government in India and on the request of the newly-elected Sri Lankan President Ranasinghe Premadasa. The last IPKF contingents left Sri Lanka in March 1990.

Background

Sri Lanka, from the early 1980s, was facing increasingly violent ethnic strife in the Sri Lankan Civil War. The origins of the Sri Lankan Civil War can be traced to the independence of Sri Lanka in 1948, after the end of British rule. At the time, a Sinhalese majority government was instituted. This government passed legislation deemed discriminatory by some against the Tamil minority in Sri Lanka.

In the 1970s, two major Tamil parties united to form the Tamil United Liberation Front (TULF), a separatist Tamil nationalist group that agitated for a separate state of Tamil Eelam in north and eastern Sri Lanka that would grant the Tamils greater autonomy within the federal structure.

However, the Sixth Amendment to the Constitution of Sri Lanka, enacted in August 1983, classified all separatist movements as unconstitutional, Outside the TULF, Tamil factions advocating more militant courses of action soon emerged, and the ethnic divisions eventually led to violent civil war.

Indian Involvement and Intervention

Initially, first under Indira Gandhi and later under Rajiv Gandhi, the Indian Government sympathized with the Tamil insurrection in Sri Lanka because of the strong support for the

Tamil cause within the Indian state of Tamil Nadu. Emboldened by this support, supporters in Tamil Nadu provided a sanctuary for the separatists and helped the LTTE smuggle arms and ammunition into Sri Lanka, making them the strongest force on the island. In fact in 1982, the LTTE supremo Prabhakran was arrested by the police in Tamil Nadu, for a shoot-out with his rival Uma Maheswaran, in the middle of the city. Both of them were arrested and later released by the police. This activity was left unchecked as India's regional and domestic interests wanted to limit foreign intervention on what was deemed as a racial issue between the Tamils and the Sinhalese. To this end, the Indira Gandhi government sought to make it clear to Sri Lankan President Junius Richard Jayewardene that armed intervention in support of the Tamil movement was an option India would consider if diplomatic solutions should fail.

The first round of civil violence flared in 1983 when the killing of 13 soldiers of the Sri Lanka Army sparked anti-Tamil pogroms—the Black July riots—in which over 3000 Tamils were killed. The riots only aided in the deterioration of the ethnic relations. Militant factions, including the LTTE, at this time recruited in large numbers and continued building on popular Tamil dissent and stepped up the guerrilla war. By May 1985, the guerrillas were strong enough to launch an attack on Anuradhapura, attacking the Bodhi Tree shrine–a sacred site for Buddhist Sinhalese–followed by a rampage through the town. At least 150 civilians died in the hour long attack.

Rajiv Gandhi's government attempted to re-establish friendly relations with the various factions in Sri Lanka while maintaining diplomatic efforts to find a solution to the conflict as well as limiting overt aid to the Tamil fighters.

The Sri Lankan government, deducing a decline in support for the Tamil rebels from India, tried to rearming itself extensively for its anti-insurgent role with support from Pakistan, Israel, Singapore, and South Africa. In 1986, the campaign against the insurgency was stepped up. In 1987, retaliating against an increasingly bloody insurgent movement, the Vadamarachchi Operation (Operation Liberation) was launched against LTTE strongholds in Jaffna Peninsula. The operation involved nearly

4,000 troops, supported by helicopter gunships as well as ground-attack aircraft. In June 1987, the Sri Lankan Army laid siege on the town of Jaffna. This resulted in large-scale civilian casualties and created a condition of humanitarian crisis. India, which had a substantial Tamil population in South India faced the prospect of a Tamil backlash at home, called on the Sri Lankan government to halt the offensive in an attempt to negotiate a political settlement. However, the Indian efforts were unheeded. Added to this, in the growing involvement of Pakistani advisers, it was necessary for Indian interest to mount a show of force. Failing to negotiate an end to the crisis with Sri Lanka, India announced on 2 June 1987 that it wound send a convoy of unarmed ships to northern Sri Lanka to provide humanitarian assistance but this was intercepted by the Sri Lankan Navy and forced to turned back.

Following the failure of the naval mission the decision was made by the Indian government to mount an airdrop of relief supplies in aid of the beleaguered civilians over the besieged city of Jaffna. On 4 June 1987, in a bid to provide relief, the Indian Air Force mounted Operation Poomalai. Five Antonov An-32s under fighter cover flew over Jaffna to airdrop 25 tons of supplies, all the time keeping well within the range of Sri Lankan radar coverage. At the same time the Sri Lankan Ambassador to New Delhi, Bernard Tilakaratna, was summoned to the Foreign Office to be informed by the Minister of State, External Affairs, K. Natwar Singh, of the ongoing operation and also indicated that the operation was expected not to be hindered by the Sri Lankan Air Force. The ultimate aim of the operation was both to demonstrate the seriousness of the domestic Tamil concern for the civilian Tamil population and reaffirming the Indian option of active intervention to the Sri Lankan government.

The Indo-Sri Lanka Accord

Following Operation Poomalai, faced with the possibility of an active Indian intervention and lacking any possible ally, the President, J. R. Jayewardene, offered to hold talks with the Rajiv Gandhi government on future moves. The siege of Jaffna was soon lifted, followed by a round of negotiations that led to the signing of the Indo-Sri Lankan Accord on July 29, 1987 that brought a temporary truce. Crucially however, the negotiations did not include the LTTE as a party to the talks.

The signing of the Indo-Sri Lankan Accord on 29 July 1987 brought a temporary truce to the Sri Lankan Civil War. Under the terms of the agreement, Colombo agreed to a devolution of power to the provinces the Sri Lankan troops were withdrawn to their barracks in the north, the Tamil rebels were to disarm.

The Mandate for the IPKF

Among the provisions undersigned by the Indo-Sri Lanka Accord was the commitment of Indian military assistance should this be requested for by the Sri Lankan Government, as well as the provision of an Indian Peace Keeping Force that would "guarantee and enforce the cessation of hostilities". It was on these grounds, and on the request of President J. R. Jayewardene, that Indian troops were inducted to Northern Sri Lanka. J N Dixit, the then Indian ambassador to Colombo, in an interview to rediff.com in 2000 described that ostensibly, Jayawardene's decision to request Indian assistance came in the face of increasing civil riots and violence within the southern Sinhala majority areas, including the capital Colombo that were initiated by the Janatha Vimukthi Peramuna and the Sri Lanka Freedom Party that necessitated the withdrawal of the Sri Lankan Army from the Tamil areas of northern Sri Lanka to maintain order.

The Indian Peace Keeping Force

Originally a reinforced division with small naval and air elements, the IPKF at its peak deployed four divisions and nearly 80,000 men with one mountain (4th) and three Infantry Divisions (36th, 54th, 57th) as well as supporting arms and services. At the peak of its operational deployment, IPKF operations also included a large Indian Paramilitary Force and Indian Special Forces elements. Indeed Sri Lanka was first theatre of active operation for the Indian Navy Commandos. The main deployment of the IPKF was in northern and eastern Sri Lanka. Upon its withdrawal from Sri Lanka the IPKF was renamed the 21st Corps and was headquartered near Bhopal and became a quick reaction force for the Indian army.

IPKF Order of Battle

Indian Army

The first Indian Army troops to be inducted into Sri Lanka were a ten thousand strong force from the 54th Infantry division, composed of elements of the Sikh Light Infantry, the Maratha Light Infantry and the Mahar Regiment which flew into Palay airbase, from July 30 onwards. This was followed later by the 36th Infantry division. By August, the 54th Infantry Division under the command of Maj Gen Harkirat Singh and the 340th Indian Inf Bde had landed in Sri Lanka. By 1987, the IPKF consisted of

- 54th Air Assault Division. (Major General Harkirat Singh (General Officer Commanding), Brigadier Kulwant Singh, Dy GOC):-Became an infantry division later due to lack of airlift capacity within the Indian armed forces.
    - o 10 Para Commando. (Jaffna)-an attached unit
    - o 65 Armoured Regiment (originally with T-54 tanks and later with T-72s).-an attached unit, it was later determined that the T55 was a better vehicle for counterinsurgency operations. Listed by some sources as an independent unit.
    - o 91 Infantry Brigade (Jaffna)
        - — 5 Madras Bn
        - — 8 Mahar Bn
        - — 1 Maratha Light Infantry Bn
    - o 76 Infantry Brigade (Brigadier I.M. Dhar) (Munnar, Vavuniya, Mulliativu)
    - o 47 Infantry Brigade (Trincomalee-Batticoloa-Amparai)
- 36 Infantry Division.
    - o 115 Infantry Brigade.(Jaffna)
        - — 5th Bn The First Gorkha Rifles.(5/1 GR).(Battle Of Urumparai,Battle Of Nallur Temple Jaffana,Battle Of Manipai)
        - — 72 Infantry Brigade.(Jaffna)
        - — 4 Bn./5 Gorkha Regiment.

— 13 Sikh LI Bn.

- o 41 Infantry Brigade. (Jaffna)
  - — 5 Rajputana Rifles

- 57th Infantry Division, trained in jungle warfare,
- 4th Mountain division, only two brigades used.
- Independent Units
  - o 340 Independent Infantry Brigade (Amphibious). (Trincomalee) The Indian Marines
  - o 18 Infantry Brigade. (Jaffna)
  - o 5 Para Battalion.

Indian Air Force

Soon after its intervention in Sri Lanka and especially after the confrontation with the LTTE, the IPKF received a substantial commitment from the Indian Air Force, mainly transport and helicopter squadrons, including:

- No. 19 Squadron-Antonov An-32s
- No 109 and No. 119 Helicopter Units-Mil Mi-8 helicopters.
- No. 125 HU-Mil Mi-24s.
- No. 664 AOP Squadron Chetak and Cheetah

Indian Navy

The Indian Navy regularly rotated naval vessels thru Sri Lanka waters, mostly smaller vessels such as patrol boats.

- Indian Naval Air Arm
  - o No. 321 Squadron of the Indian Navy-HAL Chetaks
  - o No. 310 Squadron of the Indian Navy-Breguet Alizé
- MARCOS (also the Marine Commando Force or MCF)-Took part in Operation Pawan (Hindi, "wind") in 1988 and in the raid on an LTTE base at Guru Nagar. MARCOS operators (including Lt Singh) boarded two Gemini rafts off the coast of Jaffna City and towed two wooden rafts of explosives into a channel leading to the city's Guru Nagar Jetty. Avoiding mines, eight men and two officers shifted to the wooden rafts and paddled to the jetty then

fixed demolition charges to the jetty and LTTE speedboats. The commandos were detected but laid down suppressive fire and detonated the explosives before retreating to the Geminis without taking casualties. Two nights later, commandos swam back into the harbour amidst heavy patrolling by the LTTE to destroy the remaining speedboats. They were again detected and sustained minor injuries. These actions helped recapture Trincomalee and Jaffna harbours from the LTTE. For leading these actions the 30 year old Lt. Singh became the youngest officer to receive the Maha Vir Chakra Award.

Indian paramilitary forces

- Central Reserve Police Force
- Indian Coast Guard

Combat operations

The IPKF suffered around 1,255 killed in action and several thousand wounded. After several years, the Sri Lankan Armed Forces realised the role of IPKF and proposed building a memorial to the Indian dead in Sri Lanka.

The LTTE casualties are not known reliably but number in several thousands. Some estimates state that over 7,000 cadres died in various encounters with the IPKF.

Intelligence Failures

The Indian intelligence agencies failed to consistently provide accurate information to the forces. One example is the Jaffna football ground massacre. The LTTE's disinformation machinery leaked information to the Indian army that the LTTE leader Velupillai Prabhakaran was hiding in a building near the Jaffna university football ground. The operation plan was chalked out. It was decided to airdrop commandos on the ground while subsequent movement by tank formation ensured that Prabhakaran was caught alive. It was a good plan on paper. The formation moved out. Battle-hardened commandos were selected for the operation. The commandos started moving down from helicopter. But soon a rain of bullets from the LTTE fighters and sharpshooters perched on the tree tops started to fall on the commandos. The choppers also came under fire. The fate of the tanks moving in pincer formation on the ground was not much different. The LTTE had laid anti-tank mines in the way leading to the operational zone. And the football ground massacre was complete. The irony of the entire story was that the man they were hunting for was nowhere around the area on the day of the operation.

The IPKF complained that accurate maps of the operational theatres were not made available to them by the various intelligence agencies.

There was also a case where an agent of Research and Analysis Wing (RAW) was killed in an ambush set up by the IPKF. He had been acting on orders to carry out back channel diplomacy and peacetalks with the LTTE.

Impact

The IPKF mission while having gained tactical successes, did not succeed in its intended goals. On May 21, 1991, the LTTE assassinated Rajiv Gandhi for his role in sending the IPKF to Sri Lanka.

The primary impact of the IPKF, has been that it shaped India's counter-insurgency techniques and military doctrine. On the international scene, it does not find significant mention in National or International militarv historv. The political fallout. the IPKF's casualties, as well as the deterioration of international relations has however shaped India's foreign policy towards the Sri Lankan conflict.

Assassination of Rajiv Gandhi

The decision to send the IPKF in Sri Lanka was taken by then prime-minister of India, Rajiv Gandhi, who held office until 1989. The operation in Sri Lanka was one of the factors that led to the ouster of the Rajiv Gandhi-led Congress (I) government in 1989.

Rajiv Gandhi was assassinated at a rally at Sriperumbudur on 21 May 1991, while he was campaigning for re-election during the 1991 Indian General Election, by a suicide bomber, who was a member of the LTTE, named Dhanu.

India's Foreign Policy

The debacle that was IPKF's intervention in Sri Lanka is raised at times in Indian political discourse whenever the situation in Sri Lanka shows signs of deteriorating, and there is a question of intervening; or, in Sri Lankan politics (particularly by the LTTE), when it is proposed that India, or, more broadly, other foreigners, ought to have a role in promoting peace on the island nation.

As a result, relations between India and Sri Lanka became extremely sour and India vowed never to offer any military help to Sri Lanka again. This policy has not been changed since and no defence pact has been signed between India and Sri Lanka. India has never been directly involved in the peace talks between the LTTE and Sri Lanka but has supported Norway's efforts.

Controversies

The IPKF's role in the Sri Lankan conflict was much maligned by voices both there and at home at the time. It was alleged by the LTTE to have engaged in a number of incidents of human rights violation. Some neutral organisations also alleged the IPKF and LTTE to have engaged with scant regard for civilian safety and to have violated human rights. These allegations led to considerable outcry and public resentment within Sri Lanka as well as India, especially in Tamil Nadu, where the IPKF came to be viewed as an invading and oppressing force.

Indian forces were accused of indulging in number of civilian massacres, Involuntary disappearances and rapes during their time in the Northeastern province of Sri Lanka. These include complicity in the incidents such as Valvettiturai massacre in which on 2, 3, and 4 August 1989 over 50 Tamils were massacred by the Indian Peace Keeping Force in Valvettiturai, Jaffna. In addition to the killings over 100 homes, shops and other property were also burnt and destroyed. Another notable incident was the Jaffna teaching hospital massacre on October 22, 1987, following a confrontation with Tamil militants near the hospital, IPKF quickly entered the hospital premises and massacred over 70 civilians. These civilians included patients, two doctors, three nurses and a pediatric consultant who were all in uniform. The hospital never completely recovered after this massacre. The IPKF was also accused of complicity in murder of Sinhalese civilians in the 1987 Trincomalee massacre where according to Asian Times in August 1987, a number of majority Sinhalese civilians were massacred. The then Sri Lankan government accused the Madras Regiment posted in the Trincomalee district of complicity, although the Indian officials denied responsibility, they withdrew the Madras Regiment from Trincomalee district.

Indian paramilitary forces

Central Reserve Police Force

The Central Reserve Police Force (CRPF) is a paramilitary security agency/Force functioning under the aegis of Ministry of Home Affairs(MHA), Government of India. The CRPF's primary role lies in assisting the State/Union Territories in police operations to maintain law and order and contain insurgency. It came into existence as the Crown Representative's Police on 27 July 1939. After Indian Independence, it became the Central Reserve Police Force on enactment of the CRPF Act on 28 December 1949.

The Director General of CRPF is Mr.SIS Ahmed of 1970 IPS batch,appointed on 1 March 2007 who was earlier the Director General of CISF since 6 May 2005.

Besides Law and Order and counter insurgency duties, the role of CRPF in the General Elections, held repeatedly during the past few years, has been very significant and vital. This is especially true for the trouble torn states of J&K, Bihar and in the North East. During the Parliamentary elections of September 1999, the CRPF played a major role in the security arrangements. The CRPF is one of the largest paramilitary force in the world with 200 battalions besides various establishments. Of late, CRPF contingents are also being deployed in UN missions.

History

CRPF was originally created as CRP(Crown Representative Police) on 27 July 1939, with 2 Battalions. Its primary duty at that time was to protect the British residents in sensitive states. In 1949, Sardar Patel had it renamed as CRPF under the CRPF Act. The

Sixties saw major expansion of CRPF in which many State Reserve Police Battalions were merged with CRPF. Today, the force has 200 Battalions. CRPF has been active against foreign invasion and domestic insurgency.

On 21 October 1959, Dy.S.P. Karam Singh and his 20 soldiers were attacked by the Chinese Army, at Hot Springs in Ladakh. 10 were killed and the rest were taken prisoners. 21 October is now remembered across the country as POLICE COMMEMORATION DAY.In the 1965 India-Pakistan war, two companies (approx. 150 men) of the 2nd Battalion of CRPF defeated an infantry brigade (approx. 1600 men) of Pakistan Army at Kanjar Kot in Gujarat.

The CRPF guarded the India-Pakistan border until 1965, at which point the Border Security Force was created for that purpose.

On 13 December 2001, the CRPF troopers killed all five terrorists who had entered the premises of the Indian Parliament at New Delhi.

In 2005, the CRPF troops killed all terrorists who had stormed the Ram Temple at Ayodhya.

In recent years, the Central Government has decided to follow up on recommendations of the Cabinet to use each security agency for its mandated purpose. Therefore, the counterinsurgency operations in India has been entrusted to the CRPF. The CRPF is currently charged with securing the Kashmir valley. Recently CRPF have completely relieved the Border Security Force in the Kashmir Valley of its Internal Security duties.

Organization

The CRPF is headed by Director general and is divided into ten administrative sectors headed each by an Inspector General.Each Sector consists of one or more administrative and/or Operational Ranges,headed by an officer of the rank of Deputy Inspector General of Police.Group Centres are headed by Addl DIGs. There are 200 CRPF battalions of 720 constables approximately each and commanded by an officer designated as Commandant and consists of seven CRPF companies.The Companies are in charge of Assistant Commandants.

The Rapid Action Force

The Rapid Action Force (RAF) is a specialised 10 battalion wing of the Indian Central Reserve Police Force.

It was formed in October 1992, to deal with communal riots and related civil unrest. The battalions are numbered from 99 to 108.

Weapons

CRPF uses basic Infantry weapons such as:

1. FN 35 and Glock 17 9 mm pistols
2. Heckler & Koch MP5 replacing the Carbine 1A 9 mm sub-machine guns
3. INSAS 5.56 mm assault rifles replacing the FN FAL, 1A1, 1C, AKM and V.58 7.62 mm assault rifles
4. INSAS 5.56 mm light machine guns replacing the 7.62 mm FN MAG, Bren L4 and the.50 cal Browning M2HB machine guns
5. Dragunov, Mauser SP66 and Heckler & Koch MSG-90 7.62 mm sniper rifles
6. AGS-17 Plamya 30 mm automatic grenade launcher
7. M40 RCL 106 mm and Carl Gustav 84 mm recoiless rifles. CRPF also uses landmine detectors; Light Machine-Guns and Heavy-Machine-Guns.strling carbine9mm

Women in the CPRF

The CRPF is the only Paramilitary Force in the world to have two battalions staffed entirely by women. The first battalion was raised in 1986 with its headquarters at New Delhi. The second battalion came into existence in 1996 at Gandhinagar, Gujarat.

The Green Force

Another specialised outfit of the CRPF is the Green Force. The force has been able to effectively check environmental degradation and sustain the regeneration of local flora and fauna. Every year Green Force personnel plant lakhs (hundreds of thousands) of trees in various parts of the country.

Indian Coast Guard

The Indian Coast Guard is a part of Armed forces (under Navy) of India created to guard Republic of India's vast coastline. Many people confuse the Indian Coast Guard as an Armed Force (akin to the Indian Army, Navy and Air Force) since it is placed under the Ministry of Defence. The Indian Coast Guard's structure is similar to the other Para Military Forces of India such as the Border Security Force (BSF) and the Central Industrial Security Force (CISF) which are all constituted as 'Armed Forces' of India (so is the Indian Coast Guard), wherein the 'Armed Force' means a Force which is authorised by the Government to Handle and use Arms in the legal discharge of their duties. It was created on 18 August 1978 as an independent entity as per the Coast Guard Act. It's primary objective is to guard India's vast coastline and operates under the effective control of the Ministry of Defence.

The coast guard works closely with the Indian Navy and the Indian Customs Department, and is generally headed by a naval officer of the rank of Vice-Admiral. India's coast guard has a large number of fast craft including hovercrafts and hydrofoils. They patrol the seas and river mouths. The coast guard has performed a number of commendable tasks of rescuing distressed personnel. It has also apprehended pirates on high seas and cleaned up oil spills. Heavy patrolling of sensitive areas such as Gujarat, West Bengal and Mumbai have resulted in the nabbing of a large number of smugglers and illegal immigrants.

Unfortunately, the Indian Coast Guard was unable to intercept the heavily armed terrorists who came ashore from small boats during the seaborne November 2008 Mumbai attacks. After hijacking a fishing trawler to provide cover and avoid detection by the Indian Coast Guard, terrorists showed fake identification papers to Indian Coast Guard boarding officers and were allowed to continue on their way. Terrorist teams then sailed close to the Mumbai coast and deployed in small boats laden with arms and explosives. Once ashore, they killed and wounded hundreds in a standoff battle that went on for four days. After this attack decision was taken to improve the service by providing more assets and setting up nine more stations.

India and weapons of mass destruction

India does possess nuclear weapons and maintains short-and intermediate-range ballistic missiles, nuclear-capable aircraft, surface ships, and submarines under development as possible delivery systems and platforms. Although it lacks an operational ballistic missile submarines India has ambitions of possessing a nuclear triad in the near future when INS Arihant the lead ship of India's *Arihant* class of nuclear-powered submarines formally joins the Indian Navy in 2012 after undergoing extensive sea-trials. Though India has not made any official statements about the size of its nuclear arsenal, estimates suggest that India has between 40 and 95 nuclear weapons, consistent with estimates that it has produced enough weapons-grade plutonium for up to 75-110 nuclear weapons. Production of weapons-grade plutonium production is believed to be taking place at the Bhabha Atomic Research Centre, which is home to the CIRUS reactor acquired from Canada, to the indigenous Dhruva reactor, and to a plutonium separation facility.

India is not a signatory to the 1968 Nuclear Non-Proliferation Treaty (NPT), which India argues entrenches the status quo of the existing nuclear weapons states whilst preventing general nuclear disarmament. India tested a nuclear device in 1974 (code-named "Smiling Buddha"), which it called a "peaceful nuclear explosive." The test used plutonium produced in the Canadian-supplied CIRUS reactor, and raised concerns that nuclear technology supplied for peaceful purposes could be diverted to weapons purposes. This also stimulated the early work of the Nuclear Suppliers Group. India performed further nuclear tests in 1998 (code-named "Operation Shakti").

Brief Historical Overview

As early as 26 June 1946, Pandit Jawaharlal Nehru, soon to be India's first Prime Minister, announced: As long as the world is constituted as it is, every country will have to devise and use the latest devices for its protection.

India's first Nuclear test occurred on 18 May 1974. Since then India has conducted another series of tests at the Pokhran test range in the state of Rajasthan in 1998. India has an extensive civil and military nuclear program, which includes at least 10 nuclear reactors, uranium mining and milling sites, heavy water production facilities, a uranium enrichment plant, fuel fabrication facilities, and extensive nuclear research capabilities.

In 1998, as a response to the continuing tests, the United States and Japan imposed temporary economic sanctions on India.

Current Arsenal and Estimates of Inventory

- In 2005, it was estimated that India had between 40 and 50 warheads.
- In November 2008, the Bulletin of the Atomic Scientists estimated that India has about 70 assembled nuclear warheads, with about 50 of them fully operational.
- A report by David Albright, published by the Institute for Science and International Security in 2000, estimated that India at end of 1999 had 310 kilograms of weapon grade plutonium, enough for 65 nuclear weapons. He also estimated that India had 4,200 kg of reactor grade plutonium which is enough to build 1,000 nuclear weapons. By the end of 2004, he estimates India had 445 kilograms of weapon grade plutonium which is enough for around 85 nuclear weapons considering 5 kg of plutonium required for each weapon.
- Former R&AW official J.K. Sinha, claimed that India is capable of producing 130 kilograms of weapon grade plutonium from six "unsafeguarded" reactors not included in the nuclear deal between India and the United States.

Doctrine

India has a declared nuclear no-first-use policy and is in the process of developing a nuclear doctrine based on "credible minimum deterrence." In August 1999, the Indian government released a draft of the doctrine which asserts that nuclear weapons are solely for deterrence and that India will pursue a policy of "retaliation only". The document also maintains that India "will not be the first to initiate a nuclear first strike, but will respond with punitive retaliation should deterrence fail" and that decisions to authorize the use of nuclear weapons would be made by the Prime Minister or his 'designated successor(s).'"

According to the NRDC, despite the escalation of tensions between India and Pakistan in 2001-2002, India remains committed to its nuclear no-first-use policy.

Command and Control

India's Strategic Nuclear Command was formally established in 2003, with an Air Force officer, Air Marshal Asthana, as the Commander-in-Chief. The joint services SNC is the custodian of all of India's nuclear weapons, missiles and assets. It is also responsible for executing all aspects of India's nuclear policy. However, the civil leadership, in the form of the CCS (Cabinet Committee on Security) is the only body authorized to order a nuclear strike against another offending strike: In effect, it is the Prime Minister who has his finger "on the button."

International Treaties

India is not a signatory to either the Nuclear Non-Proliferation Treaty (NPT) or the Comprehensive Test Ban Treaty (CTBT), but did accede to the Partial Test Ban Treaty in October 1963. India is a member of the International Atomic Energy Agency (IAEA), and four of its 17 nuclear reactors are subject to IAEA safeguards.

India announced its lack of intention to accede to the NPT as late as 1997 by voting against the paragraph of a General Assembly Resolution which urged all non-signatories of the treaty to accede to it at the earliest possible date.

India voted against the UN General Assembly resolution endorsing the CTBT, which was adopted on 10 September 1996. India objected to the lack of provision for universal nuclear disarmament "within a time-bound framework." India also demanded that the treaty ban laboratory simulations. In addition, India opposed the provision in Article XIV of the CTBT that requires India's ratification for the treaty to enter into force, which India argued was a violation of its sovereign right to choose whether it would sign the treaty. In early February 1997, Foreign

Minister Gujral reiterated India's opposition to the treaty, saying that "India favors any step aimed at destroying nuclear weapons, but considers that the treaty in its current form is not comprehensive and bans only certain types of tests."

In August 2008, the International Atomic Energy Agency (IAEA) approved safeguards agreement with India under which the former will gradually gain access to India's civilian nuclear reactors. In September 2008, the Nuclear Suppliers Group granted India a waiver allowing it to access civilian nuclear technology and fuel from other countries. The implementation of this waiver makes India the only known country with nuclear weapons which is not a party to the NPT but is still allowed to carry out nuclear commerce with the rest of the world.

Since the implementation of NSG waiver, India has signed nuclear deals with several countries including France, United States,, Mongolia, Namibia, and Kazakhstan while the framework for similar deals with Canada and United Kingdom are also being prepared.

Ballistic missiles

Astra

Under former president Dr. Abdul Kalam India pursued the Integrated Guided Missile Development Program (IGMDP) which was an Indian Ministry of Defence program for the development of a comprehensive range of missiles, including the intermediate range Agni missile (Surface to Surface), and short range missiles such as the Prithvi ballistic missile (Surface to Surface), Akash missile (Surface to Air), Trishul missile (Surface to Air) and Nag Missile (Anti Tank). Other projects such Indian Ballistic Missile Defence Program have derived from the IGMDP. In 2005, India became only the fourth country to have Anti Ballistic capability when India tested two systems the AAD and PAD.

India has methodically built an indigenous missile production capability, using its commercial space-launch program to develop the skills and infrastructure needed to support an offensive ballistic missile program. For example, during the 1980s, India conducted a series of space launches using the solid-fueled SLV-3 booster. Most of these launches put light satellites into near-earth orbit. Elements of the SLV-3 were subsequently incorporated into two new programs. In the first, the new polar-space launch vehicle (PSLV) was equipped with six SLV-3 motors strapped to the PSLV's first stage. The Agni IRBM technology demonstrator uses the SLV-3 booster as its first stage.

Prithvi

The Prithvi (Sanskrit: "Earth") I is mobile liquid-fueled 150 kilometer tactical missile currently deployed with army units. It is claimed that this missile is equipped only with various conventional warheads (which stay attached to the missile over the entire flight path). The missile is of particular interest to the United States (and potential buyers) in that has the capability of maneuvering in flight so as to follow one of several different pre-programmed trajectories. Based on the same design, a modified Prithvi, the Prithvi II, is essentially a longer-ranged version of the Prithvi I except that it has a 250-kilometer range and a lighter payload. It is suspected that any nuclear missions will be executed by the Prithvi II. Currently, the Prithvi II has completed development and is now in production. When fielded, it will be deployed with air force units for the purpose of deep target attacking maneuvers against objectives such as air fields.

- Prithvi I — Army Version (150 km range with a payload of 1,000 kg)
- Prithvi II — Air Force Version (250 km range with a payload of 500 kg)
- Prithvi III — Naval Version (350 km range with a payload of 500 kg)

The Prithvi missile project encompassed developing 3 variants for use by the Indian Army, Indian Air Force and the Indian Navy. The initial project framework of the Integrated Guided Missile Development Program outlines the variants in the following manner. in October 2009 India conducted 2 simultenous user trials of 350 km extended range Prithvi II to be used for strategic purposes.

Dhanush

Dhanush (Sanskrit: Bow) is a naval variant of the Prithvi missile. It can fire either the 250 km or the 350 km range missiles. Supposedly it is a customised version of the Prithvi and that the additional customizations in missile configuration are to certify it for sea worthiness. Dhanush has to be launched from a hydraulically stabilized launch pad. Its low range acts against it and thus it is seen a weapons either to be used to destroy an aircraft carrier or an enemy port. Indian Navy's K-15 Sagarika submarine-launched ballistic missile is reported to be a variant of the Dhanush missile.

The ship launched Dhanush Ballistic Missile was tested from INS Subhadra of the Sukanya class patrol craft in 2000. INS Subhadra is a vessel which was modified and the missile was launched from the reinforced helicopter deck. The 250 km variant was tested but the tests were considered partially successful. In 2004, the missile was again tested from the INS Subhadra and was this time successful. Then the following year in December the missile's 350 km version was tested from the INS Rajput and hit the land based target.

Agni

The Agni (Sanskrit: Fire) missile system comprises three missiles:

- Agni I,
- Agni II
- Agni III

Agni-I uses the SLV-3 booster (from India's space program) for its first stage and a liquid-fueled Prithvi for its second stage.

Nuclear-capable Agni-II missiles have a range of up to 3,000 km and can carry a payload of 1,000 kg. Unlike the Agni-I, the Agni-II has a solid-fueled second stage.

In July 2006, India successfully test-fired Agni-III, a two-stage nuclear-capable ballistic missile with a range of 3,000 km. Both stages of the Agni-III utilizes solid-fuel propellants and its range can be extended to 4,000 km. The missile is capable of carrying a nuclear payload within the range of 600 to 1,800 kg including decoys and other anti-ballistic counter-measures.

India's DRDO is also working on a submarine-launched ballistic missile version of the Agni-III missile, known as the Agni-III SL. This missile is expected to provide India with a credible sea-based second strike capability. According to Indian Defence sources, Agni-III SL will have a range of 3,500 km. In addition, the 5,000 km range Agni-V ICBM is expected to be tested by 2010-11.

Surya

The report of Surya ICBM has not been confirmed by officials of the Indian government and have repeatedly denied the existence of the project. The Surya ICBM is an ICBM program that has been mentioned repeatedly in the Indian press. Surya (meaning Sun in Sanskrit and many other Indian languages) is the codename for the first Intercontinental Ballistic Missile that India is reported to be developing. The DRDO is believed to have begun the project in 1994. As the missile is yet to be developed, the specifications of the missile are not known and the entire program continues to remain highly speculative. Estimates of the range of this missile vary from 5,000 kms to 10,000 kms. It is believed to be a three-stage design, with the first two stages using solid propellants and the third-stage using liquid. In 2007, the *Times of India* reported that the DRDO is yet to reveal whether India's currently proposed ICBM will be called Agni-V (or Surya-1). As of 2009 it was reported that the government had not considered an 8,000-km range ICBM.

Four decades of investments in a missile-related design, development, and manufacturing infrastructure have also made this sector less vulnerable to long-term disruption by technology denial regimes. More significantly, India's sophisticated civilian satellite launch capability makes it one of the few developing states theoretically capable of building an intercontinental ballistic missile (ICBM).

Shaurya

The Shaurya missile (Sanskrit: Valour) is a short-range surface-to-surface ballistic missile developed by DRDO of India for use by the Indian Army. It has a range of 600 km and is capable of carrying a payload of one-tonne conventional or nuclear warhead. The Shaurya missile provides India with a significant second strike capability. Shaurya Missile is considered a land version of the Sagarika. This missile is stored in a composite canister just like the BrahMos supersonic cruise missile. The composite canister makes the missile much easier to store for long periods without maintenance as well as to handle and transport. It also houses the gas generator to eject the missile from the canister before its solid propellant motors take over to hurl it at the intended target. Shaurya missiles can remain hidden or camouflaged in underground silos from enemy surveillance or satellites till they are fired from the special storage-cum-launch canisters. DRDO Defence scientists admit that given Shaurya's limited range at present, either the silos will have to be constructed closer to India's borders or longer-range missiles will have to be developed. The Shaurya system will require some more tests before it becomes fully operational in two-three years. Moreover, Defence scientists say the high-speed, two-stage Shaurya has *high maneuverability* which also makes it *less vulnerable* to existing anti-missile Defence systems.. When Anti-Ballistic Missile Systems AAD and PAD are to be tested again, the Shaurya invulnerability to anti-missile systems will be tested. The DRDO scientists also have said that if Shaurya is successful and manages to avoid anti ballistic missile radars then the missile can even be used to improve the AAD and PAD systems.

Sagarika

Sagarika (Sanskrit: Wave / Born from the Ocean) is a nuclear capable submarine-launched ballistic missile with a range of 750 km. This missile has a length of 8.5 meters, weighs seven tonnes and can carry a pay load of up to 500 kg.. The development of this missile started in 1991. The first confirmation about the missile came in 1998. The development of the underwater missile launcher know as the Project 78 (P78) was completed in 2001. This was handed over to the Indian Navy for trials. The missile was successfully test fired thrice. The Indian Navy plans to introduce the missile into service by the end of 2010. Sagarika missile is being integrated with the Advanced Technology Vessel that is expected to begin sea trials by 2009. Sagarika will form part of the triad in India's nuclear deterrence and will provide with retaliatory nuclear strike capability.

Sagarika has already been test-fired from an underwater pontoon, but now DRDO is planning a full-fledged test of the missile from a submarine and for this purpose may use the services of a Russian sub-marine.. Eventually it could be introduced into as many as 5 ballistic missile submarines.

Cruise Missiles

- Nirbhay: Nirbhay (Sanskrit "Fearless") is a long range, subsonic cruise missile being developed in India. The missile will have a range of 1,000 km and will arm three services, the Indian Army, Indian Navy and the Indian Air Force. The Nirbhay will be able to be launched from multiple platforms on land, sea and air. The first test flight of the missile is expected in the year 2009. Nirbhay will be a terrain hugging, stealth missile capable of delivering 24 different types of warheads depending on mission requirements and will use inertial navigation system for guidance.. There are plans to arm the IL-76MDs with the aerial version of the missile.
- 3M-54 Klub: India has acquired around 200 3M-54 Klub for arming Talwar class frigate, Shivalik class frigate, Kolkata class destroyer and Sindhughosh class submarine. The Russian 3M-54 Klub is a multi-role missile system developed by the Novator Design Bureau (OKB-8) with a range of 250 km-300 km and an average speed of.8 Mach with a maximum of 2.9 Mach. India has both the Klub-N and Klub-S variant to be used for Ships and Submarines respectively.. Both the Klub-N and Klub-S have been tested successfully. India currently has the 3M-54E, 3M-54E1, 91RE1 and 91RE2 variants. In addition the Navy has plans to arm the Tu-142 and Tu-22M with an air-launched version. Due to Klub's longer range than BrahMos it may also be used in the Mirage 2000 and Su-30 MKI too. The Navy has shown interest in buying more Klubs which would be incorporated on to the S-1000 submarine if bought

by India. India is also keen on other Former Soviet cruise missile such as the P-700 Granit and P-500 Bazalt.

- Popeye: India imported a large number of Israel's Rafael made Popeye Missile in late 1999.. Popeye II, an air launched cruise missile capable of carrying nuclear warheads with a range of 80 km can be launched from planes was given to India along with missile defence radars in a deal.. At that time the United States was wary of this due to its close relations with Pakistan. But due to recent military and strategic dealings between the Israel, India and the United States, it is thought that the United States has little or no objection now. The exact number transferred to India is unknown, but possibly 20 missiles to perhaps 50 missiles could have been given with possibly more being built in India. It is still not known which planes are armed with these missiles but it is thought to be the Tu-142 and Sukhoi Su-30MKI, which incorporate some Israeli technology.
- P-70 Ametist: India has Soviet P-70 Ametist submarine-launched cruise missiles.. The missile were mostly probably bought in the early 90s and may be used today as canistered launched land based cruise missiles instead of submarine launched cruise missiles. The missiles can carry nuclear warheads and have a range of 50–65 km. Although they are extremely old and incompetent due to their low range and speed, there are still reports that they are kept in reserve and can still be used due to their upgrades in the late 90s..
- Moskit: India has a number of operational Moskits. The P-270 Moskit is a Russian supersonic ramjet powered cruise missile capable of being launched from land and ships. India has most probably bought both land and ship variants which have a range of 120 km. India bought around 200 Klub missiles and now it is believed that the Moskit have been kept in reserve but can still be used.
- Brahmos: BrahMos is a supersonic cruise missile that can be launched from submarines, ships, aircraft or land. It is

a joint venture between India's Defence Research and Development Organisation (DRDO) and Russia's NPO Mashinostroeyenia who have together formed the BrahMos Aerospace Private Limited.

The acronym BrahMos is perceived as the confluence of the two nations represented by two rivers, the Brahmaputra of India and the Moskva of Russia. It travels at speeds of Mach 2.5 to 2.8 and is the world's fastest cruise missile. It is about three-and-a-half times faster than the U.S.A's subsonic Harpoon cruise missile. A hypersonic version of the missile is also presently under development (Lab Tested with 5.26 Mach Speed). BrahMos claims to have the capability of attacking surface targets as low as 10 meters in altitude. It can gain a speed of Mach 2.8, and has a maximum range of 290 km. The ship-launched and land-based missiles can carry a 200 kg warhead, whereas the aircraft-launched variant (BrahMos A) can carry a 300 kg warhead. It has a two-stage propulsion system, with a solid-propellant rocket for initial acceleration and a liquid-fueled ramjet responsible for sustained supersonic cruise. Air-breathing ramjet propulsion is much more fuel-efficient than rocket propulsion, giving the BrahMos a longer range than a pure rocket-powered missile would achieve.

The high speed of the BrahMos likely gives it better target-penetration characteristics than lighter subsonic cruise-missiles such as the Tomahawk. Being twice as heavy and almost four times faster than the Tomahawk, the BrahMos has almost 32 times the initial kinetic energy of a Tomahawk missile (although it pays for this by having only 3/5 the payload and a fraction of the range despite weighing twice as much, suggesting a different tactical paradigm to achieve the objective).

Although BrahMos is primarily an anti-ship missile, it can also engage land based targets. It can be launched either in a vertical or inclined position and is capable of covering targets over a 360 degree horizon. The BrahMos missile has an identical configuration for land, sea, and sub-sea platforms. The air-launched version has a smaller booster and additional tail fins for added stability during launch. The BrahMos is currently being configured for aerial deployment with the Su-30MKI as its carrier

Surface to Air Missile

- Akash: Akash (Hindi: Sky) is India's medium range surface-to-air missile Defence system The missile can target aircraft up to 30 km away, at altitudes up to 18,000 m. Akash can be fired from both tracked and wheeled platforms. Akash is said to be capable of both conventional and nuclear warheads, with a reported payload of 60 kg. A nuclear warhead could potentially give the missile the capability to destroy both aircraft and warheads from ballistic missiles. The missile is described as being able to strike several targets simultaneously, which could mean either separate, independently targetable warheads, or a sufficient blast to destroy a number of them.

Along with India, a limited number of other countries including the US and Russia have developed operational multi-target handling surface-to-air missile systems capable of carrying a nuclear warhead.

Delivery mechanisms

Nuclear Submarines

According to some accounts, India plans to have as many as 20 nuclear submarines capable of carrying missiles with nuclear warheads. Currently, India has built one and is building two more nuclear submarines under the Advanced Technology Vessel plan. India currently maintains six submarines of the Sindhughosh Class that can launch the nuclear-capable 3M-54 Klub cruise missiles.

- Former Leasing of Soviet submarines: In 1988 INS *Chakra* (Sanskrit: Wheel), a Charlie-class submarine was leased by the Indian Navy for three years from the Soviet Union, until 1991. The submarine was leased to India between 1988 and 1991 mainly for India to gain experience in the operations of a nuclear submarine. It was later decommissioned in 1991.
- Arihant class submarine: The Arihant class submarines (Sanskrit: Slayer of Enemies) are a class of nuclear-powered

Ballistic Missile submarines being constructed for the Indian Navy at Visakhapatnam, India under the Advanced Technology Vessel (ATV) Project The ATV is an SSBN and will be armed with ballistic missiles.

The first of these, INS Arihant was launched on 26 July 2009 The vessel, which will undergo sea-trials for up to two years, will then be equipped with an unknown number of K-15 Sagarika SLBMs.

The second and third submarines of the class may incorporate the Nirbhay as well. As of July 2007, the Sagarika missile as well as Dhanush had undergone three successful tests each.

- INS Cruise Missile Submarines: The INS Sindhuraj, INS Sindhuvir, INS Sindhuratna, INS Sindhushastra, INS Sindhukesari and INS Sindhuvijay are capable of launching 3M-54 Klub and BrahMos nuclear-capable cruise missiles.. India bought 10 Kilo class (in India known as Sindhughosh Class) submarine of which 6 have been refitted by the Russian Navy so that the they can launch cruise missiles such as nuclear capable 3M-54 Klub.
- Leasing of Russian Akula and Amur Submarines: In 2000, negotiations between India and Russia were conducted into the leasing of two incomplete *Akula* class. The Akulas were to be delivered to the Indian Navy in 2008 on a lease of at least seven years and up to ten years, in which at the end of the lease, it has an option to buy them. The acquisition was to help the Indian Navy prepare for the introduction of the ATV. The cost to India of acquiring two Akula submarines and their support infrastructure along with training of the crews had been estimated at $2 billion.. The Indian version was reportedly armed with the 300 km range 3M-54 Klub nuclear-capable missiles.. Supposedly on 9 November 2008 one of the two submarines was conducting tests, when an accident on board killed 20 sailors but no damage occurred to the submarine. Though this deal fell apart for some time due to the Indians demanding an upgrade/improvement in some of its safety features, Russia's President Dmitry Medvedev on his

official trip to New Delhi said that the deal was back on track and that "The talk is not about selling submarines into India's property, but about their rent by India's navy". However, unlike the earlier deal the modified deal states that India can only rent and not buy the subs, but defence experts state that the so-called lease agreement is only to divert international attention and that it would be eventually modified and India would inevitably keep the subs. The first submarine will be named INS Chakra.. Russia has also offered the advanced Amur Class Submarine, known as the S1000. According to GlobalSecurity India is already building the S1000 cruise missile submarines in Mazagaon Docks. The Amur will be most probably fitted with P-700 Granit or the Klub cruise missile capable of carrying nuclear warheads.

Frigates, Destroyers and Aircraft Carriers

Other than submarines, India also maintains ships such as destroyers, modified patrol crafts and frigates which can launch nuclear capable ballistic and cruise missiles.

Talwar class frigate and Shivalik class frigate are frigates of the Indian Navy that can fire nuclear capable cruise missiles. INS Tabar and INS Trishul are Talwar class vessel armed with supersonic nuclear 3M-54 Klub cruise missiles while INS Shivalik was the first vessel of the Shivalik class to incorporate the 3M-54 Klub. Other vessels of the Shivalik Class and Talwar Class are to be armed with the BrahMos and 3M-54 Klub missiles by 2009 and 2010 respectively. All these frigates are also equipped with Barak missiles or other SAMs and harbour helicopters such as the HAL Dhruv. In years to come, the Nirbhay missile is also to be incorporated into Talwar class frigates and Shivalik class frigates.

Rajput Class, Kolkata Class and Delhi Class are Destroyers of the Indian Navy that may be armed with nuclear capable missile-Nirbhay. In addition Kolkata Class will also incorporate the Russian nuclear 3M-54 Klub cruise missile.

The ship launched Dhanush Ballistic Missile was tested from INS Subhadra of the Sukanya class patrol craft in 2000. INS

Subhadra is a patrol vessel which was modified and the missile was launched from the reinforced helicopter deck. The 250 km variant was tested but the tests were considered partially successful. In 2004, the missile was again tested from the INS Subhadra and was this time successful. Then the following year in December the missile's 350 km version was tested from the INS Rajput and hit the land based target..

INS Vikramaditya Aircraft Carrier (formerly known as Admiral Gorshkov) was fitted with P-500 Bazalt nuclear capable cruise missiles of the range of 550 km. The Vikramaditya could still be armed with this after its refit. India is also a potential customer for a Slava class cruiser which also incorporates the P-500 Bazalt

Nuclear-capable Aircraft

India currently has 4.5 generation fighter jets capable of launching nuclear weapons. Nuclear-capable aircraft are also seen as a less expensive way of dropping nuclear warheads as well as being as effective.

- Fighter Jets : The Sukhoi Su-30MKI, Dassault Mirage 2000, and MiG-29 serve in the Indian Air Force and are also seen as a means to deliver nuclear weapons. In addition India maintains SEPECAT Jaguar and MiG-27M which can be used to drop gravity bombs. However, these planes would be considered useless in the 21st century as gravity bombs have little chance of accomplishing a task. On the other hand, the Su-30MKI, capable of carrying nuclear weapons and tailor-made for Indian specifications, integrates Indian systems and avionics is one of the best air superiority fighters and also consists of French and Israeli subsystems. The MKI variant features several improvements over the basic K and MK variants and is classified as a 4.5 generation fighter. Due to similar features and components, the MKI variant is often considered to be a customized Indian variant of the Sukhoi Su-35. The Mirage 2000Hs were heavily customised during the Kargil War and is the only other version, other than the French 2000N, to be able to be armed with nuclear weapons. However, the air force doesn't really see the Mirage as a nuclear strike aircraft. Though MiG-29 like the HAL Tejas after many test flights have not been tested to use nuclear weapons, they have the capacity to be armed with them. Both the HAL Tejas and Su-30MKI can travel excess of 3,000 km without refueling; this allows India to attack targets far away in an effective manner only using planes rather than delivery systems such as the Agni. The HAL Tejas is India's only indigenous plane to be armed with nuclear weapons, thus making India less dependent on Russia.

India has leased four Russian Tupolev Tu-22M3 bombers, which could carry air-launched cruise missiles. India has reportedly upgraded its Russian-built Tu-142 maritime patrol aircraft to carry air-launched cruise missiles.

Ballistic Missile Defence

India has an active ABM development effort using indigenously developed and integrated radars and locally designed missiles. In November 2006, India successfully conducted the PADE (Prithvi Air Defence Exercise) in which an Anti-ballistic missile, called the Prithvi Air Defence (PAD) an *Exoatmospheric* (outside the atmosphere) interceptor system intercepted a Prithvi-II ballistic missile. The PAD missile has the secondary stage of the Prithvi missile and can reach altitude of 80 km. During the test the target missile was intercepted at an 50 km altitude. India became the fourth nation in the world to acquire such a capability and the third nation to develop it through indigenous effort. On 6 December 2007 the Advanced Air Defence (AAD) missile system was tested successfully. This missile is an Endo atmospheric interceptor with an altitude of 30 km. According to scientist V K Saraswat of DRDO the missiles will work in tandem to ensure a hit probability of 99.8 percent. Induction of the system into services is expected to be in 2010. Two new anti ballistic missiles that can intercept IRBM/ICBMs are being developed. These high speed missiles (AD-1 and AD-2) are being developed to intercept ballistic missiles with the range of 5,000 km.

India also has Russian S300PMU-2 and it is used as an interceptor for Ballistic missiles. An indigenous nuclear tipped surface to air missile, Akash Missile is used to destroy low range missiles and is capable of destroying various targets and is one of the few of its kind systems in the world. India has also shown interest in the Russian S-400, the most advanced anti-ballistic missile.

Chemical Weapons

In 1992 India signed the Chemical Weapons Convention (CWC), stating that it did not have chemical weapons and the capacity or capability to manufacture chemical weapons. By doing this India became one of the original signatories of the Chemical Weapons Convention [CWC] in 1993, and ratified it on 2 September 1996. According to India's ex-Army Chief General Sunderji, a country having the capability of making nuclear weapons does not need to have chemical weapons, since the dread of chemical weapons could be created only in those countries that do not have nuclear weapons. Others suggested that the fact that India has found chemical weapons dispensable highlighted its confidence in the conventional weapons system at its command.

India informed the United Nations in May, 2009 that it had destroyed its stockpile of chemical weapons in compliance with the international Chemical Weapons Convention. With this India has become third country after South Korea and Albania to do so. This was cross-checked by inspectors of the United Nations.

India has an advanced commercial chemical industry, and produces the bulk of its own chemicals for domestic consumption. It is also widely acknowledged that India has an extensive civilian chemical and pharmaceutical industry and annually exports considerable quantities of chemicals to countries such as the United Kingdom, United States, and Taiwan.

Biological Warfare

India has a well-developed biotechnology infrastructure that includes numerous pharmaceutical production facilities bio-containment laboratories (including BSL-3 and BSL-4) for working with lethal pathogens. It also has highly qualified scientists with expertise in infectious diseases. Some of India's facilities are being used to support research and development for BW Defence purposes. India has ratified the BWC and pledges to abide by its obligations. There is no clear evidence, circumstantial or otherwise, that directly points toward an offensive BW program. New Delhi does possess the scientific capability and infrastructure to launch an offensive BW program, but has chosen not to do so. In terms of delivery, India also possesses the capability to produce aerosols and has numerous potential delivery systems ranging from crop dusters to sophisticated ballistic missiles.

In 2001, after Indian Postal Services received 17 "suspicious" letters believed to contain Bacillus anthracis spores, a Bio-Safety Level 2 (BSL-2) Laboratory was established to provide guidance in preparing the Indian government for a biological attack. B. anthracis is one of many pathogens studied at the institute, which also examines pathogens causing tuberculosis, typhoid, hepatitis B, rabies, yellow fever, Lassa fever, Ebola, and plague.

The Defence Research and Development Establishment (DRDE) at Gwalior is the primary establishment for studies in toxicology and biochemical pharmacology and development of antibodies against several bacterial and viral agents. Work is in progress to prepare responses to threats like Anthrax, Brucellosis, cholera and plague, viral threats like smallpox and viral hemorrhage fever and biotoxic threats like botulism. Most of the information is classified. Researchers have developed chemical/biological protective gear, including masks, suits, detectors and suitable drugs. India has a no first use policy.

India has ratified the BWC and pledges to abide by its obligations. There is no clear evidence, circumstantial or otherwise, that directly points toward an offensive BW program. New Delhi does possess the scientific capability and infrastructure to launch an offensive BW program, but has not chosen to do so. In terms of delivery, India also possesses the capability to produce aerosols and has numerous potential delivery systems ranging from crop dusters to sophisticated ballistic missiles. However, no information exists in the public domain suggesting interest by the Indian government in delivery of biological agents by these or any other means. To reiterate the latter point, in October 2002, Indian President A.P.J. Abdul Kalam asserted that "we [India] will not make biological weapons. It is cruel to human beings..."

WEAPONS OF MASS DESTRUCTION INDIA

Ballistic Missiles

a. Prithvi I-Army Version (150 km range with a payload of 1,000kg)

   Prithvi II-Air Force Version (250 km range with a payload of 500kg)

   Prithvi III-Naval Version (350 km range with a payload of 500kg)

b. Dhanush is a System consisting of stabilization platform and missiles and can fire either the 250Km or the 350Km range missiles.

   Then the following year in December the missile's 350Km version was tested from the INS Rajput and hit the land based target

c. The Agni Missile system comprises of Agni I, Agni II and the Agni III 1500 Agni I uses the SLV-3 booster (from India's Space Program) for its first stage and a liquid-fueled Prithvi for its second stage.

d. On the other hand India's Agni II missiles have a range of the 1500 to 2500 kilometers. Unlike the Agni I, the Agni II has a solid-fueled second stage. India has also tested the Agni III IRBM with a range between 3000 and 5500km kilometres which has two stages. With a normal payload of 1000kg it can travel 5000km

e. The Surya-1 and-2 will be classified as strategic weapons, extending the Indian nuclear deterrent force to targets around the world. India currently is limited by the range of the Agni-3 missile.

   The Surya-1 will have an expected range of 6000-10,000 km. It reportedly has a length of 40 m and a launch weight of 80,000 kg (some reports indicate as much as 275,000 kg. As the missile has yet to be developed, the payload and warhead are as yet unknown. It is believed to be a three-stage design, with the first two stages using solid propellants and the third-stage using liquid. The first test flight is expected in 2009, but there may be delays. The

Surya-is a longer-ranged variant of the Surya-1. It has a reported range of over 20,000 km.

f. The Shaurya missile is a short-range surface-to-surface ballistic missile developed by DRDO of India for use by the Indian Army.It has a range of 600 km and is capable of carrying a payload of one-tonne conventional or nuclear warhead.The Shaurya missile provides India with a significant second strike capability.

g. Sagarika is a nuclear capable submarine-launched ballistic missile with a range of 750 km. This missile has a length of 8.5 meters, weighs seven tonnes and can carry a pay load of up to 500 kg

CRUISE MISSILES INDIA

a. Nirbhay is a long range, subsonic cruise missile being developed in India. The missile will have a range of 1000 km and will arm three services, the Indian Army, Indian Navy and the Indian Air Force.

b. India has acquired around 200 3M-54 Klub for arming Talwar class frigate, Shivalik class frigate, Kolkata class destroyer and Sindhughosh class submarine The Russian 3M-54 Klub is a multi-role missile system developed by the Novator Design Bureau(OKB-8) with a range of 250Km-300Km and a average speed of.8 Mach with a maximum of 2.9 Mach

c. Popeye II, an air launched cruise missile capable of carrying nuclear warheads with a range of 80 Km can be launched from planes was given to India along with missile defence radars in a deal.

   The exact number transferred to India is unknown, but possibly 20 missile to perhaps 50 missiles could have been given with possibly more being built in India.

d. India has Soviet P-70 Ametist submarine-launched cruise missiles.

   The missiles can carry nuclear warheads and have a range of 50-65Km.

e. The P-270 Moskit is a Russian supersonic ramjet powered cruise missile capable of being launched from land and ships. India has most probably bought both land and ship variants which have a range of 120km.

f. Akash is India's medium range surface-to-air missile Defence system The missile can target aircraft up to 30 km away, at altitudes up to 18,000 m.Akash is said to be capable of both conventional and nuclear warheads, with a reported payload of 60kg. Akash can be fired from both tracked and wheeled platforms.

Nuclear Submarines

According to some accounts India plans to have as many as 20 nuclear submarines capable of carrying missiles with nuclear warheads. The Advanced Technology Vessel (ATV) is a Nuclear Powered Ballistic Missile Submarine being constructed for the Indian Navy at Visakhapatnam, India The ATV is an SSBN and will be armed with the ballistic missiles. Once it is completed, it can be equipped with 6-8 nuclear capable Dhanush,Sagarika or Agni SLBM ballistic missiles and upto 12 BrahMos cruise missiles. It is also to be fitted with an advanced sonar system. The second and third submarines of the class may incorporate the Nirbhay as well. As of July 2007, the Sagarika missile as well as Dhanush had undergone three successful tests each.

The ATV is to be unveiled on January 26, 2009 but trials will start later that year while induction is planned for 2010. The INS Sindhuraj, INS Sindhuvir, INS Sindhuratna, INS Sindhushastra, INS Sindhukesari and INS Sindhuvijay are capable of launching 3M-54 Klub and BrahMos nuclear-capable cruise missiles. India bought 10 Kilo class (in India known as Sindhughosh Class) submarine of which 6 have been refitted by the Russian Navy so that the they can launch cruise missiles such as nuclear capable BrahMos and 3M-54 Klub's 3M-14E variant.

The Submarine version of the BrahMos has been tested from static, underwater test stands in Russia and from the INS Sindhuvijay. As the Sinduvijay is similar to the other refitted submarines the test is considered a success.

9

Integrated Guided Missile Development Programme

The Integrated Guided Missile Development Program (IGMDP) was an Indian Ministry of Defence program between the early 1980s and 2007 for the development of a comprehensive range of missiles, including the intermediate range Agni missile (Surface to Surface), and short range missiles such as the Prithvi ballistic missile (Surface to Surface), Akash missile (Surface to Air), Trishul missile (Surface to Air) and Nag Missile (Anti Tank). The program was managed by Defence Research and Development Organization (DRDO) in partnership with other Indian government labs and research centres. One of the most prominent chief engineers on the project, Dr. Abdul Kalam went on to become the President of India.

The project was started in early 1980s and resulted in the development of several key strategic missiles. The last major missile developed under the program was Agni 3 intermediate-range ballistic missile which was successfully tested on 9 July 2007. On 8 January 2008, and after the third test of Agni-3 on 7 May 2008, the DRDO announced that it will be closing the IGMDP program formally since most of the missiles in the program have been developed and inducted into Indian armed forces. According to a statement by Dr. S Prahlada, a DRDO Director, new missile and weapons systems will be developed in new five-year programs and include both Indian private industries as well as foreign partners to lower costs. DRDO has independently continued further development work on Nag and Surya missile.

In 2008, India noted that the strategic integrated guided missile program was completed with its design objectives achieved. Follow on strategic projects are being either pursued singly (e.g. Agni project) whereas tactical systems could involve joint ventures with even foreign partners.

Missiles in Indian history

The use of rockets and missiles by Indians in modern times dates back to the 18th century, during the period of ruler Hyder Ali and Tipu Sultan. Fighting the British East India company, Tipu Sultan's Army used variety of rockets in supporting role. It was the world's first use of rockets for fighting modern wars which was later developed further by the British against. In the Second Anglo-Mysore war, at the Battle of Pollilur (10 September 1780), an entire British detachment lead by Colonel Baillie was destroyed resulting in 3,820 soldiers being taken prisoner including Colonel Baillie. At the Battle of Srirangapattana in 1792, Mysorean soldiers launched a barrage of rockets against British troops, followed by an assault of 36,000 men. Later at the battle of Srirangapattana during the fourth Anglo-Mysore war, in April 1799, British forces retreated from the battlefield when attacked by rockets and musket fire of Tipu Sultan's army.

Tipu's rockets had been fully integrated into his Army, which were under special Rocket Brigades called *Kushoons*. These were extremely effective in battle, inflicting losses on British forces. These rockets were later re-engineered by William Congreve and known in Britain as Congreve Rockets.

Twentieth Century

In the twentieth century, the government of independent India embarked on a number of plans to develop missiles which would strengthen India's defences. In 1958, the government constituted the Special Weapons Development Team which would later become the Defence Research and Development Laboratories (DRDL), to undertake the development of first-generation anti-tank missiles. In the 1970s, the Indian government decided to manufacture anti-tank missiles under license from France. At the same time, DRDL was entrusted with two other projects: Project

Valiant, which involved the development of a long-range ballistic missile; and Project devil, which was aimed at reverse engineering the Soviet SA-2 surface-to-air missile. Both projects were terminated prematurely; Project Valiant was terminated in 1974 and Project Devil met the same fate in 1980.

However, by this time, DRDL had developed some infrastructure and facilities to undertake the design and development of missiles. In 1983, under the experience and leadership of Dr. Abdul Kalam, who had previously been the project director for the SLV-3 programme at ISRO, the Indian government revived the missile program as an Integrated Guided Missile Development Program (IGMDP). As part of this program, the Interim Test Range at Balasore in Orissa was developed for missile testing.

India on Tuesday 07, 2008 announced the closing of the strategic integrated guided missile programme, and said the development and production of most of futuristic weapons systems would henceforth be taken up with foreign partnerships.

The main aim of the Integrated Guided Missile Development Program was to develop, a missile in five different categories simultaneously, namely: a short-range surface-to-air missile (*codenamed* Trishul), a medium-range surface-to-air missile (*codenamed* Akash), a third-generation anti-tank guided missile (*codenamed* Nag), a short-range surface-to-surface missile (*codenamed* Prithvi), and an intermediate-range surface-to-surface missile (*codenamed* Agni).

There were a number of failures and successes, which led to an expansion of the program in the 1990s, to develop the long range Agni missile, a ballistic missile (*codenamed* Sagarika), which would be the naval version of the Prithvi, and an inter-continental-ballistic-missile (*codenamed* Surya) with a range of 8,000-12,000 km.

In 1998, the Government of India, signed an agreement with Russia to design, develop, manufacture and market a Supersonic Cruise Missile System which has been successfully accomplished by 2006. BrahMos is a supersonic cruise missile that can be launched from submarines, ships, aircraft or land. At speeds of Mach 2.5 to 2.8, it is the world's fastest cruise missile and is about three and a half times faster than the American subsonic Harpoon cruise missile. BAPL is contemplating a hypersonic Mach 8 version of the missile, named as the BrahMos II. BrahMos II will be the first hypersonic cruise missile and is expected to be ready by 2012-13. The laboratory testing of the missile has started.(*codenamed* BrahMos).

Agni missile system

The Agni missile is an IRBM developed under the IGMDP by India. It was first tested at the Interim Test Range in Chandipur in 1989, and is capable of carrying a conventional payload of 1000 kg (2,200 lb) or a nuclear warhead. It consists of one (short range) or two stages (intermediate range). It is rail and road mobile. It is powered by solid and/or liquid propellants.

Agni-III is the third in the Agni series of missiles. The Agni I has a range of 700–800 km while the Agni-II as a range of 2,000–2,500 km. They are claimed to be a part of the "credible deterrence" against Pakistan and China. The Agni-II can only reach some parts of western China and Asia. The last test (Agni-II) took place in May 2009.

Agni III is expected to be India's nuclear deterrent against People's Republic of China. Agni III development began when relations with China were still negative. However, the rapid improvement in friendly relations between the two nations has reduced the need for rapid deployment of the missile.

An operational Agni-III was tested on July 9, 2006 from Wheeler island off the coast of the eastern state of Orissa. After the launch, it was reported that the second stage of the rocket had failed to separate and the missile had fallen well short of its target. It can hit strategic targets deep inside China, including Shanghai and Beijing with a strike range of 3,500 km. It falls short of the range of ICBMs (intercontinental ballistic missiles) which have ranges over 5000 km. As reported earlier, a new type of steel that will help to increase the range from 15 to 30% was developed. On 12 April 2007 Agni-III missile was tested successfully and again on 7 May 2008. Agni III the ninth missile in the Agni series to have been tested. The first was tested in May 1989. Agni III has been successfully tested on 7th Feb 2010. The test has met all mission parameters.

A new Agni-V missile with 5000–6000 km range is being developed. This missile is the modified version of the Agni-III missile with another stage. This missile is called the Agni-III* (Agni-III star).

Prithvi missile system

The Prithvi missile is the tactical surface-to-surface short-range ballistic missile (SRBM) developed by India under the Integrated Guided Missile Development Program. The Prithvi was India's first indigenously developed ballistic missile. Development of the Prithvi began in 1983, and it was first test-fired on February 25, 1988 from Sriharikota, SHAR Centre, Pottisreeramulu Nellore district, Andhra Pradesh. It has a range of up to 150 to 300 km. The land variant is called Prithvi while the naval operational variant of Prithvi I and Prithvi II class missiles are *codenamed* Dhanush (*meaning* Bow). Both variants are used for surface targets.

The Prithvi is said to have its propulsion technology derived from the Soviet SA-2 surface-to-air missile. Variants make use of either liquid or both liquid and solid fuels. Developed as a battlefield missile, it could carry a nuclear warhead in its role as a tactical nuclear weapon.

Variants of Prithvi

The Prithvi missile project encompassed developing three variants for use by the Indian Army, Indian Air Force and the Indian Navy, outlined in the initial project framework of the IGMDP.

- Prithvi I-Army Version (150 km range with a payload of 1000 kg)
- Prithvi II-Air Force Version (200 km range with a payload of 500 kg)
- Prithvi III-Naval Version (350 km range with a payload of 500 kg)

Over the years these specifications underwent a number of changes. While the *codename* Prithvi stands for any missile inducted by India into its armed forces in this category, the later developmental versions Prithvi II and Prithvi III were the codenames used for the Army and Air Force versions, while the versions for the Navy were spun off into separate projects. The Prithvi I class of missiles were inducted into the Indian Army in 1994, while Prithvi II with an extended range was being inducted in 2006.

Prithvi I

Prithvi I class was a single stage liquid-fuelled surface-to-surface missile with a maximum warhead payload of 100 kg and a range of 150 km. It has an accuracy of 10 – 50 metres and can be launched from Transporter erector launchers. This class of Prithvi missile was inducted into the Indian Army in 1994.

Prithvi II

Prithvi II class is also a single stage liquid-fuelled missile with maximum payload of 300 kg, but with an extended range of 200 kilometres. It was developed with the Indian Air Force being the primary user. It was first test-fired on January 27, 1996 and the development stages were completed in 2004. The Prithvi II class of missiles are in the process of induction by the Indian Airforce. It has been tested again on 12 Oct 2009 as part of User trials.

Sagarika

Prithvi III class was spun off as *Sagarika*. This is a two-stage surface-to-surface missile for launch from naval ships and submarines. The first stage is solid fuelled with a 16 metric ton force (157 kN) thrust motor. The second stage is liquid fuelled. The missile can carry a payload of 350 kg to a distance of 300 km and a 500 kg warhead.

There were a number of shortcoming in the initial version of Prithvi missiles namely, High circular error probability (CEP) of around 500 meters and volatility of the liquid-fuelled propulsion system requiring fuelling only just before launching. These shortcomings were overcome in the later developmental versions through improved navigation systems into the missiles to reduce the CEP to as low as 10 to 15 meters. Later Prithvi versions can be kept up to 10 years after fuelling.

Dhanush

The Dhanush is a Naval variant of the Prithvi short-range ballistic missile intended for launch from surface ships. The development phase included the launch of three developmental Dhanush missiles. The fourth launch was carried out successfully on March 30, 2007, with the ballistic missile performing as expected. The Indian Navy is pursuing the Dhanush as a high precision strike weapon capable of striking both sea and shore based targets to be deployed on its surface ships.The Defence Ministry is planning to make variants of Dhanush with strike ranges 250–500 km and payload up to 750 kg.The 500 km variant will have reduced payload to extend range.

Defence Ministry officials have said that the 8.53 metre-long and 0.9 meter wide Dhanush, with a strike range of 350 km and payload capacity of 500 kg, would "soon be operationalised" in the Navy. "the telemetry and tracking network have established that the technology demonstrator (missile) met its entire mission objective,". "the missile was launched from the warship near balasore off the orissa coast,". scientists and naval officers tracked the missile right from its take off till the impact point at sea. the missile, indigenously developed by the Defence Research and Development Organisation (DRDO) for the navy, was launched for the first time on April 11, 2000. the launch was the second in a series of flight tests aimed to gauge the missile's parameters. On December 13, 2009 Dhanush was re-tested by launching it from INS Subhadra.The test was hailed as a complete success.

Pradyumna Ballistic Missile

The Prithvi Air Defence missile has been named as Pradyumna Ballistic Missile.

Akash Missile System

Akash is a medium range surface-to-air missile developed as part of India's Integrated Guided Missile Development Program to achieve self-sufficiency in the area of surface-to-air missiles. It is the most expensive missile project ever undertaken by the Union government in the 20th century. Development costs skyrocketed to almost $120 million which is far more than other similar systems.

Akash is a medium-range surface-to-air missile with an intercept range of 30 km. It has a launch weight of 720 kg, a diameter of 35 cm and a length of 5.8 metres. Akash flies at supersonic speed, reaching around Mach 2.5. It can reach an altitude of 18 km. A digital proximity fuse is coupled with a 55 kg pre-fragmented warhead, while the safety arming and detonation mechanism enables a controlled detonation sequence. A self-destruct device is also integrated. It is propelled by a solid fuelled booster stage. The missile has a terminal guidance system capable of working through electronic countermeasures. The entire Akash SAM system allows for attacking multiple targets (up to 4 per Battery). The Akash missile's use of ramjet propulsion system allows it to maintain its speed without deceleration, unlike the Patriot missiles. The missile is supported by a multi-target and multi-function phased array fire control radar called the 'Rajendra' with a range of about 80 km in search, and 60 km in terms of engagement.

The missile is completely guided by the Radar, without any active guidance of its own. This allows it greater capability against jamming as the aircraft self protection jammer would have to work against the high power Rajendra, and the aircraft being attacked is not alerted by any terminal seeker on the Akash itself.

Design of the missile is similar to that of the SA-6 with four long tube ramjet inlet ducts mounted mid-body between wings. For pitch/yaw control four clipped triangular moving wings are mounted on mid-body. For roll control four inline clipped delta fins with ailerons are mounted before the tail. However, internal schema shows a completely modernised layout, including an Onboard computer with special optimized trajectories, and an all digital Proximity fuse.

The Akash system meant for the Army uses the T-72 tank chassis for its launcher and radar vehicles. The Rajendra derivative for the Army is called the Battery Level Radar-III. The Air Force version uses an Ashok Leyland truck platform to tow the missile launcher, while the Radar is on a BMP-2 chassis and is called the Battery Level Radar-II. In either case, the launchers carry three ready-to-fire Akash missiles each. The launchers are automated, autonomous and networked to a command post and the guidance radar. They are slewable in azimuth and elevation. The Akash system can be deployed by rail, road or air. The first test flight of Akash missile was conducted in 1990, with development flights up to March 1997.

The IAF has initiated the process to induct the Akash and Trishul surface-to-air missiles developed as a part of the Integrated Guided Missile Development Program. The Multiple target handling capability of Akash weapon system was demonstrated by live firing in a C4I environment during the trials. Two Akash missiles intercepted two fast moving targets in simultaneous engagement mode in 2005 itself. The Akash System's 3-D central acquisition radar (3-D car) group mode performance was then fully established.

In December,2007 Indian Air Force completed user trials for the Akash missile system. The trials, which were spread over ten days were successful and the missile hit its target on all five occasions. Before the ten day trial at Chandipur, the Akash system's ECCM Evaluation tests were carried out at Gwalior Air force base while mobility trials for the system vehicles were carried out at Pokhran. The IAF had evolved the user Trial Directive to verify the Akash's consistency in engaging targets. The following trials were conducted: Against low flying near range target, long range high altitude target, crossing and approaching target and ripple firing of two missiles from the same launcher against a low altitude receding target. Following this, the IAF declared that it would initiate the induction of 2 squadrons strength (each squadron with 2 batteries) of this missile system, to begin with. Once deliveries are complete, further orders would be placed to replace retiring SA-3 GOA (Pechora) SAM systems. In February 2010, the Indian Air Force ordered six more squadrons of the Akash system, taking orders to eight of the type. The Indian Army is also expected to order the Akash system.

Trishul missile system

Trishul is the name of a short range surface-to-air missile developed by India as a part of the Integrated Guided Missile Development Program. It has a range of 9 km and is fitted with a 5.5 kg warhead. Designed to be used against low-level (sea skimming) targets at short range, the system has been developed to defend naval vessels against missiles and also as a short range surface to air missile on land. Guidance consists of three different guiding beams, with the guidance handed over progressively to a narrower beam as the missile approaches the target.

According to reports, the range of the missile is 12 km and is fitted with a 15 kg warhead. The weight of the missile is 130 kg. The length of the missile is 3.1 m.

Development costs of the missile touched almost $70 million to the taxpayers.India had Officially shut down Trishul Missile project on February 27, 2008. The programme of surface-to-air Trishul missile, one of the five missiles being developed by Defence Research and Development Organization, is being shelved. Defence Minister George Fernandes indicated in Rajya Sabha when he said Trishul missile had been delinked from user service, though it would be continued as a technology demonstrator.

Nag missile system

Nag is India's third generation "Fire-and-forget" anti-tank missile. It is an all weather, top attack missile with a range of 3 to 7 km.

The missile uses an 8 kg tandem HEAT warhead capable of defeating modern armour including ERA (Explosive Reactive Armour) and composite armour. Nag uses Imaging Infra-Red (IIR) guidance with day and night capability. Mode of launch for the IIR seeker is LOBL (Lock On Before Launch). Nag can be mounted on an infantry vehicle; a helicopter launched version will also be available with integration work being carried out with the HAL Dhruv.

Separate versions for the Army and the Air Force are being developed. For the Army, the missiles will be carried by specialist carrier vehicles (NAMICA-Nag Missile Carrier) equipped with a thermal imager for target acquisition.

NAMICA is a modified BMP-1 ICV licence produced as "Sarath" in India. The carriers are capable of carrying four ready-to-fire missiles in the observation/launch platform which can be elevated with more missiles available for reload within the carrier. For the Air Force, a nose-mounted thermal imaging system has been developed for guiding the missile's trajectory. The missile has a complete fiberglass structure and weighs around 42 kg.

Nag was test fired for the 45th time on March 19, 2005 from the Test Range at Ahmednagar (Maharastra), signalling the completion of the developmental phase. It will now enter production phase, subject to user trials and acceptance by the Indian Army.

Further versions of the missile may make use of an all-weather Milli Metric Wave (MMW) seeker as an additional option. This seeker has reportedly been developed and efforts are on to integrate it into the missile.

Specifications (Nag Missile)

Total length: 1.90 m (6.23 ft)

Diameter: 190 mm (7.5 in)

Wingspan:-

Weight: 42 kg (93 lb)

Warhead Weight: 8 kg (17.6 lb)

Propellant: Tandem Propulsion solid (Nitramine based smokeless extruded double band sustainer propellant)

Maximum effective range: 4 km (Guidance mode: IIR (Imaging infra-red)), 7 km for air-launched variant

Attack Mode: Lock-on-before-Launch-Top attack

Seeker: IIR cadmium zinc telluride

Single-shot hit probability: 0.77

CEP: 0.9 m R.S

Shaurya Missile System

The Shaurya missile is a short-range surface-to-surface ballistic missile developed by DRDO for use by the Indian Army. Capable of hypersonic speeds, it has a range of 600 km and is capable of carrying a payload of one-tonne conventional or nuclear warhead. It can hit targets deep inside Pakistan and China,both nations having unsettled disputes with India. The Shaurya missile provides India with a significant second strike capability. The missile was tested in November 2008

Shaurya missile is a land version of the under-water launched K-15 missile, Sagarika. This missile is stored in a composite canister just like the BrahMos supersonic cruise missile. The composite canister makes the missile much easier to store for long periods without maintenance as well as to handle and transport. It also houses the gas generator to eject the missile from the canister before its solid propellant motors take over to hurl it at the intended target. Shaurya missiles can remain hidden or camouflaged in underground silos from enemy surveillance or satellites till they are fired from the special storage-cum-launch canisters. DRDO Defence scientists admit that given Shaurya's limited range at present, either the silos will have to be constructed closer to India's borders or longer-range canisterised missiles will have to be developed. The Shaurya system will require some more tests before it becomes fully operational in two-three years. Moreover, defence scientists say the high-speed, two-stage Shaurya has *high manoeuvrability* which also makes it *less vulnerable* to existing anti-missile defence systems.

Other Developments

The expertise and technology developed through the IGMDP is also used in the new Anti ballistic missile called the *Exoatmospheric interceptor system* which successfully intercepted a Prithvi-II ballistic missile.

India became the fourth nation in the world to acquire such a capability and the third nation to develop it through indigenous effort. In December 2007, India successfully tested the Endoatmospheric version which destroyed a modified Prithvi-II missile at 15 km altitude with text-book perfection thereby completing what is known as Multi-layered Theatrical Wide-area Air Defence system that can successfully target and destroy all kinds of Aerial threats from low flying cruise missiles, supersonic short-range, intermediate-range and intercontinental ballistic missiles at altitudes of 15 to 50+ km at any angle and azimuth.

India is said to be in the intermediate stages of developing a new cruise missile, Nirbhay. The subsonic Nirbhay is said to be 6 m in length with a 520 mm diameter, weigh 1,000 kg and have a 1,000 km range with a speed of 0.7 mach. The technology demonstrator flight is planned for end-2009.

So far in the case of ABM system there has been three successful tests. This can lead to the possibility of an antimissile shield system.After the third test in early 2009, it was concluded that one or two more anti ballistic missile tests were needed after which operationlization could take another 4 years.

In September 2008, Indian scientists developed a path-breaking technology that has the potential to increase the range of missiles and satellite launch vehicles by at least 40%.The enhanced range is made possible by adding a special-purpose coating of chromium metal to the blunt nose cone of missiles and launch vehicles. This would add-up on the stated range.

10

Indian Army's Modernisation Plans

Modernising the Indian Infantry

Why has it taken the Army so long to conceive an upgrade package for the oldest, most potent and intensely employed fighting arm, the Infantry, even after the so-called revolution in military affairs? The foot soldier, the original and most versatile weapon system that is always taken for granted, has emerged from the dubious shock and awe strategy of recent campaigns as its ultimate arbiter. India has paid dearly for the neglect of its infantry in terms of cost, casualties and over-stretch of battle. But the Infantry has never let us down. Kargil was its finest hour. Gen VP Malik, the Army Chief of the time, wryly noted: "We will fight with what we have.

So when for the first time an international conference of Army and defence industry was launched last week to put the forgotten soldier centre-stage, some misgivings were natural. While Army Chief Gen JJ Singh outlined his vision for the soldier system of the future, the conspicuous and total absence of Government-MoD-robbed the conference of any sanctity. In sharp contrast, for a MoD-sponsored defence finance seminar earlier in the month, Government officials and ministers were stepping over each other at Vigyan Bhavan.

Free India's Army came into being in 1947 and within weeks, the Infantry soldiers landed in Srinagar to save J&K from being gobbled up by Pakistani tribal raiders. Since then, the Infantry has not ceased fighting proxy wars there and later, elsewhere too. A former Army Chief, Gen SR Choudhury, who was not from the Infantry, described the Infantry as the Army and vice versa. Field Marshal Montgomery said: An army is considered only as good as its Infantry.

The experience of four wars, several border skirmishes, two out-of-area missions, the ceaseless campaign to counter cross-border terrorism in Kashmir, numerous other insurgencies in the North-East, internal stability operations elsewhere in the country and UN peace keeping operations make the Indian Infantry the most battle-hardened and combat rich force in the world. The simple and uncomplaining infantryman has given so much to so many for so little. The modernisation of the infantry was first attempted-halfheartedly-in the mid-1980s by the Perspective Planning branch of the Army Headquarters. The bias for mechanised warfare, zealously pursued by Gen Sundarji, was so pronounced that the Infantry modernisation plan was skipped altogether. Guns, tanks, APCs were the weapons in demand. The Infantry was ignored. Had a modest upgrade package been undertaken at that time, infantry would have been more combat contemporary and effective.

Instead, till recently, some soldiers were still using World War II equipment and clothing. Shameful as it was, soldiers had to buy rucksacks and other accoutrements from the market. DRDO is still to come out with a light bulletproof vest. The Army failed to accurately visualize the nature of combat it would fight in the future. Pakistan-sponsored insurgency in Punjab did not alert the nation and the Army to the proxy war brewing in J&K. We defaulted on both counts-anticipating low intensity conflict and cross border terrorism and preparing the Infantry for it.

Despite the sustained counter-insurgency and counter-terrorism campaign in J&K and the North-East since the 1990s, the Army was sluggish in investing in the infantry. The first Gulf War reintroduced the fiction that wars could be won from the air. The air campaigns in Bosnia and Kosovo temporarily turned fiction into reality. But 9/11 broke the myth of supremacy of air power. Operation Enduring Freedom in Afghanistan lasted 76 days; 65 of these were air operations.

The 11-day land offensive secured a temporary and incomplete victory against the Taliban. Operation Iraqi Freedom on the other hand, fought for 20 days was bereft of any preparatory air campaign though a secret air war preceded it. Unhappily for the US/NATO-led coalition forces, despite their pyrrhic military victories, low intensity wars in Afghanistan and Iraq are continuing in full blaze.

The recent 34-day war in Lebanon and the ongoing campaign in Gaza demonstrate the limits of Israel's military power. Used to decisive victories in less than 10 days, Israeli Defence Forces (IDF) were badgered by Hassan Nasrallah's jihadi militia. Reliance on air power, tanks and guns in Lebanon as substitute for ground troops-infantry-was motivated by casualty aversion. We too have to be sensitive to casualties.

The wars in Lebanon, Iraq and Afghanistan spurred by the growing cult of Osama bin Laden and Hassan Nasrallah require a redefinition of the concept of power and military success. Success would necessarily be an inclusive military victory encompassing post-conflict stability and reconstruction. For this we need Infantry.

The Indian Army should not get overly seduced by high-sounding warfare like 'netcentric' that the West is being diverted into. This is not to suggest we ignore the strides in high-tech warfare. But as a former US NATO Commander noted recently: "This netcentric stuff is great but our men in Baghdad are being blown up with their Humvees by IEDs." He suggested that we address the battle we are fighting before switching to the one we will fight in the future.

India's supreme operational challenge is and will be the maintenance of internal security. Just last month, Prime Minister Manmohan Singh stated this ground reality. The Infantry is at the heart of counterinsurgency and counter-terrorism operations and may well get sucked into anti-Naxal operations as well. Keeping the Army operationally ready for both conventional and unconventional missions is imperative but the emphasis has to be on the business of the day: CI and CT.

The Indian Infantry is belatedly embarking on a modernisation programme to enhance its combat skills through increased lethality, communications, surveillance, mobility and suvivability. These force multipliers will enable the soldier to fight all-weather, 24x7 and on any terrain in the right battle-configuration albeit with the accent on LIC.

The GSQR for the Future-Infantry-Soldier-As a System (F-INSAS) must empower not encumber the soldier. DRDO must compete with domestic and international industry. DRDO has one more chance to make amends for its omissions and commissions. F-INSAS must strike the right balance between the surge of technology and sensibility of the soldier keeping the battle of the future in mind. Defence Minister AK Antony should accord F-INSAS the highest strategic priority.

Revolution in Military Affairs

Despite the army leadership's best efforts, the ongoing Revolution in Military Affairs (RMA) had, till recently, almost completely bypassed the Indian Army. For well over a decade the army's efforts to modernise had been thwarted due to political neglect and lack of adequate budgetary support. The funds made available for modernisation are extremely limited and a large portion of these funds is surrendered year after year. For Financial Year 2006-07, a sum of Rs 3,000 crore was surrendered as unspent. The fact that 155 mm ammunition for the Bofors howitzer had to be imported from South Africa during the Kargil conflict in 1999 tells its own tale of persistent shortages. Had the conflict not been confined to the 150 km frontage of the Kargil sector, T-72 and 130 mm medium gun ammunition too would have run short and it would have been politically embarrassing for the government as well as the army. In the plains the army would have had to fight with obsolete Vijayant tanks and several other vintage equipment that were unsuitable for combat. However, sustained efforts by Army HQ have now borne fruit and the army's modernisation drive is once again well underway.

In the prevailing era of strategic uncertainty, while terrorism has become the primary threat, the external and internal threats and challenges faced by India are such that a large army is still required to be maintained. Also, a high degree of preparation and operational readiness is still necessary as conventional war, though improbable, cannot be categorically ruled out. At the same time, heavy capital investments in modern defence equipment are undoubtedly a drain on a developing economy that is ill-equipped to handle the burgeoning defence expenditure. Several eminent analysts have recommended that qualitative upgradation should be accompanied by quantitative downsizing of personnel strength of the army. However, given its responsibilities for border management and the manpower-intensive low intensity conflict that the army is involved in, this is easier said than done.

Future conventional conflict on the Indian sub-continent will in all probability result from the ongoing low-intensity limited war on the Line of Control (LoC) with Pakistan or the unresolved territorial and boundary dispute with China and will be predominantly a land conflict. The Indian Army seriously lacks a potent firepower punch, especially in the mountain sector. Precision-guided munitions (PGMs) have still to enter service in numbers large enough to make a real difference. The reconnaissance, surveillance and target acquisition (RSTA) assets necessary for the optimum exploitation of even the existing firepower assets are grossly inadequate. Automated command and control and decision support systems have been on the drawing boards for several decades but are yet to mature.

In a future conventional war that will be fought under the nuclear shadow, manoeuvre will be extremely limited. This restriction will lead to much greater emphasis being placed on firepower to achieve the laid down military aim.

Hence, it is imperative that artillery modernisation is undertaken with alacrity so as to generate firepower asymmetries on the future battlefield. After a long spell of keeping the powder dry, action on modernisation of the Indian artillery is livening up once again. Since January 2008, the Ministry of Defence (MoD) has issued three global tenders for 155mm guns and howitzers for the mountains, the plains and self-propelled guns for the deserts. Summer and winter trials are expected to be held over the next one year and, red tape permitting, contracts may be awarded as early as in the first half of 2010.

Artillery firepower had paved the way for victory during the Kargil conflict. Despite the lessons learnt in Kargil, modernisation of the artillery had continued to lag behind. The last major acquisition of towed gun-howitzers was that of about 400 pieces of 39-calibre 155mm FH-77B howitzers form Bofors of Sweden in the mid-1980s. This gun had proved its mettle in the Kargil conflict. Just when a contract for 120 tracked and 180 wheeled self-propelled (SP) 155mm guns was about to be concluded after years of protracted trials, South African arms manufacturer Denel, a leading contender for the contract, was alleged to have been involved in a corruption scam in an earlier deal for anti-material rifles (AMRs). The other two howitzers in contention, from Soltam of Israel and BAE (Bofors) of Sweden did not meet the laid down criteria according to the COAS and Army HQ recommended fresh trials, setting the programme back at least three to four years. Another key issue was that the howitzers that had been offered were technology demonstration models and not guns that were in actual service with the home country armies.

The probability of the next conventional war breaking out in the mountains is far higher than that of a war in the plains. With this in view, the artillery recently conceptualised a requirement for a light-weight towed howitzer of 155mm calibre for employment in the mountains. Neither the present Bofors howitzer nor its replacement will be capable of operations in the mountains. A light-weight 45-calibre 155mm howitzer weighing less than 5,000 kg, with a light but adequately powered prime mover, is ideal for the mountains. The gun-train should be capable of negotiating sharp road bends without the need to unhook the gun from the prime mover. The two British 45-calibre 155mm howitzers that competed for the US contract for a similar howitzer some years ago – the UFH (Ultra-lightweight Field Howitzer) and the LTH (Light-weight Towed Howitzer) – could be considered for licensed production with transfer of technology.

In January 2008, the MoD floated a Request for Proposal (RfP) for 140 pieces of ultra-light 39 calibre 155mm towed howitzers for use by the Indian Army's mountain formations and, presumably, by its rapid reaction divisions – as and when these are raised as it will be easy to transport by air. 140 howitzers will be adequate to equip seven medium artillery regiments and will cost approximately Rs 3,000 crore. The RfP has been reportedly issued to UK's BAE Systems (which now owns Bofors), for the M777 howitzer claimed to be the lightest in the world at under 4,220 kg, and to Singapore Technologies for the Pegasus SLWH.

India has floated a global tender for the purchase of 400 155mm towed artillery guns for the Army, to be followed by indigenous manufacture of another 1,100 howitzers, in a project worth a whopping Rs 8,000 crore. The RFP was issued to eight prospective bidders including BAE, General Dynamics, Nexter (France), Rhinemetall (Germany) and Samsung (South Korea). An RfP has also been issued for 180 wheeled self-propelled guns for around Rs 4,700 crore for employment by mechanised forces in the plains and semi-desert sectors.

Since the Bofors 155mm Howitzer was introduced into service, the indigenously designed and manufactured 105 mm Indian Field Gun (IFG) and its (not so) light version, the Light Field Gun (LFG), have joined the 75/24 Indian Mountain Gun, the 100mm Russian field gun and the 122mm Russian howitzer on the obsolescence list. Approximately 180 pieces of 130mm M46 Russian medium guns have been successfully "up-gunned" to 155mm calibre with ordnance supplied by Soltam of Israel. The new barrel length of 45 calibres has enhanced the range of the gun to about 40 km with extended range ammunition.

A contract for the acquisition of two regiments of the 12-tube, 300mm Smerch multi-barrel rocket launcher (MBRL) system with 90 km range was reported to have been signed with Russia's Rosoboronexport in early-2006. This will be a major boost for the long-range firepower capabilities of the army. If this weapon system had been available during the Kargil conflict, Pakistan's brigade HQ and forward airfield at Skardu and other targets deep inside POK could have been hit with impunity. Extended range (ER) rockets are being introduced for the 122 mm Grad MBRL that has been in service for over three decades. The ER rockets will enhance the weapon system's range from 22 to about 40 km. A Rs 5,000 crore contract has also been signed for the serial production of the Pinaka MBRL weapon system, another DRDO project plagued by time delays and completed with help from Larsen and Toubro and the Tatas.

The modernisation plan of tube artillery alone is likely to cost Rs 13,000 crore. The major acquisitions will be of initial lots of 400 towed howitzers of 155mm calibre, with a barrel length of 52 calibres, costing about Rs 4,000 crore, 140 ultra-light weight 155mm towed howitzers, with a barrel length of 45 calibres, costing Rs 3,000 crore and 180 SP 155mm howitzers costing Rs 5,000 crore. The "Shakti" project for a command and control systems for the artillery, called Artillery Combat Command and Control System (ACCCS), has reached the stage of maturity and is now being fielded up to the regimental level.

The BrahMos supersonic cruise missile (Mach 2.8 to 3.0), with a precision strike capability, very high kill energy and range of 290 km, was inducted into the army in July 2007. It is a versatile missile that can be launched from TATRA mobile launchers and silos on land, aircraft and ships and, perhaps in future, also from submarines. Fifty BrahMos missiles are expected to be produced every year. Efforts are underway to further increase its strike range. BrahMos Aerospace has orders worth Rs 3,500 crore from the army and the navy, which has opted for the anti-ship as well as the land attack cruise missile (LACM) versions. These terrain hugging missiles are virtually immune to counter measures due to their high speed and very low radar cross section and are far superior to sub-sonic cruise missiles like Pakistan's Babur. Chile, Kuwait, Malaysia and South Africa have shown interest in acquiring this missile.

The Indian army is extensively engaged in ongoing internal security (IS) and counter-insurgency operations (CI) and simultaneously needs to prepare itself for a future border conflict that may spill over to a larger conventional war in the plains. In keeping with these twin requirements, Army HQ have apparently decided to upgrade the IS and CI capabilities of infantry battalions as well as enhance their Infantry firepower-mobility-EW (electronic warfare) punch for a possible war in the plains against Pakistan or in the mountains against China. The Army Chief's modernisation vision is to "adapt to high-end technology, improve night-fighting capability... (and) information technology, information warfare and network centric warfare." Despite its large-scale employment on border management and extensive commitments in Internal Security and Counter Insurgency operations, infantry modernisation had been languishing for several decades when the Ministry of Defence (MoD) finally cleared a visionary plan to modernise the army's infantry battalions by according "in principle" approval in the form of Modification 4B to the war establishment (WE) of a standard infantry battalion in 1998. However, no funds were specially sanctioned for this purpose till the BJP-led NDA government approved the expenditure of Rs 3,500 crore in September 2003. Thereafter, approval had to be sought on file for each new weapon system or piece of equipment on a "case-by-case" basis as has become the norm. It is by now well-known how each such case chronicles the saga of an uphill struggle to get approval first from the MoD, then MoD (Finance) and, finally, the Ministry of Finance (MoF). All this is only possible after the DRDO has first certified that the weapon system or equipment in question cannot be developed and manufactured indigenously and such a certificate is hard to come by.

While 250 Kornet-E anti-tank guided missiles (ATGMs) with thermal imaging sights have substantially increased the anti-tank capability of infantry battalions, most efforts to modernise the equipment held by infantry and Rashtriya Rifles (RR) units are aimed at enhancing their capability for surveillance and target acquisition at night and boosting their firepower for precise retaliation against infiltrating columns and terrorists holed up in built-up areas. About 200 hand-held BFSRs with practical ranges up to seven to eight km where clear line of sight is available, 2,000 hand-held thermal imaging devices (HHTIs) with ranges up to 2,000 metres for observation at night and stand-alone infra-red, seismic and acoustic sensors with varying capabilities have enabled infantrymen to dominate the Line of Control so completely that infiltration has come down to almost a trickle.

The newly acquired weapons, which complement these surveillance and observation devices, include: 1,500x84 mm rocket launchers, including some disposable ones; 1,000 AMRs (anti-material rifles); 8,000 UBGLs (under-barrel grenade launchers); 4,000 new generation carbines; 300 bullet proof vehicles; and, several hundred accurate sniper rifles. However, the numbers acquired and the ammunition stocks are still inadequate and need to be made up more rapidly. While the INSAS 5.56 mm assault rifles have now been in service for almost 10 years and proved to be effective, the light machine gun (LNG) version is still facing teething problems and the carbine version for close quarter battle has not found favour with the army. New 5.56 mm assault rifles of bull-pup design with an integrated laser range finder and grenade launcher are under development. Efforts are also being made to provide infantry platoons and sections with integrated GPS-based navigation system, secure light-weight walkie-talkie radio sets and better protective gear with a helmet that incorporates a built-in head-up display.

The mechanised infantry is now equipped with the BMP-2 ICV Sarath of which over 1,000 have been built since 1987. A new variant is the 81 mm Carrier Mortar Tracked Vehicle (CMTV) that is based on the chassis of the Sarath ICV and has been indigenously developed to enhance the integral firepower available to mechanised infantry battalions. Other variants include a command post, an ambulance, armoured dozer and engineer and reconnaissance vehicles. Mechanised reconnaissance and support battalions need better surveillance radars, fire-and-forget ATGMs and effective night fighting capability. However, their capabilities can be upgraded on a lower priority compared with infantry battalions that are engaged in border management and IS/CI operations.

The army's infantry battalions also need their own mini or micro UAVs like Elbit's Skylark or Rafael's Skylite, among others, to partly reduce the extent of patrolling necessary in internal security environment and to improve their surveillance capability in conventional conflict. These UAVs should have a range of about 10 to 15 km, should be light-weight (less than 10 kg), hand-launched, carry a single payload, e.g. a daylight video camera or infra-red camera for night operations, and should be inexpensive enough to be dispensable. A mini ground control station should be authorized at battalion HQ for planning and control. Ideally, these should be indigenously designed and developed and locally manufactured.

A new DRDO project, that is reported to be ongoing, aims to equip future soldiers with lightweight force multipliers. Soldiers of the future will have miniaturised communication and GPS systems, small power packs, weapon platforms and smart vests with fibre-optic sensors. The soldiers will also have better and lighter combat fatigues, boots, belts, ammunition pouches, rucksacks and rations in the form of meals-ready-to-eat. Though somewhat akin to the US Army's Land Warrior programme, the Indian Army programme for modernisation of infantry battalions will result in only incremental changes. However, these would be significant enough to make a difference on the battlefields of the Indian sub-continent. The infantryman's average combat load is approximately 27 kg, including the 3.06 kg 5.56 mm INSAS assault rifle and its "on weapon" ammunition. If this can be reduced by even a few kg, it will enable the soldier to improve his agility in battle and counter-insurgency operations. Ultimately an infantryman has to be prepared to engage in hand-to-hand combat and agility can make a difference between life and death.

For over 350 infantry battalions, plus about 150 Rashtriya Rifles, Assam Rifles and Territorial Army battalions, these major changes will be extremely costly to implement and will spill over at least 10 to 12 years – that is, if the funds can be found. What is certain is that there is no alternative to making the financial commitment that is necessary to enhance the operational capabilities of the army's infantry battalions. Without modernising this cutting edge of its sword, the army will soon begin to resemble the armies of India's lesser neighbours.

The indigenously designed Arjun main battle tank (MBT) has been in the pipeline for over two decades. Though the tank has many good features, it has consistently failed to meet the army's GSQR for an MBT and orders have been placed for only 124 tanks to be manufactured. The lack of progress on the Arjun MBT had slowed down the pace of armour modernisation. India then signed a deal with Russia to acquire 310 T-90S tanks in the year 2000. Subsequently, India began to assemble these tanks at Avadi. It has recently been reported that in addition to these, India has decided to acquire another 347 T-90S tanks and assemble them within the country.

The first Indian assembled T-90S (Bhishma) rolled off the production line on January 8, 2004. While T-90S Russian tanks have provided new teeth to India's strike formations in the plains and corrected the imbalance that had resulted from Pakistan's acquisition of T-80 UD from Ukraine and the Al Khalid tanks jointly designed with China, a large number of T-72 (Ajeya) tanks are still awaiting modernisation. The lack of a suitable fire control system and night fighting capability are major handicaps. As soon as the obsolescent Vijayanta tanks are phased out of service, it will be time to also discard the old T-55s as well as they can no longer be either upgraded or modernised. Armour modernisation is now proceeding apace and can be classified as a success story.

The air defence (AD) of mechanised forces is another area that is crying for attention. The Kvadrat missile system that has been the backbone of AD for strike formations since the early 1970s are now ageing and need urgent replacement. With the DRDO's indigenous Akash medium-range and Trishul short-range missile projects not making major headway, it is time to start looking at import substitutes. In fact, the assets of Army Air Defence corps of the army are grossly inadequate to provide effective protection against enemy aircraft during war. This young corps requires substantial capital infusion to really come into its own.

Another DRDO project that is way behind schedule is the Nag anti-tank missile system. The antiquated Jonga-mounted SS-11 B1 anti-tank guided missile (ATGM) system has been replaced in missile battalions by MILAN shoulder-fired ATGMs. However, a vehicle-mounted missile system like the Nag is definitely necessary for reconnaissance and attrition tasks. The experimental Plan AREN tactical communications system for strike formations needs early replacement. The ability to carry broadband data needs to be enhanced in particular. Even the more recent static communications network called ASCON lacks ISDN capability for the real-time transmission of maps and streaming video.

While some Stentor long-range BFSRs have been in service for over a decade, medium-range radars are still to be acquired. At least about 30 to 40 weapon locating radars (WLRs) are required for effective counter-bombardment, especially in the plains, and only a few have been procured so far. Israeli Searcher-I unmanned aerial vehicles (UAVs) have been introduced into service but these are few in number and it will be a long time before these will really make a difference by providing a real-time surveillance capability so that ground forces can initiate action even as a fresh input is received. Only a small number of Searcher – II UAVs, with an upper ceiling that makes them suitable for the mountains, have been acquired.

An automated command and control and decision support system for use by the General Staff is still a far cry and so are supporting systems like the battlefield surveillance system and air space management system. The urgent requirement of real-time satellite reconnaissance systems has still not been accepted despite the nuclear overhang under which the armed forces now operate. Even though the cameras on India's remote sensing and cartographic satellites now have sharply enhanced resolutions, less than one metre, military-grade photographs of still better resolution are needed to be purchased from the open market. These sources may dry up quickly during war.

A "system of systems" approach must be followed so that scarce RSTA and communications resources can be synergistically configured and optimally exploited. The war in Iraq fought in March-April 2003 was based on the concept of "network-centric warfare" in which surveillance sensors, targeting systems and "shooters" are fused together in a seamless "system of systems" that reduced response time between the acquisition of a target and its destruction to 15 to 20 minutes. While such a system may take over a decade to establish, a beginning must be made right away.

PGMs are increasingly gaining currency as weapons of choice in conflict on land, both to accurately destroy critical hard targets quickly as well as to avoid or at least minimise collateral damage. During the Gulf War I in 1991, despite all the CNN-generated hype of smart bombs flying unerringly through ventilators, PGMs formed less than 10 percent of the total high explosive dropped over Iraq and were rather inaccurate. The "collateral" destruction of an air raid shelter harbouring women and children has been too well documented to bear recounting. The coalition forces did not destroy a single Iraqi Scud missile launcher. In Kosovo, PGMs accounted for about 30 per cent of the ordnance dropped and accuracies had improved considerably by 1999. In the post-September 11, 2001 retribution inflicted on the Taliban militia and its al Qaeda supporters in Afghanistan, the share of PGMs had risen to nearly 60 percent. In Gulf War II in Iraq, the ratio of PGMs went up to nearly 70 per cent. The Indian artillery does not have any PGMs worth the name. Only limited quantities of the Russian Krasnopol PGM have been imported for the Bofors 155 mm howitzer. Among others, the Bofors Bonus PGM is a suitable candidate, subject to successful trials in the deserts and the mountains.

Finally, the approach to army modernisation must be more focused; the priorities must be clearly established and then adhered to. The government must give a firm commitment in terms of funds and the Ministry of Defence must streamline its procedures and processes for speedy procurement of high priority weapons and equipment. It is time to institute a rolling, non-lapsable defence modernisation fund of Rs. 25,000 crores as a viable method of ensuring that defence procurement is not subjected to the vagaries of annual budgets. The present situation is disturbing and, if allowed to go on indefinitely, will seriously compromise the army's preparedness to fight the next border war that inimical neighbours like Pakistan can be expected to thrust on India.

Bibliography

Alperovitz, Gar. The Decision to Use the Atomic Bomb. New York: Vintage Books, 1996.

Arend, A.: International Law and the Use of Military, London, Routledge, 1993.

Damrosch, L.F.: Law and Force in the New International Order, Boulder, Westview Press, 1991.

Friedman, G.: The Future of War: Power, Technology and American World Dominance in the 21st Century, N.Y., Random House, 1996.

Huntington, S.P.: The China Modernisation Military and the State, N.Y., Vintage Books, 1964.

Jones, W.H.: The Government and Politics of Indian Military, London, Hutchinson, 1971.

Authority, Cambridge, Belknap Press, 1985.

Posen, B.R.: The Sources of Modernization Military, Ithaca, 1984, Cornell Univ. Press.

Rhodes, Richard, The Making of the Atomic Bomb, New York: Simon and Schuster, 1988.

Rosen, P.: Societies and Military Power: India and its Armies, Ithaca, Cornell University Press, 1996.

Index

□□□